PREPARING TOMORROW'S GLOBAL LEADERS

Honors International Education

PREPARING TOMORROW'S GLOBAL LEADERS

Honors International Education

Edited by **Mary Kay Mulvaney** and **Kim Klein**

Series Editor | Jeffrey A. Portnoy

National Collegiate Honors Council
Monograph Series

Manufactured in the United States

National Collegiate Honors Council
100 Neihardt Residence Center
University of Nebraska-Lincoln
540 N. 16th Street
Lincoln, NE 68588-0627
www.ncnchonors.org

Production Editors | Cliff Jefferson and Mitch Pruitt
Wake Up Graphics LLC

Cover and Text Design | 47 Journals LLC

International Standard Book Number
978-0-9835457-7-4

TABLE OF CONTENTS

INTRODUCTION

Mary Kay Mulvaney
Elmhurst College

Kim Klein
Shippensburg University

We constantly hear the term "globalization" in any number of contexts, from the growth of international trade networks and the increasing diversification of populations in traditionally homogeneous European nations to the transnational exchange of pop culture. The flatness of our increasingly interconnected world is touted in texts and television shows. Media abound with striking international news: the bloody fight for democratic freedom throughout the Arab Spring; the economic dilemmas of the European Union; the continuing Afghan conflict; and the increasingly influential Chinese, Indian, and Brazilian economies.

The accelerating pace of globalization is also reflected in trends in higher education. Once a privilege of the elite, international study among all U.S. college students is rising. According to the Institute of International Education, slightly more than 1/4 million American undergraduates study abroad annually ("Open Doors").

In our diverse and interconnected world, expanding our students' horizons beyond the classrooms and laboratories of our home campuses is increasingly important. Even some of the brightest honors students remain naïve to the causes and ramifications of current world events and lack the necessary intercultural skills to become effective ethical leaders with a global consciousness. They function extremely well in a generational zone of instant technology via iPhones, YouTube, and Facebook, but much of that merely contextualizes the ordinary, the bizarre, and the local or momentarily provides glimpses into the often unreal world of pop culture. Developing the academic as well as intercultural competence of our students is no longer a luxury: it is an obligation. Indeed, as education researcher George D. Kuh discusses in the 2008 and 2013 AAC&U reports, *High-Impact Educational Practices* and *Ensuring Quality & Taking High-Impact Practices to Scale*, respectively, there is a growing endorsement of experiential education and recognition of the necessity for fast-paced educational offerings, including study abroad programming. In light of this expanding vision, we recognized a gap in the valuable offerings of NCHC monographs. While NCHC's monographs examine program development, pedagogy, and other important aspects of honors education, no NCHC resource addresses the needs of honors administrators and faculty endeavoring to internationalize their programs. This monograph attempts to fill that gap.

OVERALL DESIGN

Because the issues are broad and the models and the expertise of our members are widely and creatively varied, this monograph is an edited collection of scholarly essays highlighting critical components of quality honors international education. The collection is divided into three major sections: philosophical and pedagogical issues, programmatic elements and challenges, and practical tips from the annals of experienced faculty. These three sections are followed by a fourth section, which provides the details of eleven honors international courses that vary in length, location, and focus. These sample honors courses function as models for possible honors international courses in other venues; they can be tailored to fit the needs of a wide variety of honors programs and colleges. Because honors education clearly has no monopoly on study abroad programming, the chapter authors and model courses emphasize the components that are distinctly honors.

The first section, entitled "Transformative Pedagogies," comprises seven chapters. It begins with Elizabeth Baigent's discussion of teaching and learning strategies that will ensure honors students move beyond the status of "academic tourists" to become true "scholars abroad." In the second chapter, A. Minh Nguyen examines the "classical philosophical underpinnings of honors international education" and ways to design international experiences to cultivate critical and creative thinkers equipped to face the challenges of the twenty-first century. The next five chapters provide models of integrating experiential learning into honors study abroad programs. Mary Kay Mulvaney explains how and why she combines two high-impact educational practices—City as Text™ pedagogy and undergraduate research—in her honors study abroad programs in Europe. John Zubizaretta, Christine Hait, Corinne Mann, Marca Wolfensberger, and their students offer further suggestions for enriching the City as Text™ model through international collaboration. The final three chapters in this section describe model honors international service-learning and research programs. Phame Camarena and Helen Collins examine the development of a service-learning program in Mexico, designed specifically for first-year honors students. Kevin W. Dean and Michael B. Jendzurski assess how honors students' leadership development, research skills, and commitment to global service are fostered through West Chester University's decade-long service-learning partnership in South Africa. Mary Ann Studer describes the transformative impact of community-based research projects on her students and university and on communities around the world.

The second section, "Programmatic Elements and Challenges," consists of eight chapters addressing a wide array of issues central to developing successful honors international education programs. Bernice Braid examines the first important step in this process: preparing faculty to lead effective honors study abroad programs. Next, Phillip Krummrich and Kayla Burton identify the most important obstacles that prevent honors students from studying abroad and offer strategies for overcoming these barriers. The following chapter by Kim Klein and Mary Kay Mulvaney offers additional strategies for addressing the financial obstacles to studying abroad. Following faculty and student recruitment, a critical component of pre-departure planning involves ensuring travelers' safety in these increasingly tumultuous times. In her second contribution to the monograph, Mary Ann Studer offers time-tested advice for keeping students and faculty safe in international environments. Lisa Markus,

Jill McKinney, and Anne M. Wilson explore the links between their students' study abroad experiences and their honors undergraduate theses and offer suggestions to enhance the synergies between these two high-impact educational practices. Advocating stronger institutional commitment to international education, Christopher J. Frost, Timothy L. Hulsey, and Karey Sabol provide their perspectives on internationalizing honors programs. Recognizing the specific curricular challenges faced by honors students in professional fields, Ellen B. Buckner and Lygia Holcomb address the needs of those who are interested in developing international research and service-learning programs for students in the health professions. Finally, Cecile Houry examines the growing population of international students at American universities and provides strategies for successfully involving international students in study abroad programs organized by U.S. honors programs and colleges.

The third section, "Advice from Experienced Faculty Leaders," does exactly as readers would expect. Karl M. Petruso provides his "Top Ten List" of tips for honors study abroad program directors. Recognizing the unique challenges posed by short-term study abroad programs, Karen Lyons offers advice on "Maximizing the Short-Term Study Abroad Experience" for students and faculty alike.

The monograph concludes by offering eleven distinct models of honors international courses. The model courses include destinations in Asia, Africa, Europe, and Latin America. The disciplines represented range from art and archaeology to linguistics and leadership; the majority incorporate the perspectives of multiple disciplines. All are infused with distinctly honors teaching and learning strategies that can inspire honors faculty and administrators who are developing or reinvigorating their honors international course offerings.

The hard work of our many talented contributors who have years of experience designing and teaching honors courses overseas have made this monograph a reality. We sincerely hope that this publication is a valuable resource for honors faculty, administrators, and all who are committed to providing the exceptional international academic opportunities that will prepare students to compete and lead on the global stage.

We would like to thank the NCHC Publications Board and the International Education Committee for encouraging us to undertake this project and for supporting our efforts. In particular, we would like to thank Jeffrey Portnoy for guiding us through the publication process and carefully editing the manuscript. A final thank you is for our families, especially Nicholas, Mark, and John, who have been unfailingly patient and supportive as we have worked on this project.

Works Cited

Kuh, George D. *High-Impact Educational Practices: What They Are, Who Has Access to Them, and Why They Matter.* Washington, D.C.: Association of American Colleges and Universities, 2008. Print.

Kuh, George D., and Ken O'Donnell. *Ensuring Quality & Taking High-Impact Practices to Scale.* Washington, D.C.: Association of American Colleges and Universities, 2013. Print.

"Open Doors Report 2010." Institute of International Education. *Institute of International Education.* 15 Nov. 2010. Web. 30 July 2011.

PREPARING TOMORROW'S GLOBAL LEADERS

Honors International Education

PART I:
TRANSFORMATIVE PEDAGOGIES

CHAPTER 1

Academic Tourist or Scholar Abroad: Deep Approaches to Learning

Elizabeth Baigent
University of Oxford

"Hey, these ruins are inhabited," a youthful American visitor memorably exclaimed when he met a faculty member in an Oxford University college (qtd. in Beadle 120). Deceived by the ivy, crumbling stonework, and general sense of antiquity, he had assumed the university buildings were vestiges of a previous culture and had little to do with modern life (ctd. in Beadle 120). Countless other visitors come already armed with what Edward W. Said terms "imaginative geographies" of Oxford: they arrive with a way of seeing and conceptualizing Oxford and themselves in relation to and because of Oxford (49). Oxford is also a destination for what Nicola Watson terms "literary tourism." Literary tourists come in search of a city seen through the eyes of authors such as Matthew Arnold, Lewis Carroll, Evelyn Waugh, Dorothy L. Sayers, C. S. Lewis, Philip Pullman, or J. K. Rowling, or film characters such as Inspector Morse. Many leave having interacted with the place only superficially and with their assumptions and imaginative geographies intact. Others brush aside the ivy to transcend their preconceptions and literary associations: they leave with a deep understanding of the place, their homes, and themselves.

THE LOCATION OF CULTURE

Helping students to penetrate the ivy, to confront their imaginative geographies of both home and away, is the challenge for study abroad program leaders in Oxford, as well as in Paris, Bologna, Leiden, Edinburgh, and other cities with ancient universities, long histories, and a strong literary presence. The task is made easier because the primary motivation for students to study abroad is to experience other cultures, at least in the case of students who come from developed countries.[1] In some respects the challenge for students is similar to that faced by all visitors to other cultures; Robert Hewison characterizes it as learning to distinguish history from "heritage-ism." He asks how people can be encouraged critically to explore other cultures from which they are separated by time, place, or both by asking awkward questions about them and about their own culture, in the manner of the historian, and to reject the anodyne, sanitized, or romanticized version of other cultures, which is presented by what he terms the "heritage industry." Similarly, Homi Bhabha challenges the assumption that authentic culture is confined to a small number of apparently canonical sites, such as Oxford, of which other cultures are imitations. Rather, he argues, each site presents its own cultural geography, and the centers of Great Tradition or canonical authority remain elusive (x–xi). If explorers of supposedly canonical sites move beyond the stereotype, the canon, and the ivy, they can accept their reaction to both the visited place and home as authentic. As Bhabha says, "I went to Oxford [as a student] to embellish the antique charms of the armoire: I ended up realizing how much I desired street food" (x). Bhabha's acceptance of this realization made his experience transformative: a rejection of it would have left his preconceptions intact and his experience superficial (and him smug, congratulating himself for being an Oxonian and unlike other men). If study

4

abroad students return home from Oxford knowing only that home is different from Oxford, then their program leaders have not given them a transformative experience. Rather, they have provided a temporary experience of another place, one which is contingent on being in that place, and they have not equipped students to think differently about home or to challenge the simple binary of home and away.

THE DEATH OF GEOGRAPHY

This kind of deep understanding of another culture and consequently of self is the traditional aim of study abroad programs, though, regrettably, too little high-quality research exists on whether they achieve this aim.[2] It could be argued, however, that study abroad programs that bring academically able students from the USA to the University of Oxford should instead focus on engagement with academic values and ambitions that have little to do with living in a particular place and everything to do with being part of the international research culture, something that Karen Arnold suggests in fact occurs with Rhodes Scholars in Oxford (12). (Such programs may also promote integration into the international socio-economic elite although whether that is desirable is another matter.) Certainly from the point of view of the host institution rather than the individual student, it is hard to disagree with Maidi Brown's assessment that academic achievement is judged much more important than cultural engagement, experiential learning, or anything else (11), and in a top-rank research university "academic achievement" means confident entry into the culture and conversation of the international group of elite universities.

Such elite universities are global rather than local; they are the educational equivalents of what Saskia Sassen describes as "global cities" that are culturally more akin to and better connected to other global cities, wherever situated, than to their own geographical hinterlands. As digitized information flows negate the influence of distance, it can be argued that what defines proximity is connectivity, not longitude and latitude. The consequences allow Peter Martin to claim that geography is dead (11) and Frances Cairncross to assert that the era is characterized by the "death of distance." The defining feature of global or international universities is the creation of high-quality information, and membership in one of them radically reduces the distance to all the others since members have privileged access to high-quality information generated at other leading institutions and stored in digitized, subscription-only journals, databases, and archives. Thus students from smaller or less selective U.S. higher education institutions who come to the University of Oxford end up close to Harvard, Princeton, and Berkeley, in the sense of being intimately connected to the information created in and circulated by them, even though the number of miles separating them from those elite U.S. institutions will probably have increased. The most academically able of the students also end up culturally close to Harvard, Princeton, and Berkeley; that is, they share similar academic values and ambitions, are embedded in the same research process, participate in the same scholarly conversations, and operate at the same intellectual level. What is important to them, it can be argued, has nothing to do with Oxford's local culture but everything to do with its being a global university. It is true that unequal access to information increasingly defines global geography, and top-rank universities increasingly operate on a world scale in terms of the pool of students and scholars from which they recruit. They see themselves as part of a single international research culture (K. D. Arnold; International Alliance of Research Universities). It is also true that many study abroad students come to Oxford to test themselves against the standard of a top-rank university and to ease their passage into graduate school at another top-rank university at home. They could agree with the student who candidly remarked, "I'm not interested in England in the same way as my friend who's a Spanish major is interested in Spain: sure I like to find out about England, but I'm really at Oxford to get into a top grad school at home."[3]

Ideas of global universities and global cities, however, risk reinventing Bhabha's canonical cultural sites, which prove elusive; and it may be that reports of the death of geography have been greatly exaggerated, as Kevin Morgan has argued, not least because place remains crucially important in fostering what Etienne Wenger terms "communities of practice" and in transmitting tacit knowledge that is context-dependent and can be transmitted only, or at least best, through face-to-face interaction.[4] Moreover, a flourishing focus of research in the history of science argues that a geography of science and scholarship exists and that ideas are produced and consumed differently in different places.[5] Thus, while some study abroad students in Oxford share the view of the visiting student quoted above who saw Oxford largely as a way into a global system, others agree with the student who said, "I'm a British studies major; I really want to understand England better." Still others find that being removed from home shapes their receptiveness to new ideas, while the experience of being in a new place changes how, what, and why they learn. Many study abroad students in Oxford speak of the effect of the place on their learning. "Experiencing old buildings was enriching in a way I didn't expect; . . . the sense of history reminds you how small you are, that you are in a place where so many have gone before. This was not something I even knew was on the agenda," said one, while another echoed, "standing in physical places, not just looking at the pictures [I know I'm] part of a great tradition." While program leaders in Oxford should not assume that engaging with local culture is the students' main aspiration, some exposure to local culture is inevitable, and program leaders must help students do it well, that is, thoughtfully, as part of their overall pedagogical goal of fostering critical faculties and inculcating the sense that learning does not stop at the tutorial room door.

DEEP AND SURFACE APPROACHES TO LEARNING

A study abroad program in Oxford should help students participate in the international and perhaps placeless culture of high-level scholarship and simultaneously foster a critical exploration of the particular culture of the place that allows students to transcend preconceptions and reflect on their home cultures. Voicing this aspiration is doubtless easier than meeting it, but help may come from recent research on learning that describes all true learning using the same word that the most perceptive students use to describe their study abroad experience: "transformative." Derived from empirical phenomenographic research by Ference Marton and Roger Säljö and developed by European and Australian authors, this research distinguishes a deep from a surface approach to learning.[6] The focus in the educational experience is not on how teachers teach but on how students learn, and the research brings insight to education in all fields: that is, it can help in the design of courses for students who are learning about literary criticism and about what it is like to live in a city built for feet and bicycles rather than cars, or about Plato and about why houses in England look as they do. The research provides a way of thinking about teaching and learning that can help students to have an intellectually stimulating experience in their chosen academic fields and to understand why the place that is their home for one or two semesters is as it is. The key is the students' approach to learning, which is summarized in Table 1 from Paul Ramsden's *Learning to Teach in Higher Education*.

Put another way, Roger Säljö suggests that "learning" can mean:

1. A quantitative increase in knowledge, that is, acquiring information or "knowing a lot."

2. Memorizing or storing information that can be reproduced.

3. Acquiring facts, skills, and methods that can be retained and used as necessary.

4. Making sense or abstracting meaning, relating parts of the subject matter to one another and to the real world. [or]

5. Interpreting and understanding reality in a different way or comprehending the world by reinterpreting knowledge. (ctd. in Ramsden 27–28; Biggs)

Items 1, 2, and 3 are views that underpin a surface approach to learning, and 4 and 5 relate to deep approaches to learning.

Some learning is transformative because it involves understanding and reinterpretation, while other learning is merely reproductive. This difference exists regardless of the subject matter of study, so honors students abroad can be encouraged to have a deep approach to learning both as they do their library study and as they

TABLE 1: APPROACHES TO LEARNING (RAMSDEN 47)

Deep Approach	Surface Approach
Intention to understand Student maintains structure of task	Intention only to complete task requirements Student distorts structure of task
Focus is on "what is signified" (e.g., the author's argument, or the concepts applicable to solving the problem)	Focus is on "the signs" (e.g., the words and sentences of the text, or unthinkingly on the formula needed to solve the problem)
Relate previous knowledge to new knowledge	Focus on unrelated parts of the task
Relate knowledge from different courses	Memorize information for assessments
Relate theoretical ideas to everyday experience	Associate facts and concepts unreflectively
Relate and distinguish evidence and argument	Fail to distinguish principles from examples
Organize and structure content into a coherent whole	Treat the task as an external imposition
Internal emphasis: to help the student see and make sense of his/her world (Entwistle and Marton)	External emphasis: demands of assessments, knowledge cut off from everyday reality

live in the city. They can approach critically the imaginative geography of a place in the same way they approach a literary text or a philosophical problem.

The Oxford study abroad program of which I am the Senior Tutor discourages a surface approach to learning by avoiding:

- busy work ("At home there is so much work that's just a drag to get through.");

- assessment based on simple recall or rehearsal of trivial detail ("I just hate the quizzes we have at the end of courses.");

- cynical comments about the subject matter and students' performance;[7]

- making clear that the students do not have to please their tutors ("At home the professors are so personally invested in you, you feel you've got to do well for their sake, to give them what they expect. Here the conversation is different, always critical of the ideas, never about you, and somehow you have the freedom to say what you want.").

The program fosters a deep approach to learning by:

- planning an appropriate institutional structure: our students are Registered Visiting Students of the University of Oxford. As such, they have the same rights to attend lectures; use libraries; access online resources; and benefit from computing, language-learning, and other facilities as do students who are matriculated for degrees from Oxford. The difference between being a Registered Visiting Student and simply being a visiting student is mostly unclear to study abroad students when they arrive, but what is clear to faculty is that students cannot be full participants in the international research culture they come to explore if they are excluded from many of the conversations and resources that characterize that culture. ("It was just so exciting in the library to say I need that book and it would just be there, whatever it was. It was just so exhilarating. It felt like there were no limits. I could get anything I wanted.")

- designing courses to foster student learning: Oxford students benefit from individual tutorials that have as their primary goal teaching students to think, not getting them to acquire information or skills, although they do these latter things to an impressive extent along the way since no argument can withstand intelligent scrutiny unless based on extensive knowledge skillfully acquired and deployed (Palfreyman 19–20). The wide choice of tutorials maximizes the opportunities for students to study what they want and pursue their chosen topics at an appropriate level: Ramsden reports that these things have been shown empirically to be conducive to deep learning. An appropriate level in Oxford terms is one that demands detailed and focused study of research-based findings, and this is much appreciated by the students. ("At home I'd come to the point where I knew a little about a lot and that's not enough." "It's time to skip the *Wikipedia* and get to details.")

- encouraging students to think critically about how they might approach their learning and about what they are doing by explaining the point of program activities. Michael Prosser and Keith Trigwell report that empirical studies show that the effects of such explanations are less effective than one would hope, but they do promote some improvement (100). Being clear about the nature of the academic program, how each aspect contributes to the whole, and what the expectations are in terms of approach by students and tutors all help students to take a deep approach to their learning.

- developing good assessment practices: rapid, detailed, and frequent feedback on written work, focusing on what the student should do to develop (Nicol and Macfarlane-Dick 209–10). In particular verbal feedback in tutorials (eight weekly meetings of one student and one tutor during the semester) or supervisions can help students engage deeply with the material (Palfreyman 19–20; Gibb and Simpson). ("It was the immediate feedback, and sustained over eight meetings which really made it for me." "That was the good thing about the tutorials. There was constant feedback.") That summative assessment for tutorials is based on tutor evaluation, not cumulative scores, means that students can experiment intellectually. ("I liked the fact that you could take risks.")

- learning outside the classroom: encouraging learning as a critical and enquiring way of life, fostered in conversation and experience, as well as in the lecture hall or library (McAlpine 121). This practice means encouraging but not compelling conversation among students, for example, by organizing food groups in student houses, so that social contexts become intellectual forums. ("For the first time in my life I get to talk about philosophy over dinner, not the latest football game. I don't have to pretend that studies are just a drag to get through.") The program also takes students on field trips to both classic tourist sites, such as the Georgian city of Bath, and less superficially attractive destinations, such as the Imperial War Museum in London, or Coventry, a city nearly obliterated by Nazi bombing. At attractive sites the point is not just to gawk and photograph, but to exercise critical judgment: in Bath, for example, students join faculty in examining the city landscape as a mix of international Palladian taste adapted to local geology and topography, mediated by differing conceptions of the British nation.

- retaining a sense of humor. Opper, Carlson and Teichler remind us that even the most assiduous and intellectually enquiring students have come on study abroad programs in part to enjoy themselves, and Prosser and Trigwell report empirical studies which confirm that a supportive and enjoyable context encourages students to take a deep approach to their learning. More importantly, program activities should not suggest that enjoyment happens when learning stops, but rather the reverse. Critically enjoying the absurdities of the host culture is one way to do this, provided it is led by native program leaders. This area is one in which study abroad programs led by the students' home institution staff may have some difficulties.[8] SCIO, the organizing institution of this program, addresses this issue by having a multinational staff in which native Britons are joined by U.S., Australian, and Ghanaian citizens, all of whom have lived in Oxford for many years.

Student satisfaction surveys (2004–2012) suggest that almost all students leave satisfied. More important to the staff are reflections given by students after they leave, either through correspondence ("In Oxford I first encountered a world of scholarship and inquiry and knew that this was where I felt at home"; "In Oxford I learned to push myself") or through alumni surveys (2007–2012), which substantially replicate the findings of the exit evaluations, although response rates were much lower. The choices regarding graduate school made by ex-students, many going to top international research institutions, and comments by their professors at home, many of whom describe our ex-students as "unteachable," meaning not willing to settle for easy answers after they get home, bear this out. ("I always used to write nice tidy answers, with all my points all neat and tidy: at Oxford I learned to enjoy the messiness and complexity of [my chosen field of inquiry].")

CONCLUSION

For a study abroad program in a beautiful city such as Oxford to relish and emphasize the uniqueness of the place is important. Oxford is, after all, still Oxford, Matthew Arnold's "city with her dreaming spires," rather than any other place, and study abroad program leaders in the city must recognize that they benefit from the raised expectations of self that living and working in beautiful places engender in some students ("Thyrsis" 19). ("It was just the beauty of the place and the antiquity. It was overwhelming. I just had to try my best to live up to it.") Although Arnold's phrase about "dreaming spires" is generally quoted to imply timeless tradition, the poem from which it is taken is in fact about change. Change is what study abroad programs should foster in their participants, students and leaders alike. By helping students cultivate a deep approach to learning inside the classroom and out, program leaders should send them home more critical and more reflective and with attitudes to learning that are not geographically dependent, but transferable across space and time. Whether students enter the world of international scholarship or settle down in their home town, if study abroad has been successful, they will see themselves and their surroundings with changed eyes.

NOTES

[1] For greater detail on the motivations of students from developed nations who chose to study abroad see the studies of Gabrielle Parker and Annie Rouxeville; Susan Opper, Jerry Carlson, and Ulrich Teichler; S. A. Lamet and Maryelise Lamet; and James Forney Pelowski.

[2] For detailed discussions of the impact of study abroad on students' intercultural knowledge and self-awareness, see the research studies of Elinor G. Barber; James A. Coleman; Susan Opper, Jerry Carlson, and Ulrich Teichler; and Deborah K. Sell.

[3] All quotations are responses given by students on the Scholars' Semester in Oxford program in interviews, focus groups, correspondence, student satisfaction surveys on exit, and alumni surveys from 2004 to the present. Quotations are used with permission and are rendered anonymous to protect the identity of the respondents. I extend warm thanks to all student participants and to colleagues at SCIO, which runs the above program, and the Oxford Learning Institute.

[4] For further discussion of the nature of tacit knowledge and its role in knowledge creation, see the works of Harald Bathelt, Anders Malmberg, and Peter Maskell and that of Meric S. Gertler, as well as Michael Polanyi's work on "personal knowledge."

[5] For further discussion of how place shapes knowledge, see the works of David N. Livingstone; James A. Secord; and *Cultures of Knowledge.*

[6] The concept of deep vs. surface approaches to learning is discussed in the works of Noel J. Entwistle; Entwistle and Marton; Paul Ramsden; and Marton and Säljö.

[7]See Gina Wisker for discussion of good practice in dealing with international students; see Michael Prosser and Keith Trigwell for discussion of good practice in higher education, and see Graham Gibbs and Claire Simpson's discussion of employing assessment strategies to support student learning.

[8]See M. Battsek's discussion of this difficulty and other possible areas of concern.

WORKS CITED

Arnold, Karen D. "Generating Leaders in an Age of Diversity: Fifty Years of U.S. Rhodes Scholars." *Oxford Centre for Higher Education Policy Studies Occasional Paper 26*. Oxford: OxCHEPS, 2005. Print.

Arnold, Matthew. "Thyrsis: A Monody, to Commemorate the Author's Friend, Arthur Hugh Clough." *Macmillan's Magazine*, Apr. 1866. Web. 24 June 2011.

Barber, Elinor G. "The Impact of Foreign Educational Experience on Individuals." *ISECSI Bulletin of International Interchanges* 20 (1983): 7–10. Print.

Bathelt, Harald, Anders Malmberg, and Peter Maskell. "Clusters and Knowledge: Local Buzz, Global Pipelines and the Process of Knowledge Creation." *Progress in Human Geography* 28 (2004): 31–56. Print.

Battsek, M. "A Practical Analysis of Some Aspects of Study Abroad." *Journal of General Education* 13 (1962): 225–42. Print.

Beadle, Muriel. *These Ruins are Inhabited*. London: Robert Hale, 1961. Print.

Bhabha, Homi. *The Location of Culture*. London: Routledge, 1994. Print.

Biggs, John B. *Teaching for Quality Learning at University: What the Student Does*. Buckingham, UK: Society for Research into Higher Education, 1999. Print.

Brown, Maidi. "Do We Need a Strategic Development Function in Universities?" *Good Practice Working with International Students.* Ed. Gina Wisker. Birmingham, UK: Staff and Educational Development Association, 2000. 7–20. Print.

Cairncross, Frances. *The Death of Distance 2.0: How the Communications Revolution Will Change Our Lives.* London: Texere, 2001. Print.

Coleman, James A. "The Current State of Knowledge Concerning Student Residence Abroad." *The "Year Abroad": Preparation, Monitoring, Evaluation: Current Research and Development.* Ed. Gabrielle Parker and Annie Rouxeville. London: Association for French Language Studies, 1995. 17–42. Print.

Cultures of Knowledge: An Intellectual Geography of the Seventeenth-Century Republic of Letters. U of Oxford. Web. 24 June 2011.

Entwistle, Noel J. *Teaching for Understanding at University: Deep Approaches and Distinctive Ways of Thinking.* Basingstoke, UK: Palgrave Macmillan, 2009. Print.

Entwistle, Noel J., and Ference Marton. "Changing Conceptions of Learning and Research." *The Experience of Learning: Implications for Teaching and Studying in Higher Education.* Ed. Ference Marton, Dai Hounsell, and Noel J. Entwistle. Edinburgh: Scottish Academic P, 1997. Print.

Gertler, Meric S. "The Undefinable Tacitness of Being (There): Tacit Knowledge and the Economic Geography of Context." *Journal of Economic Geography* 3 (2003): 75–99. Print.

Gibbs, Graham, and Claire Simpson. "Conditions Under Which Assessment Supports Student Learning. *Learning and Teaching in Higher Education* 1 (2004): 3–31. Print.

Hewison, Robert. *The Heritage Industry: Britain in a Climate of Decline.* London: Methuen, 1987. Print.

International Alliance of Research Universities. Web. 24 June 2011.

Lamet, S. A., and Maryelise Lamet. "The Effects of Study Abroad on Students." National Association of Foreign Student Advisers. Seattle, WA. May 1982. Conference Presentation.

Livingstone, David N. "Science, Text and Space: Thoughts on the Geography of Reading." *Transactions of the Institute of British Geographers* 30.4 (2005) 391–401. Print.

Martin, Peter. "The Death of Geography." *Financial Times* 22 Feb. 1996. Print.

Marton, Ference, and Roger Säljö. "On Qualitative Differences in Learning—1: Outcome and Process." *British Journal of Educational Psychology* 46 (1976): 4–11. Print.

—. "On Qualitative Differences in Learning—2: Outcome as a Function of the Learner's Conception of the Task." *British Journal of Educational Psychology* 46 (1976): 115–27. Print.

McAlpine, Lynn. "Designing Learning as Well as Teaching: A Research-Based Model for Instruction That Emphasizes Learner Practice." *Active Learning in Higher Education* 5.2 (2004): 119–34. Print.

Morgan, Kevin. "The Exaggerated Death of Geography: Learning, Proximity, and Territorial Innovation Systems." *Journal of Economic Geography* 4 (2004): 3–21. Print.

Nicol, David J., and Debra Macfarlane-Dick. "Formative Assessment and Self-Regulated Learning: A Model and Seven Principles of Good Feedback Practice." *Studies in Higher Education* 31.2 (2006): 199–218. Print.

Opper, Susan, Jerry Carlson, and Ulrich Teichler. *Impacts of Study Abroad Programmes on Students and Graduates.* London: Jessica Kingsley, 1990. Print.

Palfreyman, David, ed. *The Oxford Tutorial: "Thanks, You Taught Me How to Think."* 2nd ed. Oxford: OxCHEPS, 2008. Print.

Parker, Gabrielle, and Annie Rouxeville, eds. *The "Year Abroad": Preparation, Monitoring, Evaluation: Current Research and Development.* London: Association for French Language Studies, 1995. Print.

Pelowski, James Forney. "A Study of the Impact of the Cross-Cultural Education Program, the Winter Term Abroad, on the Alumnae of Lake Erie College for Women from 1953 through 1978." Diss. Michigan State U, 1979. Print.

Polanyi, Michael. *Personal Knowledge: Towards a Post-Critical Philosophy.* London: Routledge, 1998. Print.

Prosser, Michael, and Keith Trigwell. *Understanding Learning and Teaching: The Experience in Higher Education.* Buckingham, UK: Society for Research into Higher Education, 1999. Print.

Ramsden, Paul. *Learning to Teach in Higher Education.* 2nd ed. London: Routledge Falmer, 2003. Print.

Said, Edward W. *Orientalism.* London: Routledge and Kegan Paul, 1978. Print.

Säljö, Roger. "Learning in the Learner's Perspective. I. Some Common-Sense Conceptions." *Reports from the Institute of Education.* U of Gothenburg, 76 (1979). Print.

Sassen, Saskia. *The Global City: New York, London, Tokyo.* Princeton: Princeton UP, 1991. Print.

Secord, James A. *Victorian Sensation: The Extraordinary Publication, Reception, and Secret Authorship of "Vestiges of the Natural History of Creation."* Chicago: U of Chicago P, 2000. Print.

Sell, Deborah Kay. "Research on Attitude Change in U.S. Students Who Participate in Foreign Study Experiences: Past Findings and Suggestions for Future Research." *International Journal of Intercultural Relations* 7.2 (1983): 131–47. Print.

Watson, Nicola J. *The Literary Tourist: Readers and Places in Romantic and Victorian Britain.* Basingstoke, UK: Palgrave, 2006. Print.

Wenger, Etienne. *Communities of Practice: Learning, Meaning, and Identity*. New York: Cambridge UP, 1998. Print.

Wisker, Gina, ed. *Good Practice Working with International Students*. Birmingham, UK: Staff and Educational Development Association, 2000. Print.

CHAPTER 2

Transformation through Study Abroad: Critical Thinking and World Citizenship

A. Minh Nguyen

Eastern Kentucky University

An earlier version of this essay, "Study Abroad's Contribution to Critical Thinking and World Citizenship," was published in Think *11.31 (June 2012). 27–40. Print.*

Honors education is often associated with classical traditions, acknowledging the influence of ancient Greek and Roman philosophers on Western thought and endorsing the continued relevance of these classical roots for the modern student. This chapter articulates and defends two theses espoused by contemporary educational theorists Richard Paul and Linda Elder, related to this tradition. Creative thought and critical thought cannot be separated, and the intellectual traits constitutive of critical thinking are interdependent. The twin theses, combined with certain impact studies, demonstrate that study abroad enhances both creativity and criticality. The primary value of such gains resides in their potential to realize not only the Socratic ideal of rationality but also the Diogenean ideal of cosmopolitanism. The former consists in the cultivation of fair-minded, creative, and critical individuals and societies, whereas the latter consists in the cultivation of citizens of the world and the single community to which they belong. Developing and establishing these two theses, this chapter explores the classical philosophical underpinnings of honors international education and the intellectual growth it fosters and concludes with several recommendations that ensure the desired gain.

THE BENEFITS OF STUDY ABROAD

Study abroad is typically described as life changing. A defining moment, or so participants say, study abroad shapes a participant's life for years after the experience. In 2002, the Institute for the International Education of Students (IES) conducted the largest quantitative survey of study abroad alumni ever. Over 3,700 participants responded to questions regarding personal development, intercultural development, academic commitment, and career development. This data, which the Institute gathered from respondents who took part in IES-sponsored study abroad programs between the academic years of 1950–1951 and 1999–2000, is discussed by IES executives Mary M. Dwyer and Courtney K. Peters in *Transitions Abroad*. The results clearly show that study abroad "positively and unequivocally" influences the maturity, education, and career path of participating students (56).

Highlights of this extensive IES alumni survey, as reported by Dwyer and Peters, include the following:

- When asked about personal development, 96 percent said study abroad increased their self-confidence, 89 percent said it empowered them to tolerate ambiguity, and 84 percent said it caused them to modify their sociopolitical positions.

- When questioned about intercultural development, 98 percent said study abroad expanded their understanding of their own cultural values and biases, 82 percent said it helped them to develop a more refined way of looking at the world, and

90 percent said it inspired them to cultivate a more diverse circle of friends.

- When queried about academic commitment, 80 percent said study abroad raised their interest in academic study, 86 percent said it strengthened their commitment to foreign language study, and 64 percent said it influenced their decision to attend graduate school.

- When asked about career development, 62 percent said study abroad triggered an interest in a career direction pursued thereafter, 76 percent said it enabled them to acquire skill sets that influenced their career path, and 48 percent said it prompted them to engage in international work or volunteerism. (ctd. in Dwyer and Peters 56–57)

In a more lengthy discussion of this survey offered in *Frontiers: The Interdisciplinary Journal of Study Abroad*, Dwyer concludes "that study abroad has a significant impact on students in the areas of continued language use, academic attainment measures, intercultural and personal development, and career choices. Most importantly, the study illustrates that this impact can be sustained over a period as long as 50 years" (161).

BEYOND THE CULTURAL AND LINGUISTIC BENEFITS

How reliable are the self-report data just described? Given people's temptation to over report good behavior and underreport bad behavior, could the high percentage of respondents who claimed to have been positively transformed by their study abroad experience be an artifact of social desirability bias? While such a possibility cannot be ruled out, its actuality is yet to be established. Besides, a number of studies employ objective measurement tools, such as the pretest and posttest of specific skills, to confirm the advantages of study abroad beyond the cultural and linguistic benefits. Considering the improvement of creative thinking and communication skills, Tracy Rundstrom Williams shows that students who study abroad generally demonstrate a greater increase in intercultural communication skills after their time abroad than students who stay on campus ("Exploring" 356). Exposure to various cultures, furthermore, is the most reliable indicator of such skills.

Irvine Clarke, III, et al. show that students who participate in study abroad programs not only improve their intercultural communication skills to a greater degree than those who do not but also achieve a "significantly higher level of intercultural communication" after the experience than their stay-at-home counterparts (176). In addition, the former become more globally engaged and more open to cultural diversity than the latter.

Finally, living abroad boosts creativity. In a series of five studies, William W. Maddux and Adam D. Galinsky find a robust correlation between living overseas and enhanced creativity, identifying adaptation as the critical mechanism that underlies this linkage:

> Adaptation may be the key psychological element that explains why living abroad is associated with creativity. Because culture is such a pervasive force, impacting and shaping every aspect of one's life, adapting oneself to a new culture—learning how to behave and think in [a] different way—may make individuals chronically aware of multiple perspectives and approaches when dealing with mundane and novel situations and, thus, may be associated with increased creativity. (1054)

While traveling overseas might not enhance creative tendencies or capabilities for participants, living in a foreign land and adapting to a new culture would. To the extent that study abroad augments the chance of cultural adaptation, participants are poised to gain from enhanced creativity.

THE INSEPARABILITY OF CREATIVITY AND CRITICALITY

Study abroad promotes the development of not only creative thinking but also critical thinking for two reasons. According to the commonly accepted model of critical thinking designed and developed by Paul and Elder, critical thinking and creative thinking, writes Paul, are "so interwoven that neither can be separated from the other without an essential loss to both" (3–4).[1] Also, in line with the Paul-Elder Model, certain traits of mind, several of which study abroad has been shown to advance, constitute critical thinking, and the traits are interdependent. In other words, the acquisition, possession, retention, employment, development, and enrichment of one requires the acquisition, possession, retention, employment, development, and enrichment of the others, and critical thinking will be compromised if people are severely lacking in any of these traits (*Critical Thinking* 21–22). Because of the inseparability of critical thought and creative thought, as well as the interdependence of the intellectual traits constitutive of critical thinking, to the extent that study abroad promotes the development of creative thinking and constitutive traits such as intellectual humility and intellectual empathy, study abroad promotes the development of critical thinking.

Thinking, whether creative or critical, is a cognitive achievement. A deployment of mental abilities, thinking is something that the mind must work to attain. Creative thinking involves a process of molding and shaping, whereas critical thinking involves a process of judging and selecting. When engaged in sound thinking, especially in a self-reflective manner, people cannot help performing the creative and critical functions simultaneously. A mature mind cannot form high-quality thoughts without ascertaining their worth, and such ascertaining includes a critical component. Nor can the mind provide well-reasoned critiques absent creative effort because it has to envision alternative possibilities and craft the analyses and interpretations involved. To produce is to appraise; to evaluate is to generate. Creativity thus requires criticality, and vice versa. Overlapping and interacting with each other, they are integrated and inseparable aspects of excellence of thought. Insofar as the creative implies the critical, an improvement in creative thinking implies an improvement in critical thinking.

Some may oppose the Inseparability Thesis because it fails to delineate important distinctions and ultimately conflates two different ways of thinking. Opponents may invoke the following passage from Barry K. Beyer to justify their stance:

> Whereas creative thinking is divergent, critical thinking is convergent; whereas creative thinking tries to create something new, critical thinking seeks to assess worth or validity in something that exists; whereas creative thinking is carried on by violating accepted principles, critical thinking is carried on by applying accepted principles. Although creative and critical thinking may very well be different sides of the same coin, they are not identical. (35)

There are three reasons for rejecting the critique just outlined. First of all, to maintain the Inseparability Thesis is not to identify creativity with criticality. Inseparability is not identity. That Helen of Troy is inseparable from her lover Paris does not mean that they are numerically or qualitatively identical. Pursuing the analogy one step further, scholars may affirm, consistently with the Inseparability Thesis, the following propositions: that while all are blessed with some measure of creativity and criticality, people tend to have more of one than the other, sometimes in the extreme; that the extent to which the former can be deliberately cultivated is more limited than the latter; and that the twin qualities can be instantiated or activated to produce entirely different and unrelated end results.

Secondly, Beyer's objection assumes that the creative/critical distinction maps neatly onto the divergent/convergent distinction, but this assumption is tendentious. Logicians, mathematicians, and scientists can engage in convergent thinking by attempting to solve problems that admit one and only one solution, and do so in a creative manner. Isaac Newton invented differential and integral calculus in order to advance his inquiries into motion and gravitation and to solve the problems thereof. Similarly, writers, composers, and artists can engage in divergent thinking by forging new ideas and new inventions in a critical manner. Leonardo da Vinci's greatness as a painter and a sculptor was due in no small part to his profound analysis and interpretation of human anatomy. Newton's critical thinking is crucially divergent, whereas da Vinci's creative thinking is crucially convergent. This conclusion is consonant with both Joy Paul Guilford's hypothesis that divergent thinking and convergent thinking are two major components of the creative process and the finding that creative people deploy both forms of thinking well (46ff). Mihaly Csikszentmihalyi, who has extensively studied creative people, writes: "Divergent thinking is not much use without the ability to tell a good idea from a bad one—and this selectivity involves convergent thinking" (60–61).

Lastly, in the aptly titled essay "Mystery and Creation," Giorgio de Chirico, a Surrealist Italian painter, observes: "To become truly immortal, a work of art must escape all human limits: logic and common sense will only interfere. But once these barriers are broken, it will enter the realms of childhood visions and dreams" (58). This passage is reminiscent of Beyer's contention that "whereas creative thinking is carried on by violating accepted principles, critical thinking is carried on by applying accepted principles" (35). With all due respect to Beyer and de Chirico, even if artists somehow succeed in their deliberate attempt to defy logic or elude rationality in order to create a truly immortal work of art, their consciousness of what they are trying to defy or elude, together with their means-ends reasoning, indicate that whatever else it may be, their endeavor is still an exercise in critical thinking.

An inseparable connection exists between creativity and criticality. One is an indispensable component of rather than a subsidiary complement to the other. Since the acquisition, possession, retention, employment, development, and enrichment of one requires the same of the other, teachers cannot afford to educate their students on the unfounded assumption that creative thinking and critical thinking are segregated without compromising their ability to attain both. A cognitively integrated and holistic approach to education is recommended. Furthermore, creativity and critical-ity should be concurrently and conjointly cultivated across the cur-riculum. All else being equal, a course or program of study should not be favored or disfavored simply because it is more creative than critical, or more critical than creative, as traditionally conceived. Creative thinking and critical thinking function best in tandem.

THE INTERDEPENDENCE OF INTELLECTUAL TRAITS

Paul and Elder conceive of critical thinking as "the art of ana-lyzing and evaluating thinking with a view to improving it" (*Miniature Guide* 2). Requiring "rigorous standards of excellence and mindful command of their use," critical thinking, they write, is "self-directed, self-disciplined, self-monitored, and self-corrective thinking" (*Miniature Guide* 2). Their conception of critical think-ing as an art notwithstanding, Paul and Elder insist that it is more than just mastering a certain set of skills. Since it defines one's char-acter, critical thinking involves the possession of a certain set of traits, the habit of exercising these traits, and the commitment to accept and employ the results thereof to guide one's behavior. In accordance with the Paul-Elder Model, the traits characteristically present in critical thinkers include intellectual humility, intellec-tual courage, intellectual empathy, intellectual perseverance, intel-lectual integrity, intellectual autonomy, confidence in reason, and fair-mindedness.[2]

Establishing the Interdependence Thesis is complicated. Intel-lectual humility, for example, consists in the Socratic knowledge of one's own ignorance. To realize what they know and do not know, people need both intellectual integrity and intellectual courage. Intellectual integrity enables them to be true to their own thinking and to recognize the limits of their knowledge as well as the limita-tions of their point of view, whereas intellectual courage enables them to squarely face their own biases, prejudices, and whatever else is responsible for their own cognitive shortcomings. Intellec-tual integrity and intellectual courage, in turn, require intellectual autonomy and intellectual empathy, respectively.

The reason intellectual integrity requires intellectual autonomy is that intellectual integrity consists in being true to one's own thinking, being consistent in the application of the standards one uses to assess one's own thinking, holding oneself to the same robust standards of evidence one expects others to meet, and acknowledging inconsistencies in one's own thought-feeling-action matrix. These are nothing but different forms of thinking for oneself in accordance with standards of rationality, and such thinking for oneself constitutes intellectual autonomy. Since thinking for oneself in accordance with standards of rationality is challenging, especially when one must face and address ideas toward which one has strong negative emotions and to which one has yet to give a serious hearing, intellectual autonomy and thus intellectual integrity require intellectual courage. Both also require intellectual perseverance: because of the demands of thinking for oneself and taking responsibility for one's own thinking, one constantly needs to stick to the true and the relevant and use one's knowledge and insight to the optimum level despite obstacles and difficulties, especially when the struggle with uncertainty and confusion may persist for an extended period.

As asserted above, intellectual courage requires intellectual empathy. To discover their own biases and prejudices, people often must entertain views that differ from their own and reason from premises with which they disagree. Like intellectual autonomy and intellectual integrity, intellectual empathy requires intellectual perseverance in addition to the generosity and flexibility of mind that enables people to switch from one perspective to another. Penetrating a paradigm toward which they harbor hostility takes time and effort. The same holds true for rectifying if not eradicating people's egocentric and sociocentric penchant for identifying truth with their own immediate perceptions or longstanding beliefs.[3]

Likewise, intellectual empathy requires confidence in reason and fair-mindedness, in addition to creativity and imagination. People's attempt to put themselves in the place of others to understand their ideas will be unwarranted unless they have sufficient trust in reason to believe they will not be contaminated by whatever is false or misleading in the alternative perspective under consideration.

Faith in reason and the conviction that they will not be harmed by considering novel or foreign viewpoints are not sufficient, however, to motivate most people to consider them seriously. The motivation must also derive from an intellectual sense of justice.

All viewpoints are equal in the sense that they face the same tribunal of reason and are subject to the same standards of rationality. Fair-minded thinkers do not discriminate against any viewpoint because of their own feelings or vested interests, or the feelings or vested interests of members of any group to which they belong. Applying the same intellectual standards through and through, they treat all viewpoints alike, without reference to their own advantage or the advantage of any of their groups. Consequently, if people are committed to the fair play of reason, they have to be just to the views they oppose and consider them in their strongest form so as not to dismiss or disparage them out of ignorance or bias. To discharge this duty, people need intellectual humility.

THE CULTIVATION OF CRITICAL THINKING

The empirical data presented above supports the claim that study abroad spurs the growth of a number of intellectual traits. Again, as Dwyer and Peters report, the survey conducted by the Institute for the International Education of Students, which elicited feedback from 3,723 study abroad alumni, noted that 98 percent said study abroad expanded their understanding of their own cultural biases, and 82 percent said it helped them to develop a more sophisticated way of looking at the world. In addition, 84 percent said it caused them to modify their sociopolitical positions, and 64 percent said it encouraged them to explore cultures different from their own. Eighty-nine percent said it empowered them to tolerate ambiguity, and 90 percent said it inspired them to cultivate a more diverse circle of friends. Eighty-six percent said it strengthened their commitment to foreign language study, and 64 percent said it influenced their decision to attend graduate school (56–57). This evidence supports the hypothesis that study abroad furthers the development of intellectual humility, intellectual courage, intellectual empathy, and intellectual perseverance, respectively.

The results of Williams's impact study, which relies on more than just self-report measures, indicate that study abroad students generally demonstrate an increase or enhancement in each of the following: understanding of international and cultural issues; flexibility and adaptability in new environments; tolerance toward and comfortability with people of culturally diverse backgrounds; open-mindedness and curiosity; and critical skills such as resourcefulness, creative thinking, problem solving, decision making, socialization, negotiation, leadership, and teamwork in culturally diverse settings ("Reflective Model" 289–306).[4]

Given the interdependence of intellectual traits, if study abroad furthers the development of intellectual humility, intellectual courage, intellectual empathy, and intellectual perseverance, it also furthers the development of intellectual integrity, intellectual autonomy, confidence in reason, and fair-mindedness. All intellectual traits involved in critical thinking are thus enhanced, and so is critical thinking itself. The constitutive relation between intellectual traits and critical thinking makes it a category mistake to think that one could enhance the former without enhancing the latter. The mistake is akin to the logical or conceptual confusion that visitors to the National Mall in Washington, D.C., exhibit when, after having seen the polished black granite panels with the names etched on them of over 58,000 men and women in the U.S. military who were either killed or missing in action during the Vietnam War, they ask to be shown the Vietnam Veterans Memorial. To cultivate the critical traits of mind in students, as Elder and Paul assert, is to cultivate critical thinkers (35).

THE SOCRATIC IDEAL OF RATIONALITY

Scholars widely acknowledge that Socrates was a critical thinker *par excellence*.[5] As evidenced by Plato's Dialogues, Socrates manifested all intellectual traits constitutive of critical thinking. He demonstrated intellectual humility by professing ignorance of the truth of the matter under discussion, whether it be piety (*Euthyphro*), justice (*Republic*), friendship (*Lysis*), or knowledge (*Theaetetus*).[6] He demonstrated intellectual courage by challenging the prevailing ideas and practices of his day, whether they be about temperance (*Charmides*), love (*Symposium*), beauty (*Hippias Major*), or courage (*Laches*). He demonstrated intellectual empathy by accurately stating, developing, and refining the positions with which he disagreed, all the while making respectful references to other cultures such as Egypt (*Phaedrus*), Persia (*Laws* and *Phaedrus*), and of course Atlantis (*Critias* and *Timaeus*). He demonstrated intellectual perseverance by struggling with substantive and difficult issues such as the above and adhering to rational principles despite irrational resistance from others.

A nonconformist with a penchant for questioning the status quo, Socrates displayed intellectual autonomy by thinking through issues on his own rather than uncritically accepting what he was told by his peers or established theological heavyweights such as Homer and Hesiod. A single-standard advocate striving to lead an examined life, he displayed intellectual integrity by holding himself to the same set of principles by which he expected others to abide. A man of reason eager to give up his own view when another is shown to be more reasonable and hostile to the idea of privileging any party's interests including his own, he displayed fair-mindedness by considering all relevant alternatives and thinking within such standpoints in order to appreciate them and be swayed by them when the evidence warranted it. An archenemy of sophistry and disputation, he displayed confidence in reason by observing the principles of sound reasoning when persuading others of his position and deeming it less important to win an argument than to see the issue from a logical point of view and in all its complexity.

The upshot of the preceding considerations is that Socrates was both a proponent and an exemplar of a quite demanding paradigm of critical thinking. In augmenting critical thinking, therefore, study abroad makes a contribution to the realization of the Socratic ideal of rationality. Such a contribution consists in cultivating fair-minded, creative, and critical individuals and societies. Socrates incarnates individual criticality or critical thinking in a person. Here is William Graham Sumner's oft-quoted characterization of a critical society:

The critical habit of thought, if usual in a society, will pervade all its mores, because it is a way of taking up the problems of life. Men educated in it cannot be stampeded by stump orators. . . . They are slow to believe. They can hold things as possible or probable in all degrees, without certainty and without pain. They can wait for evidence and weigh evidence, uninfluenced by the emphasis or confidence with which assertions are made. . . . They can resist appeals to their dearest prejudices and all kinds of cajolery. Education in the critical faculty is the only education . . . that . . . makes good citizens. (633)

Since critical thinking is "a prime condition of human welfare" and "our only guarantee against delusion, deception, superstition, and misapprehension," Sumner concludes that "education is good just so far as it produces [a] well-developed critical faculty" (633).

THE DIOGENEAN IDEAL OF COSMOPOLITANISM

In addition to fostering critical individuals and societies, study abroad cultivates citizens of the world and the single community to which they belong. Study abroad thus makes a contribution to the realization of the Diogenean ideal of cosmopolitanism, so named in honor of Diogenes the Cynic, a Socratically inspired Greek philosopher credited with being the first thinker in the West to have called himself, according to Pauline Kleingeld and Eric Brown, a "citizen of the world [*kosmopolitês*]" (par. 5). Just as certain traits and habits characterize the critical way of life, so too certain virtues and commitments exemplify the cosmopolitan mode of being. Just as study abroad develops the critical traits and habits, so too it fosters the cosmopolitan virtues and commitments.

In *Cosmopolitanism: Ethics in a World of Strangers*, Kwame Anthony Appiah articulates and defends an attractive cosmopolitan position, which he dubs "partial" or "rooted" cosmopolitanism (xvii). Partial cosmopolitans, observes Appiah, "take sides neither with the nationalist who abandons all foreigners nor with the hardcore cosmopolitan who regards her friends and fellow citizens with icy impartiality" (xvi–xvii), while rooted cosmopolitans affirm that "loyalties and local allegiances . . . determine who we are" and that "a creed that disdains partialities of kinfolk and community may have a past, but it has no future" (xviii). In accordance with Appiah's crisp formulation of cosmopolitanism as "universality plus difference" (151), cosmopolitan virtues include concern for others on account of shared humanity and respect for legitimate differences in thought and action (xv), whereas cosmopolitan commitments include commitments to universal truth, tolerance, pluralism, and fallibilism (144). Pluralism, he asserts, is the view that "there are many values worth living by and that you cannot live by all of them"; for pluralists, it is neither surprising nor undesirable that different people and different societies subscribe to different values (144). Fallibilism, which Appiah also calls "epistemic humility," is the view that "our knowledge is imperfect, provisional, subject to revision in the face of new evidence"; knowing they do not have all the answers, fallibilists are humble enough to think they may learn from others (144). Since Appiah-style commitments to universal truth, tolerance, pluralism, and fallibilism (epistemic humility) share a strong family resemblance to confidence in reason, intellectual empathy, intellectual integrity, and intellectual humility *à la* Paul and Elder, respectively, to the extent that study abroad enables participants to develop these traits of mind, it strengthens their cosmopolitan commitments and therefore helps realize not only the Socratic ideal but also the Diogenean ideal (cf. Nussbaum, *Cultivating Humanity*, 15–84; Nussbaum, *Not for Profit*, 47–94).

In the spirit of global learning, a broadened frame of reference demonstrates that study abroad also realizes the Confucian ideal of self-cultivation and the Daoist ideal of transcending oppositions. Confucius advocates critical thinking in *Analects* 2:15 and 4:15 because, for him, reflection on the materials of knowledge and reflection on oneself are both essential to learning (Kim 71; Richey, par. 17; Riegel, par. 20).[7] Because of its idealization of wholeness plus independence as well as commitment to what Erica Brindley calls "cosmic and holistic individualism" (130), religious studies scholar Ninian Smart argues that Daoism bears some affinity to the universality-plus-difference cosmopolitan thinking that stipulates global obligations and celebrates local diversities (142).

MODEST PROPOSALS

I would like to conclude with several schematic proposals for ensuring intellectual growth in study abroad students. Study abroad, while not inexpensive, fosters the development of "informed, critical, and creative thinkers who communicate effectively," to borrow a signature phrase from my university's Quality Enhancement Plan (*QEP Executive Summary*). Since such development is crucial at all levels of education, subject to the relevant budgetary constraints, study abroad ought to be part of any significant institutional effort to promote critical and creative thinking, with its operations integrated into and aligned with the institution's strategy, structure, and processes so as to achieve high levels of logistical performance. Additionally, educators ought to develop strategies for recruiting and retaining a large and varied pool of participants so that, providing all are in good academic and disciplinary standing as well as in good physical and mental health, both students who want to study abroad and students who need to study abroad are encouraged to participate, with the latter accorded priority. Furthermore, global learning ought to be integrated into general education courses and generally throughout the curriculum such that students' coursework, internships, and service experiences enhance their preparation for the study abroad experience, which then becomes a kind of capstone in the general education curriculum.

Because adaptation is the critical mechanism that underlies the robust correlation between living overseas and enhanced creativity, study abroad curricula and programs ought to be structured in such a way as to increase participants' chance for adapting to the culture of the host country. If participants form a hermetic community in which they live and interact primarily with others from their own culture, and being in too large a group from one's own country often encourages this behavior, they may fail to take full advantage of the opportunity to improve their creative and thus critical thinking. Conversely, host institutions should make every effort to help visiting international students, scholars, and their families adapt to the local culture so that they all gain from enhanced creativity and criticality.[8]

The ideas of classical thinkers from Socrates and Diogenes to Confucius and Lao-Tzu provide philosophical underpinnings for international education in general and honors international education in particular. Honors education, as C. Grey Austin defines it, "consists of the total means by which a college or university seeks to meet the educational needs of its ablest and most highly motivated students" (5). That a wide array of contemporary social, political, economic, and environmental problems can be solved only on a global scale is increasingly clear. Such problems require a new generation of critical and creative thinkers who cultivate an appropriately cosmopolitan consciousness and approach the problems through that lens. Highly able, highly motivated, and highly likely to succeed, honors students who partake in study abroad programs and attune themselves to the vibrations of international life are uniquely positioned to lead and serve in the vanguard of global change.[9]

NOTES

[1]For other models of critical thinking, see Beyer; Burden and Byrd; Ennis; Facione; Halpern; Moore and Parker; Nosich; and Stahl and Stahl. That these models are not necessarily incompatible with one another is worth noting; indeed, they may very well be complementary. Making that case would require considerable work and go beyond the scope of this paper.

[2]A comment about terminology is in order. In their extensive body of work on critical thinking, Paul and Elder use the following expressions synonymously: "intellectual traits," "intellectual virtues," "traits of mind," "virtues of mind," and "habits of mind." I prefer "intellectual virtues" and "virtues of mind" to the rest because virtues are excellences and hence admirable qualities, whereas traits and habits can be good or bad. In what follows, I will use "intellectual traits" and "traits of mind" because Paul and Elder favor them and I want my usage to align with theirs to avoid confusion.

[3]Since intellectual empathy is one of the essential traits of a critical thinker, critical thinking encompasses not only creative thinking but also empathetic thinking. Critical thinking involves distancing oneself from the objects of critical thought and assessing them according to rigorous standards of excellence, thereby helping one decenter and overcome egocentric or otherwise faulty thinking. The maintenance of such distance, however, does not preclude empathetic engagement with alternative perspectives. Far from necessitating unconcern or detachment, taking a step back from one's own mental states plays a vital role in expanding one's circle of thinking about thinking and feeling about feeling and enabling one to think what others think and feel what others feel from their vantage point. Through exposure to other cultures and people, one can come to critically and empathetically engage with alternative ways of being that were once inscrutable and elicited indifference if not contempt.

[4]For other useful discussions of the impact of study abroad, see the essay by Doug Reilly and Stefan Senders, which focuses upon critical and global perspectives and the development of global citizenship; Karen Rodriguez's exploration of values development through study abroad; and Atsuko Sajiki's study of intellectual empathy.

[5]For discussions of the Socratic method and its value in undergraduate education today, see Elder's "Reason to Live," William Hare's discussion of the notion of Socratic open-mindedness, and Martha C. Nussbaum's extensive discussion of the Socratic method in her text, *Cultivating Humanity: A Classical Defense of Reform in Liberal Education*.

[6]Strictly speaking, I should have used "Plato's Socrates" instead of "Socrates," since it is doubtful that Plato's portrayal of his teacher is historically accurate. As a matter of fact, one Socrates scholar, Debra Nails, has gone so far as to say that "all our information about him is second-hand and most of it vigorously disputed" (par. 1). To avoid prolixity, however, I shall continue to use the truncated expression.

[7]Compare the following teaching of the Buddha:

> It is fitting for you to be perplexed, . . . it is fitting for you to be in doubt. . . . Do not go by oral tradition, by lineage of teaching, by hearsay, by a collection of scriptures, by logical reasoning, by inferential reasoning, by reflection on reasons, by the acceptance of a view after pondering it, by the seeming competence of a speaker, or because you think, "The ascetic is our teacher." But when you know for yourselves, "These things are unwholesome; these things are blamable; these things are censured by the wise; these things, if undertaken and practiced, lead to harm and suffering," then you should abandon them. (Thera and Bodhi 65)

What is striking about the above passage is that it encourages critical thinking even about logical reasoning, inferential reasoning, and reflection on reasons.

[8]By and large, winter and summer study abroad programs are relatively brief, intensive, and hermetic. While great fun and not particularly unaffordable, they tend not to make much life-changing difference. In contrast, semester-long and year-long exchange student programs typically require immersion and enculturation. Such long-term adjustments are likely to matter more. Of course, short-term service-learning projects with visits to Nike factories in Bangladesh, cholera clinics in Haiti, or AIDS orphanages in Zimbabwe may nonetheless be high-impact for some participants, whether they visit and serve such communities for the first time or step back and realize that similar problems exist at home. The difference is one of degree and not of kind. Properly designed and implemented, both short-term and long-term study abroad programs cultivate excellence. As Manzan Dohaku, a Japanese Soto Zen master, puts it, "One minute of sitting, one inch of Buddha" (qtd. in Stryk and Ikemoto 35). Similarly, one month of study abroad, one yard of excellence; one semester, several yards; one year, many yards. It is worth pointing out in this connection that there are many legitimate ways to develop critical and cosmopolitan thinking. One is to study abroad. Another is to major or minor in Global or International Studies. Less

complicated, expensive, and time-consuming albeit less impactful is to watch one movie with subtitles a month, as Appiah advises today's youth (Aguila, par. 1). In sum, we need both types of study abroad because—academic, financial, medical, psychological, and personal issues aside—some people just want to get their feet wet. It is good to do so, but it is better, all else being equal, to go and stay, and not surround oneself with too many compatriots too often.

[9]I would like to thank the following individuals for their generous assistance during the research and writing of this essay: Ogechi Anyanwu, Mike Austin, Hal Blythe, Lisa Day-Lindsey, Laura Earles, Yaw Frimpong-Mansoh, Dana Fritz, Sanford Goldberg, Todd Gooch, Michele Gore, Anne Gossage, Todd Hartch, Samuel Hinton, Alban Holyoke, Barbara Hussey, Manyul Im, Mustapha Jourdini, Steve Kilburn, Paula Kristofik, Hung Le, Erik Liddell, Dana McClain, Joshua McKeown, Marianella Machado, Cuong Mai, Amy Martin, Aaron Pardieu, Gyan Pradhan, Patrick Puckett, Jeff Richey, Fred Ruppel, Bob Sandmeyer, Bernardo Scarambone, Rob Sica, Justin Smith, John Taylor, Abraham Vélez, David Weberman, Kate Williams, Steffen Wilson, Matthew Winslow, and Sara Zeigler. Special thanks to the Editors—Kim Klein and Mary Kay Mulvaney—as well as Jeffrey Portnoy, Frank Williams, Neil Wright, and particularly Nhi Huynh, all of whom read multiple drafts, for their patience, support, and encouragement.

WORKS CITED

Aguila, Sissi. "Kwame Appiah Discusses 'World Citizenship' at FIU." *FIU News* 23 Apr. 2010. Web. 23 July 2013.

Appiah, Kwame Anthony. *Cosmopolitanism: Ethics in a World of Strangers*. New York: Norton, 2006. Print.

Austin, C. Grey. "Orientation to Honors Education." *Fostering Academic Excellence Through Honors Programs*. Ed. Paul G. Friedman and Reva C. Jenkins-Friedman. New Directions for Teaching and Learning, No. 25. San Francisco: Jossey-Bass, 1986. 5–16. Print.

Beyer, Barry K. *Practical Strategies for the Teaching of Thinking.* Boston: Allyn and Bacon, 1987. Print.

Brindley, Erica. *Individualism in Early China: Human Agency and the Self in Thought and Politics.* Honolulu: U of Hawaii P, 2010. Print.

Burden, Paul R., and David M. Byrd. *Methods for Effective Teaching: Meeting the Needs of All Students.* 5th ed. Boston: Allyn and Bacon, 2009. Print.

Clarke III, Irvine, et al. "Student Intercultural Proficiency from Study Abroad Programs." *Journal of Marketing Education* 31.2 (2009): 173–81. Print.

Confucius. *Analects with Selections from Traditional Commentaries.* Trans. Edward G. Slingerland. Indianapolis, IN: Hackett, 2003. Print.

Csikszentmihalyi, Mihaly. *Creativity: Flow and the Psychology of Discovery and Invention.* New York: Harper, 1996. Print.

de Chirico, Giorgio. "Mystery and Creation." *Art in Theory, 1900-2000: An Anthology of Changing Ideas.* 2nd ed. Ed. Charles Harrison and Paul Wood. Malden, MA: Blackwell, 2002. 58. Print.

Dwyer, Mary M. "More Is Better: The Impact of Study Abroad Program Duration." *Frontiers: The Interdisciplinary Journal of Study Abroad* 10 (2004): 151–63. Print.

Dwyer, Mary M., and Courtney K. Peters. "The Benefits of Study Abroad: New Study Confirms Significant Gains." *Transitions Abroad* 27.5 (2004): 56–57. Print.

Elder, Linda. "Reason to Live." *Times Higher Education* 18 Feb. 2009. Web. 28 June 2011.

Elder, Linda, and Richard Paul. "Critical Thinking: Developing Intellectual Traits." *Journal of Developmental Education* 21.3 (1998): 34–35. Print.

Ennis, Robert H. *Critical Thinking.* Upper Saddle River, NJ: Prentice Hall, 1995. Print.

Facione, Peter A. *Critical Thinking: A Statement of Expert Consensus for Purposes of Educational Assessment and Instruction.* Millbrae, CA: California Academic, 1990. Print.

Guilford, Joy Paul. *The Nature of Human Intelligence.* New York: McGraw-Hill, 1967. Print.

Halpern, Diane F. *Thought and Knowledge: An Introduction to Critical Thinking.* 4th ed. Mahwah, NJ: Lawrence Erlbaum, 2003. Print.

Hare, William. "Socratic Open-Mindedness." *Paideusis* 18.1 (2009): 5–16. Print.

Kim, Hye-Kyung. "Critical Thinking, Learning and Confucius: A Positive Assessment." *Journal of Philosophy of Education* 37.1 (2003): 71–87. Print.

Kleingeld, Pauline, and Eric Brown. "Cosmopolitanism." *The Stanford Encyclopedia of Philosophy.* Ed. Edward N. Zalta. Stanford U, 2011. Web. 28 June 2011.

Maddux, William W., and Adam D. Galinsky. "Cultural Borders and Mental Barriers: The Relationship Between Living Abroad and Creativity." *Journal of Personality and Social Psychology* 96.5 (2009): 1047–61. Print.

Moore, Brooke Noel, and Richard Parker. *Critical Thinking.* 10th ed. New York: McGraw-Hill, 2011. Print.

Nails, Debra. "Socrates." *The Stanford Encyclopedia of Philosophy.* Ed. Edward N. Zalta. Stanford U, 2010. Web. 28 June 2011.

Nguyen, A. Minh. "Study Abroad's Contribution to Critical Thinking and World Citizenship." *Think* 11.31 (June 2012). 27–40. Print.

Nosich, Gerald M. *Learning to Think Things Through: A Guide to Critical Thinking Across the Curriculum.* 4th ed. Upper Saddle River, NJ: Prentice Hall, 2011. Print.

Nussbaum, Martha C. *Cultivating Humanity: A Classical Defense of Reform in Liberal Education.* Cambridge: Harvard UP, 1997. Print.

—. *Not for Profit: Why Democracy Needs the Humanities.* Princeton, NJ: Princeton UP, 2010. Print.

Paul, Richard. *The Thinker's Guide to the Nature and Functions of Critical and Creative Thinking.* Dillon Beach, CA: Foundation for Critical Thinking, 2008. Print.

Paul, Richard, and Linda Elder. *Critical Thinking: Tools for Taking Charge of Your Learning and Your Life.* 2nd ed. Upper Saddle River, NJ: Prentice Hall, 2005. Print.

—. *The Miniature Guide to Critical Thinking: Concepts and Tools.* 6th ed. Tomales, CA: Foundation for Critical Thinking, 2009. Print.

QEP Executive Summary. Eastern Kentucky University, 2007. Web. 18 May 2013.

Reilly, Doug, and Stefan Senders. "Becoming the Change We Want to See: Critical Study Abroad for a Tumultuous World." *Frontiers: The Interdisciplinary Journal of Study Abroad* 18 (2009): 241–67. Print.

Richey, Jeffrey. "Confucius." *The Internet Encyclopedia of Philosophy.* Ed. James Fieser and Bradley Dowden. U of Tennessee at Martin, 2003. Web. 5 Aug. 2011.

Riegel, Jeffrey. "Confucius." *The Stanford Encyclopedia of Philosophy.* Ed. Edward N. Zalta. Stanford U, 2011. Web. 5 Aug. 2011.

Rodriguez, Karen. "Cultivating Empathy and Empowerment among Cultural Others: Values Education and Study Abroad." *Journal of College and Character* 4.4 (2003). NASPA Foundation. Web. 28 June 2011.

Sajiki, Atsuko. *Intellectual Empathy as a Tool of Cross-Cultural Learning: United States Students in Study Abroad Program in Japan.* Diss. Indiana U. Ann Arbor: ProQuest/UMI, 2006. Publication No. AAT 3215207. Print.

Smart, Ninian. *World Philosophies.* New York: Routledge, 1999. Print.

Stahl, Nancy N., and Robert J. Stahl. "We Can Agree after All! Achieving Consensus for a Critical Thinking Component of a Gifted Program Using the Delphi Technique." *Roeper Review* 14.2 (1991): 79–88. Print.

Stryk, Lucien, and Takashi Ikemoto, eds. and trans. *Zen Poetry: Let the Spring Breeze Enter.* New York: Grove, 1995. Print.

Sumner, William Graham. *Folkways: A Study of the Sociological Importance of Usages, Manners, Customs, Mores, and Morals.* Boston: Ginn, 1906. Print.

Thera, Nyanaponika, and Bhikkhu Bodhi, trans. *Numerical Discourses of the Buddha: An Anthology of Suttas from the Anguttara Nikāya.* Walnut Creek, CA: AltaMira, 1999. Print.

Williams, Tracy Rundstrom. "Exploring the Impact of Study Abroad on Students' Intercultural Communication Skills: Adaptability and Sensitivity." *Journal of Studies in International Education* 9.4 (2005): 356–71. Print.

—. "The Reflective Model of Intercultural Competency: A Multidimensional, Qualitative Approach to Study Abroad Assessment." *Frontiers: The Interdisciplinary Journal of Study Abroad* 18 (2009): 289–306. Print.

CHAPTER 3

Short-Term International City as Text™ Pedagogy: A High-Impact Educational Practice

Mary Kay Mulvaney
Elmhurst College

For anyone who has ever taught a study abroad course, establishing anecdotally the powerful impact of the experience on students is not difficult. They frequently report learning more than they thought possible, wishing they had stayed longer, and gaining greater self-confidence for approaching new situations. Educators can further enrich an international setting, which offers the irreplaceable value of exploring a new culture firsthand, through the utilization of City as Text™ pedagogy, yielding both academic and personal development benefits. Combining that approach with onsite undergraduate research constitutes a "high-impact educational practice," in the sense defined by the American Association of Colleges & Universities (Kuh 1). Such practices, increasingly widespread on campuses across the nation, include undergraduate research, service learning, and internships. These practices, which promote genuine or deep learning, are commonly characterized by six hallmarks, according to Susan Elrod, Diane Husic, and Jillian Kinzie, "that demand meaningful faculty and peer interaction; help students connect their learning to real world settings; occur in the context of a coherent and challenging curriculum; provide students with frequent feedback; require time on task; and challenge students to think in new ways and respond to novel situations" (5). Quality international study experiences reflect most or all of these hallmarks. Consequently, they require detailed planning and careful attention to rigor throughout.

This chapter reviews the City as Text™ approach and its theoretical underpinnings, considers the combination of City as Text™ pedagogy with undergraduate research as an exemplification of such a high-impact educational practice, and focuses upon this combination in a course taught in London and Oxford.

Much has been written about City as Text™ pedagogy as a method of active, experiential, or applied learning, particularly in *Place as Text: Approaches to Active Learning*, an earlier publication in the NCHC Monograph Series. And certainly, City as Text™ is familiar to NCHC members as a significant component of the annual conference, a major structural feature of Honors Semesters, and the essence of Faculty Summer Institutes, in which faculty simultaneously research and implement this valuable pedagogy in cities across the nation. Adapting this approach as a frame for an international honors course is flexible and highly rewarding for faculty and students alike.

Understanding a city as a text to be read with the same attention to detail that any worthy text deserves requires paying attention to language, faces, customs, and nuances. One of my recent student participants observed in an exit response: "City as Text™ courses really encourage you to explore and interact with your surroundings at a new level. You're reading the city like a book, so you pay attention to every little detail—the inscriptions on statues, the clothing style of the guy next to you on the Tube, the headlines on the daily newspaper." In short, City as Text™ requires participants to slowly discover the values, reveal the priorities, and recognize the history layered within a given place.

A significant element of the City as Text™ pedagogy is the use of "walkabouts," explained in detail by Bernice Braid in *Place as Text: Approaches to Active Learning*. Essentially, walkabouts are pre-planned explorations that provide enough structure for small groups of participants to have a sense of purpose within a specific location for a four- or five-hour period, and yet, enough lack of structure to allow for genuine discovery and idiosyncratic observations along the way. This process enables students to create a mental and physical map of an area and to begin gathering details and data that later will be articulated in journal reflections and then into synthesized observations and hypotheses as students proceed to read and characterize the given place as a text—written upon by years, perhaps centuries, of human interaction, preservation, destruction, invention, and re-invention.

As Braid points out, such walkabouts, typically performed in small groups of three to five, allow for both personal and collaborative investigations, onsite interpretations, and collegial support. Participants are directed to a specific neighborhood or area, and they usually determine the path to it by using public transportation. This element is a particularly valuable, even if occasionally frustrating, aspect of international travel because of the popularity of public transportation in most major cities abroad. The walkabout brings students, writes Braid, into "uncharted territory" to observe as first-timers the characteristics and activities of a site ("City as Text™" 23). Walkabouts should include time for purchasing meals along the way since observing local customs and conversations over the exchange of food and money can provide valuable insights into a city's personality and values. Students are always encouraged to observe and reflect on the textual meaning of locals' behaviors, such as lingering over a glass of wine in sidewalk cafes facing the Champs Élysées or pouring over the daily newspapers on the subway in Berlin or adhering to the custom of afternoon cream tea in Oxford.

While participating in the NCHC Faculty Institute in Chicago in 2010, I recall being struck by the rich detail that results from an opportunity to read a city during a walkabout. Sent as a team to an older Chicago near north-side neighborhood known as Logan Square, our group learned the value of paying close attention to detail within the first few blocks. Exiting the CTA Blue Line at the Logan Square stop, I immediately noticed two fascinating indicators of the evolving history of this area. Directly across from the subway entrance stood an aging brick church, the Norwegian Lutheran Memorial Church, with a cornerstone date of 1912. I recalled from a Chicago history article that this neighborhood was originally settled by Scandinavian immigrants beginning in the late nineteenth century. Today, directly in front of the church, just outside the subway steps, a tiny garden holds a sign in Spanish, *prohibido pisar el césped*. The request to passersby to avoid the grass obviously takes for granted viewers read Spanish. In fact, this area has supported a large Puerto Rican population for the past thirty years or so, bringing vastly different traditions than its Scandinavian predecessors.

Heading across the square, we stopped to examine the large stone obelisk reminiscent of early twentieth-century American patriotic fervor, which we discovered commemorates the 1918 State of Illinois Centennial. The classic American eagle atop the obelisk towered over a stone frieze that depicted scenes of strong Nordic- and Aryan-looking men tilling the fields, defending the soil, and crushing the American Indians who initially inhabited this prairie land. We were struck by the irony of this contrast of the celebration of this male-dominated, white, ethnocentric, isolationist culture of early twentieth-century America, side-by-side with the obvious embrace of generations of multi-cultural changes. This irony was further complicated upon our stroll across the square to the tiny, heavily populated Lula Café, where we soon entered into a fascinating conversation with a middle-aged couple who were café regulars and longtime residents of this neighborhood. They clearly embraced the rich diversity of the area, ignored the occasional gang activity, and indicated their disdain for the encroaching yuppies currently in the process of gentrifying this largely working-class neighborhood. Within an hour or so of close observation, we were gradually unraveling the rich and complex history of this small section of the city, a section not routinely visited by tourists, who typically concentrate largely on the downtown lakefront or world-famous attractions like the Art Institute or the Field Museum. In the course of our walkabout, we were learning about the real Chicago, where people lived and worked, battled urban challenges, passed along traditions, and reinforced values for good or ill. Indeed, the potential of urban walkabouts is nearly limitless. Echoing Elrod, Husic, and Kinzie, walkabouts provide "meaningful faculty and student interaction . . . challeng[ing] students to think in new ways and respond to novel situations" (5). City as Text™ teaches students to be attentive to detail, to search for connections, and to reflect upon observations in writing, and then to compare observations and synthesize reactions.

Follow-up time for written reflection is extremely important in a City as Text™ course. Students keep a daily journal, continually re-assessing exactly what they have observed and gradually building a characterization of a place, a people, and a culture. They understand a place as a rich mosaic of history, contemporary challenges, and the concurrent mindless business of everyday existence that gradually coalesces into a fascinating human tale. Providing frequent feedback to students and facilitating group discussions to synthesize observations are imperative to the success of a course like this and, indeed, to any high-impact educational practice. Discussions inevitably provoke additional observations, arming the next day's teams' mini-ethnographic forays with an increasingly complex lens through which to observe and simultaneously participate in the local culture at hand. Gradually, students' writing will become more informed and more insightful and provoke curiosity, launching more complex research. Replicating this structure is possible in nearly any location; understanding the theoretical underpinnings of this pedagogy enriches faculty preparation and ultimately enhances the educational experience of students.

City as Text™ pedagogy sits comfortably within today's increasing emphasis on applied learning, experiential education, an interdisciplinary approach to the social construction of knowledge, and the notion of "high-impact educational practices" (Kuh 1). At least four important aspects of learning theory clearly inform this pedagogy: (1) experiential learning as defined by David A. Kolb, who relied upon the psychology, philosophy, and learning theories of Lev Vygotsky and John Dewey, two early twentieth-century theorists whose work has enjoyed considerable re-emphasis and adaptation during the past several decades; (2) learning conceived as a dialogic process as defined by Mikhail Bakhtin; (3) learning as envisioned in the tradition of late twentieth-century cultural anthropology, especially in the work of Clifford Geertz; and (4) learning encouraged as a collaborative act, fostering the legacy of Kenneth Bruffee, but offering a somewhat unique peripatetic approach in the centuries-old tradition of the ancient Greek philosophers.[1]

The notion of experiential learning is hardly new, nor exclusive to a City as Text™ approach. Kolb's theories in *Experiential Learning: Experience as a Source of Learning and Development* are readily evident, explains Robert Strikwerda, within City as Text™ pedagogy. Of course, Kolb's learning theory has been widely cited and adapted across disciplines. One simple search in Academic Search Complete of "experiential learning-higher education-Kolb" yields nearly 800 scholarly articles published since 2000 across fields as diverse as engineering, adult education, and sports training. Kolb posits a model of learning as a circular process moving from "concrete experience" to "observation and reflection" to "formation of abstract concepts and generalizations" to "testing implications of concepts in new situations" and then repeating the cycle (qtd. in Strikwerda 100). As Kolb writes, "learning, change, and growth are seen to be facilitated best by an integrated process that *begins* with here-and-now experience followed by collection of data and observations about that experience" (*Collaborative Learning* 21).

Kolb readily credits the influence of Dewey, who is well known for maintaining that learning necessarily involves an interaction of knowledge and skills with experience.[2] Echoing the social cognitivists referenced below, Dewey maintains that for learning there must be social involvement he labels "contagion" (*How We Think* 224). Kolb specifically acknowledges that notion, recognizing that "the experiential learning cycle [is] a spiral, filling each episode of experience with the potential for movement, from blind impulse to a life of choice and purpose" (132). Such learning epitomizes City as Text™ pedagogy.

Kolb also points to the important work of Vygotsky, the Soviet cognitive theorist, for his discussions of learning as a social process responsible for individual development. Vygotsky insists that genuine learning always occurs as an external to internal process; individuals learn through external social interactions and gradually construct meaning or internal knowledge as an inter-to-intra psychological process.[3] Replicating this view, Kolb contends that it "is the process of learning from experience that shapes and actualizes developmental potentialities" (133). These are the kind of experiences that occur within an international City as Text™ course.

Interestingly, Vygotsky points to the ontogenetic process of language acquisition as a paradigm for all learning and subsequently for a pedagogical model. Retaining two major concepts is important. In learning to speak, young children clearly use imitation; their instruction is quite obviously ahead of their development. Gradually, they internalize what they hear and imitate the sounds. Initially, they utilize their new information in a spontaneous sense with only a tacit understanding of performance. Eventually, words evolve to the level of true word meanings, such as generalizations or genuine concepts, and they are able to use language as an abstract sign system in a conscious manner. In other words, usage precedes genuine comprehension; the challenging instruction results in a maturation, just as exposure to and usage of a city will precede more complex comprehension. Learning precedes development and provides for its advancement.

In other words, Vygotskian pedagogy or a Kolb-based approach encourages students to work together in small conversational groups on tasks that will challenge them to find solutions, allow more capable students to assist their peers in modeling problem-solving that can be imitated, and involve the students' personal socio-cultural history by encouraging them to relate their school instruction to the history they already carry to the classroom or to the city being explored. Genuine learning occurs as a kind of "enculturation," a process of becoming familiar with the language, customs, and conventions of a particular community until the learner, according to Vygotsky, functions as a member of that community and solves problems through "the formation of new concepts" (*Thought and Language* 100). This process typically occurs during a City as Text™ course.

Throughout such a course, students interact with their environments, observe, reflect, synthesize, and then gradually internalize as they learn new concepts, customs, and processes and draw conclusions about a place and culture, only to test and re-test them as they encounter subsequent external experiences. In that sense, the learning reflects a dialogic process in accordance with the work of Bakhtin, the oft-quoted Soviet sociolinguist and theorist. For Bakhtin, knowledge derives from the myriad possibilities presented by language. As Lucille McCarthy and Stephen Fishman point out, Bakhtin identifies learning with "trying on new language" or "struggling for a new language" (420). Figuratively, and often literally, within a City as Text™ course, a student is learning a new language when negotiating new territory. Bakhtin insists that language, and by extension, knowledge, always occurs in simultaneity—in other words, in a combination of self and other. In other words, learning, like language, is inherently dialogic in nature. Learning occurs in a City as Text™ course as students interact with their environment in a meaningful hands-on manner; they engage in dialog with the new environment through making observations; participating in local activities; and informally interviewing local residents in museums, cafes, and grocery stores. As students interact they gradually internalize the personality of the city: its values, priorities, and history. The place in turn responds to the City as Text™ participants, furthering the dialogic relationship and, in Bakhtinian terms, the learning process.

City as Text™ methodology, Braid explains, also echoes the work of cultural anthropologist, Clifford Geertz: "Geertz helps us grasp the importance of the cross-cultural and interdisciplinary nature" of City as Text™ courses ("Field-Based Education" 96). Geertz argues that in order to understand the increasingly complex nature of human thought through the vast array of intellectual disciplines, people must see those frames "as social activities in a social world" (14). Clearly, the core learning for City as Text™ courses occurs within social activities in a real-world setting, another of the hallmarks of high-impact educational practices. As Braid explains, the students are "actively scanning and organizing into patterns" and then actually "constructing the world by interpreting what they have beheld" ("Field-Based Education" 96). Interpretation occurs with firsthand engagement with the environment, the local culture, customs, and the people as students participate, according to Braid, in "'mapping culture' [as] NCHC calls it, or as Geertz puts it, 'charting that passage'" ("Field-Based Education" 96).

Geertz justifies the very existence of City as Text™ pedagogy by advocating a broad postmodern definition of text, in this case, inviting students to read a "place" as a "text." He argues for the "great virtue of the extension of the notion of text beyond things written on paper or carved into stone," insisting that extension allows for a much broader interpretation of human events (31). In fact, Geertz maintains that to "see social institutions, social customs, social changes as in some sense 'readable' is to alter our whole sense of what such interpretation is and shift it towards modes of thought rather more familiar to the translator, the exegete, or the iconographer than to the test giver, the factor analyst, or the pollster" (31). Further, he contends that understanding of human action is best accomplished through "noting expressions and inspecting them" (i.e., the activities of City as Text™ courses) rather than through "postulating forces and measuring them" (34). In other words, this pedagogy, observes Elrod, Husic, and Kinzie, "challenges students to think in new ways," in the tradition of the AAC&U high-impact educational practices (5). Student journal entries, written onsite, frequently reflect such thinking, often revealing a broadened perspective that recognizes American views are not universally held.

Geertz's notion of the construction of thought and cultural understanding through engaged activity is related to another neo-Vygotskian development, namely the notion of situated cognition. Situated cognition, or contextualized activity, has been discussed in the work of anthropologists and social theorists, such as Jean Lave and Etienne Wagner; numerous educational researchers, such as John Seeley Brown, Allan Collins, and Paul Duguid; and cognitive psychologists, such as Marlene Scardamalia, Carl Bereiter, and others during the past several decades. Indebted to Dewey and his recognition of the social construction of knowledge, these contemporary theorists argue for the necessity of situated learning, that is, learning concepts, not in abstract isolation, but within appropriately contextualized tasks, including exploring a city neighborhood. Learning, which is often achieved primarily through the mediation of language, is best accomplished when it is highly contextualized or situated, for example, when deciphering a memorial during a walkabout conversation. In their theory of situated cognition, Brown, Collins, and Duguid emphasize the role of activity in learning, arguing that activity and perception are always prior to conceptualization. For example, in a City as Text™ course, students' activity is prior to genuine knowledge of a culture, but it provides a crucial way into the culture. This understanding of learning as a social, contextualized activity aligns with today's growing emphasis on the value of experiential and collaborative learning and points to a fourth distinctive feature of City as Text™ courses: the extended use of collaboration.

As Braid emphasizes, City as Text™ course participants, faculty and students, collaborate from day one, exploring, mapping, and charting their new spaces together ("Field-Based Education"). They compare observations and discoveries, and then after individually composing their written reflections, they compare those to begin the process of synthesizing and expanding their understanding of the new culture. This aspect of City as Text™ pedagogy is not new, nor exclusive to this approach. As Bruffee articulates in his seminal

1984 essay "Collaborative Learning and the Conversation of the Mankind," "learning is a social and not an individual process" (646). Bruffee argues vigorously for the social construction of thought and knowledge: "Knowledge is the product of human beings in a state of continual negotiation or conversation" (646–47). "Collaborative learning," Bruffee continues, "is an arena in which students can negotiate their way into that conversation" (647). This type of learning is readily apparent in the City as Text™ approach.

Since the 1980s, collaborative learning has been increasingly utilized and validated within higher education as a valuable and highly effective means of constructing knowledge. Educators, writes Braid, recognize that collaborative learning "becomes a vehicle for bonding" though it also presents "challenges" ("Field-Based Education" 96). It can also advance students' sense of ownership of their academic experience as they jointly generate and synthesize course material. As Braid observes, field-based activities provide multiple "forms of collaborative learning that range from strangers-in-a-strange-land banding together to teams of investigators charting a course" ("Field-Based Education" 100). Furthermore, Celia C. Lo's 2010 study of student learning and satisfaction asserts that collaborative learning is "well suited to the millennial generation" (241). David Johnson, Roger Johnson, and Karl Smith concur: "There can now be little doubt that cooperative learning is appropriate to higher education: it works" (27–28). Interestingly, throughout the past several decades, the corporate and political spheres have increasingly used the collaborative model, and arguably, collaboration is a defining characteristic of twenty-first-century communication in the ever-growing world of social media and instantly alterable digital discourse exchanges.

City as Text™ courses employ collaboration throughout the walkabouts. Strikwerda discusses this somewhat unconventional use of collaboration as a teaching strategy as having obvious, though perhaps overlooked, links to the peripatetic tradition of the Ancients who frequently taught their students as they ambled through the countryside or wandered through flourishing olive groves. While the Ancients may have been traversing more familiar territory than participants in international City as Text™ courses, both groups share the experience of the thought-provoking and bonding benefit of combining teaching with the activity of walking and its inevitable and gradual changing of scenery. As Strikwerda notes, the approach "slows us down, giving us time to notice, then to reflect, and then to walk some more" (102). As the group members slow down, they become "peripatetic friends" (102). Strikwerda observes: "A stroll together can open us up to differences as we realize that the literature major, the business major, the biology major do not notice the same things—just like their professors—and we can share our learning as process and result" (102). That has certainly been my experience during my City as Text™ courses. I have co-designed and taught such courses in recent years in several different cities. Details of one of these short-term international courses in the fascinating cities of London and Oxford follow below. (See Appendix for the course syllabus.)

The course (eleven days abroad if it is a two-semester-hour course or twenty-one days abroad if it is a four-semester-hour course) begins with two different two-hour preparatory classes on campus. These preparatory sessions cover course expectations and the logistics of international travel, including the basic itinerary, safety issues, and the inevitable questions regarding currency exchange and cell phone usage. More importantly, the sessions begin with a mini-City as Text™ exercise. Student teams depart for a ½-hour walkabout to specific locations on campus with instructions to observe activities, clientele, general atmosphere, and landmarks. Upon returning to the classroom, they share observations and draw conclusions about the places observed. Interestingly, although most of the students have walked through these spaces numerous times before, they always notice new things, and they always arrive at conclusions that they never before articulated about the personality of the campus. Thus, in a short period of time, the stage is set for the notion of reading a place as a text, of mapping an environment, of observing and reflecting and synthesizing reactions. This exercise also introduces the crucial elements of collaboration and bonding.

The actual overseas course begins at Heathrow Airport in London. Despite their jetlag, students immediately notice the British accents, the different currency, and, of course, the ever-so-logical British signage with exits marked as the "Way Out" and the Baggage Claim entitled, more appropriately, the "Baggage Reclaim." The international City as Text™ adventure begins as the participants make their way to the Tube connection that will bring them to the hotel. Inevitably, several students are neither conversant nor comfortable with the notion of public transportation, and so, the first significant City as Text™ lesson occurs. Coverage of universal subway basics like the naming of the line by the last stop, determining which direction to take by reading network maps, and negotiating ticket usage for entry and exit is followed by a reminder of common-sense protection of personal property. All of these topics blur as students absorb initial impressions created by subway advertisements, locals' behaviors, and the ever-present "Mind the Gap" announcements at each stop.

Once settled in the London hotel, everyone heads back to the Tube for a group excursion to Westminster Abbey, which generally provides for a perfect City as Text™ exercise. After exploring this complex site and its surroundings for several hours, students complete written reflections. Subsequent discussions generally reveal their attention to key characteristics of London: the layers of history, the cultural emphasis on literature and the arts, and the blatant blurring of Church and State. Thus, the mapping of the culture begins.

Days are filled with a combination of group events, such as viewing the Rosetta Stone at the British Museum, delighting in a performance of *Macbeth* at the Globe, grimacing at the beheading site at the Tower of London, and taking structured small-team walkabouts. Locations such as Covent Garden, Piccadilly Circus, Trafalgar Square, Kensington Gardens, and other walkabout destinations become the classrooms of the day. Journal entries and synthesizing discussions become richer and more complex as students collaboratively negotiate their paths to their day's assignment and daily readjust their lens to chart an understanding of this fascinating city. Discussions always include recognition, usually with an element of surprise, of the immense diversity of the London population today. Discussions of the evidence of British imperialism, which they find in monuments, gate inscriptions, and, of course, some wonderful Indian restaurants, inevitably ensue.

Obviously, this course could be expanded with a variety of supplemental readings and faculty onsite lectures, but this course relies upon City as Text™ techniques almost exclusively during our early days in London. Soon the honors students exercise well-tuned observational powers, their adulation of London is effusive, and they embrace all things British: especially requisite visits to Platform 9¾ at King's Cross, Abbey Road, and pub stops for fish 'n chips or jacket potatoes. Then we tear them away reluctantly and travel through the countryside to settle in Oxford for the bulk of the course. At this point, we build upon the initial City as Text™ approach and intensify the academic components of the course.

As a centuries-old seat of learning, rich in history, literature, myth, and culture, including complex town-gown relations, Oxford is an ideal city for employing the valuable experiential-learning pedagogy of City as Text™.[4] Students investigate the complex city of Oxford, which is layered as a sort of palimpsest, through first-hand examination of the numerous colleges composing the university, the museums, the marketplaces, and the landmarks like the famous Bodleian Library.

Obviously the walkabouts continue, and the city's smaller scale and slower pace are conducive to adding a research component that focuses this course on famous historical figures. Students spend considerable time on this component of the course. Drawing heavily upon David Horan's *Oxford: A Cultural and Literary Companion*, from the Cities of the Imagination Series, we direct student pairs to select one key figure in Oxford's history to research. The choices are primarily literary figures, such as Oscar Wilde, Percy B. Shelley, Lewis Carroll, and J. R. R. Tolkien. The course always emphasizes the historical context of all figures. Each team conducts library-based research on its figure and in continuing City as Text™ fashion also conducts field research, locating sites with significant links to the figure and observing alterations in the site over generations as well as contemporary uses of space.

A group investigating the patron saint of Oxford, the medieval abbess St. Frideswide, for example, researches her official history and its attendant myths. The students inevitably discuss the visual preservation of those stories in the famous nineteenth-century Edward Burne-Jones stained glass window in the Latin chapel of the magnificent Christ Church College and then explain to the class the role of St. Frideswide in Oxfordian history and the complexities of the church-gown relationships. After viewing this detailed glass narrative, students usually discover as well the window on the opposite side of the main altar that sits in counterpoint to the St. Frideswide window. This opposite window honors St. Catherine, who is depicted with the angelic face of Edith Liddell, sister of the famed Alice Liddell, the young girl whom famed Christ Church alumnus Lewis Carroll used as his model for the Wonderland character. Thus, this venture becomes a link for the group researching Lewis Carroll.

The team researching Carroll, of course, also eagerly leads the group to the grand dining hall of Christ Church, perhaps not so much to view the Lewis Carroll portrait amidst countless other political, literary, and historic icons, as to catch a glimpse of Harry Potter's evening venue. Oxford's rich layers of history gradually unravel as the students conduct their onsite research. Site explorations, journal entries, and advancing research lead to discussions of the four ever-present overlapping themes in Oxford: town, gown, church, and crown. Relating these to the investigation of literary history through a City as Text™ approach provides a unique and powerful learning experience.

The team researching Percy B. Shelley, for example, quickly learns that his illustrious career in Oxford, as a student at University College, was cut short when he was linked to the anonymous posting of a religious diatribe perceived to be heretical. With varied success, given the whims of the protective college porters, students negotiate or pay for a visit to the highly romanticized marble statue of Shelley, ensconced behind an iron gate within a private corridor of University College. The figure of the drowned Shelley washed ashore is surrounded by engraved lines of his poetry. That the memorial is simultaneously hidden and glorified adds to the mystique—and perhaps to the hypocrisy—of commemorating this famed nineteenth-century figure who was expelled from University College. Of course, the group discusses everything from historical variations on the notion of academic freedom to the intricacies of church and gown power plays to the manipulation of contemporary audiences lured into adulation for this college having such a famous alumnus.

In addition to conducting this collaborative City as Text™-enhanced research focused on specific historical figures associated with Oxford, students must analyze and critique a literary work, fiction or non-fiction, set in Oxford. Teams may select Simon Winchester's *Professor and the Madman: The Story of the Oxford English Dictionary*, Kingsley Amis's *Lucky Jim*, Colin Dexter's *The Dead of Jericho*, Thomas Hardy's *Jude the Obscure*, or Evelyn Waugh's *Brideshead Revisited*. (See the Appendix.) Once again, a blend of traditional pedagogy and City as Text™ pedagogy is employed. Discussion may begin over dinner with a somewhat traditional literary analysis of key themes, characters, or plot twists, but it continues during the expedition. For example, one team recently chose Dorothy Sayers's *Gaudy Night*, a mystery that is set in the fictional "Shrewsbury College" but is actually modeled after Somerville College, Sayers's alma mater. A site exploration of Somerville reveals obvious links to key scenes in the novel and also inevitably acts as a springboard for discussions of the *avant garde* feminism prevalent in the 1935 novel. Ironically, in 1915, Sayers completed the requirements of a first-class honors degree in modern language at Somerville, an all-women's college and, not surprisingly, the only option for women at that time in Oxford, but was not awarded her BA and MA retroactively until 1920, when the University of Oxford finally consented to grant women degrees. The impact of the discriminatory practices is especially intense for our students as they walk in the footsteps of Sayers herself. Obviously, Oxford has advanced in the area of gender equality. The last of the all-women's colleges, St. Hilda's, finally went co-educational in 2006, and today nearly half of the university student body is female; however, discrimination within this elite academic institution still exists.

Tensions between town and gown have centuries-old roots relating to noticeable discrepancies between the lifestyles of the academic elite who inhabit the beautiful walled courtyards of the numerous colleges and those who service the daily needs of the colleges, operate the local restaurants and train station, and sell the kebabs and chips from temporary street carts. This contrast is quickly revealed with a walkabout down Cowley Road, an extremely diverse section of the city, just beyond the tranquil isolation and wealth of the Magdalene College gardens where Tolkien and friends wandered seeking authorial inspiration. Filled with delightful ethnic restaurants bespeaking the area's diverse immigrant population, Cowley Road also evidences struggles of its working-class population with its grocery stores advertising specials on inexpensive cuts of meat and its re-sale clothing shops beckoning consumers. The contrast to the ivy-covered courtyards of the colleges is stark. Once again, the benefits of learning how to read a city, which students repeatedly list as one of the three most important things they learned from this course, surface.

This course and potentially any international City as Text™ research course squarely based upon credible learning theory, embody all of the hallmarks, according to Elrod, Husic, and Kinzie, of an AAC&U-espoused high-impact educational practice. Students are involved repeatedly in activities that demand "meaningful faculty and peer interaction," and they are obviously forced to "connect their learning to real-world settings" (Elrod, Husic, and Kinzie 5). Combining City as Text™ pedagogy with appropriate reading and research assignments creates a "context of a coherent and challenging curriculum" (Elrod, Husic, and Kinzie 5). Of course, it is imperative for a genuine learning experience that students are provided with "frequent feedback," a crucial aspect of this approach (Elrod, Husic, and Kinzie 5). Clearly, the walkabouts require significant "time on task," and the idiosyncrasies of specific locations and encounters "challenge students to think in new ways and respond to novel situations" (Elrod, Husic, and Kinzie 5).

Repeatedly, my colleagues and I have witnessed the positive impact of the approach described. Thus, while always pleased, I am never surprised to read the following in a student's exit response: "I enjoyed everything we did/saw. I liked the texts we read and how we divided into multiple group projects that were activity/exploration-based, which made them more interesting. . . . I recommend [the course] to anyone and everyone." Yet as educators we know that a high-impact educational practice must, of course, not only be enjoyable and satisfying for students, it should also contribute to the broad goal of creating reflective thinkers who will continually challenge themselves, expand their comfort zones, understand the necessity and frustration of compromise in a world of competing viewpoints, and embrace the value of ever-shifting perspectives. When students experience the complex, ever-shifting, external lens of a City as Text™ international research course, their own personal lens and context is unalterably changed. Because the future of the world sits squarely in the hands of students, educators must do anything they can to ensure that that future is led by reflective thinkers who value lifelong learning and embrace a multiplicity of perspectives with a critical lens. A short-term international research-focused experience is undeniably a good place to initiate that process.

NOTES

[1]Bruffee continued to expand upon these ideas throughout his career; see *Collaborative Learning: Higher Education, Interdependence, and the Authority of Knowledge,* 2nd ed.

[2]Dewey was an early advocate of experiential learning. For details of his views, see his 1938 publication, *Experience and Education.*

[3]See Vygotsky's *Thought and Language* and his *Mind in Society* for a detailed discussion of this inter-to-intra psychological process of knowledge acquisition.

⁴Although this course is taught as an honors English elective, it is open to all majors; students from business, education, political science, and other disciplines have participated. Largely because of its active-learning approach, I would argue that the course's appeal and impact are widespread because of the City as Text™ methodology.

WORKS CITED

Bakhtin, Mikhail. *Speech Genres and Other Late Essays.* Trans. Vern W. McGee. Ed. Caryl Emerson and Michael Holquist. Austin: U of Texas P, 1986. Print.

Braid, Bernice. "City as Text™." *Place as Text: Approaches to Active Learning.* Ed. Bernice Braid and Ada Long. 2nd ed. Lincoln: National Collegiate Honors Council, 2010. 51–54. NCHC Monograph Series. Print.

—. "Field-Based Education in 'Semesters.'" *Thought and Action: The NEA Higher Education Journal* (Spring 1990): 93–105. Print.

Brodkey, Linda. "On the Subjects of Class and Gender in 'The Literacy Letters.'" *College English* 51.2 (1989): 125–41. Print.

Brown, John Seely, Allan Collins, and Paul Duguid. "Situated Cognition and the Culture of Learning." *Educational Researcher* 18.1 (1989): 32–42. Print.

Bruffee, Kenneth. "Collaborative Learning and the Conversation of Mankind." *College English* 46.7 (1984): 635–52. Print.

—. *Collaborative Learning: Higher Education, Interdependence, and the Authority of Knowledge,* 2nd ed. Baltimore: Johns Hopkins UP, 2000. Print.

Cabrera, Alberto, et al. "Collaborative Learning: Its Impact on College Students' Development and Diversity." *Journal of College Student Development* 43.1 (2002): 20–34. Print.

Dewey, John. *Experience and Education.* 1938. New York: Touchstone, 1997. Print.

—. *How We Think.* 1910. New York: Prometheus Books, 1991. Print.

Elrod, Susan, Diane Husic, and Jillian Kinzie. "Research and Discovery Across the Curriculum." *Peer Review* 12.2 (2010): 4–8. Print.

Geertz, Clifford. *Local Knowledge: Further Essays in Interpretive Anthropology.* New York: Basic Books, 1983. Print.

Horan, David. *Oxford: A Cultural and Literary Companion.* Brooklyn, NY: Interlink Books, 2000. The Cities of the Imagination Series. Print.

Johnson, David, Roger Johnson, and Karl Smith. "Cooperative Learning Returns to College: What Evidence is There That It Works?" *Change* 20.4 (1998): 26–35. Print.

Kolb, David A. *Experiential Learning: Experience as the Source of Learning and Development.* Englewood Cliffs, NJ: Prentice Hall, 1984. Print.

Kuh, George D. *High-Impact Educational Practices: What They Are, Who Has Access to Them, and Why They Matter.* Washington, D.C.: Association of American Colleges and Universities, 2008. Print.

Lave, Jean, and Etienne Wegner. *Situated Learning: Legitimate Peripheral Participation.* Cambridge: Cambridge UP, 1991. Print.

Lo, Celia C. "Student Learning and Student Satisfaction in an Interactive Classroom." *The Journal of General Education* 59.4 (2010): 238–63. Print.

McCarthy, Lucille, and Stephen Fishman. "Boundary Conversations: Conflicting Ways of Knowing in Philosophy and Interdisciplinary Research." *Research in the Teaching of English* 25 (Dec. 1991): 419–68. Print.

Place as Text: Approaches to Active Learning. Ed. Bernice Braid and Ada Long. 2nd ed. Lincoln: National Collegiate Honors Council, 2010. NCHC Monograph Series. Print.

Scardamalia, Marlene, and Carl Bereiter. "Knowledge Building: Theory, Pedagogy, and Technology." *Cambridge Handbook of the Learning Sciences.* Ed. K. Sawyer. New York: Cambridge UP, 2006. 97–118. Print.

Strikwerda, Robert. "Experiential Learning and City as Text™: Reflections on Kolb and Kolb." *Journal of the National Collegiate Honors Council* 8.1 (2006): 99–105. Print.

Vygotsky, Lev. *Mind in Society: The Development of Higher Psychological Processes.* Cambridge: Harvard UP, 1978. Print.

—. *Thought and Language.* Ed. Alex Kozulin. Cambridge: MIT P, 1986. Print.

APPENDIX

Course Syllabus and Itinerary

ENG 350H—10 Special Topics
Oxford: City as Text™
COURSE SYLLABUS and COURSE ITINERARY
Spring 2010

Dr. Ted Lerud   \<tedl@elmhurst.edu\>   ext. 3661

Dr. Mary Kay Mulvaney   \<marym@elmhurst.edu\>   ext. 6479

COURSE DESCRIPTION

Employing a City as Text™ pedagogy in the tradition of the National Collegiate Honors Council (NCHC), students will investigate the complex city of Oxford with its rich history, literature, architecture, and diverse cultures. The investigation will develop through firsthand examination of city museums, college libraries, marketplaces, and so forth; through lectures and discussion led by both the Elmhurst College professors and professors of the Center for Medieval and Renaissance Studies (CMRS); through extensive field trips with follow-up reflective components within the city centre and beyond, as well as trips to significant surrounding areas: London and Stratford-Upon-Avon; and through reading, discussing, and writing analytically in response to the course texts focused on the literary history and literature of Oxford.

COURSE GOALS

1. To broaden students' intercultural skills by participating in a different culture and examining customs and traditions firsthand.

2. To enable a short-term study abroad experience in the hopes of peaking student interest for longer future experiences.

3. To understand the place of Oxford within a larger cultural history of Britain.

4. To explore and analyze a centuries-old center of higher learning firsthand using City as Text™ methodology.

5. To investigate the literary history of Oxford through written and oral texts.

6. To analyze representative texts of British literature as cultural artifacts.

COURSE TEXTS/MATERIALS

Articles

Braid, Bernice. "Field-Based Education in 'Semesters.'" *Thought and Action: The NEA Higher Education Journal* (Spring 1990): 93–105.

Strikwerda, Robert. "Experiential Learning and City as Text™: Reflections on Kolb and Kolb." *Journal of the National Collegiate Honors Council* (2007): 99–105.

Books

Horan, David. *Oxford: A Cultural and Literary Companion*. Cities of the Imagination Series. Interlink Publishing, 1999.

Shakespeare, William. *Antony and Cleopatra*.

COURSE ASSIGNMENTS AND ASSESSMENT

- Attendance and active participation in pre-seminar classes—**APRIL 13 & MAY 11, 4:15 P.M.–6:00 P.M., CH 103 AND** all lectures, tours, and discussions on site . . . 20%

- Journal of ***daily observations*** followed by synthesizing, analytical reflections 15%

- Careful reading and preparation of all course texts 10%

- Team research presentation on a key Oxford figure, delivered at applicable sites 20%

- Team presentation on a literary work set in Oxford 15%

- Integrative essay (details TBA) due June 15th electronically to Drs. Lerud and Mulvaney 20%

Team Assignments:

1. Literary Discussion Assignment (conducted over dinner at CMRS—see the calendar)

Team member responsibilities:

- Carefully read your novel of choice.

- Discuss the text with your partner and determine how best to present it to the entire group.

- Lead a discussion over dinner on the date assigned.

- Write a 2–3 page analysis paper on the text.

Others:

- Read as much of the other groups' texts as possible.

- Participate in the discussions.

Date of Dinner Book Chats	Book	Team Members
Monday, 5-31	Winchester	Book Team 1
Tuesday, 6-1	Sayers	Book Team 2
Friday, 6-4	Dexter	Book Team 3

__Literary Selections__

(Each book discussion team should select **ONE** of the following literary texts set in Oxford.):

Amis, Kingsley. *Lucky Jim.*

Dexter, Colin. *The Dead of Jericho.*

Hardy, Thomas. *Jude the Obscure.*

Sayers, D.L. *Gaudy Night.*

Snow, C.P. *The Masters.*

Wain, John. *Where the Rivers Meet.*

Waugh, Evelyn. *Brideshead Revisited.*

Winchester, Simon. *Professor and the Madman*

2. "Researched Site Session" Assignment

Team member responsibilities:

- Carefully read all sections of Horan regarding your figure.

- Explore the places that relate to the figure–look for connections in multiple ways.

- Research beyond the text, connecting to broader Oxford scene.

- Plan a 2-hour session with your partner, leading the entire group to significant sites to share your findings.

- Prepare a 1-page handout of highlights regarding your figure for each trip member (there are 11 of us).

Others:

- Read the Horan text carefully.

- Actively participate in the site sessions.

Date of On-site Presentation	Topic	Team Members
Sun., 5-30	St. Frideswide	Drs. Lerud and Mulvaney
Wed., 6-2	Samuel Johnson	Student Research Team A
Fri., 6-4	Percy B. Shelley	Student Research Team B
Sat., 6-5, a.m.	Oscar Wilde	Student Research Team C
Sat., 6-5, p.m.	Lewis and the Inklings	Student Research Team D

Important Oxford Figures

(Teams should select a key figure; research related individuals as well.)

Thomas Cramer (1489–1556)

King Charles I (1600–1649)

Samuel Johnson (1709–1784)

Percy Shelley (1791–1822)

Cardinal Newman (1801–1890)

Oscar Wilde (1855–1900)

C.S. Lewis & the Inklings (1898–1963)

Service Component: (optional opportunity)
Explore the life of the underserved in the town of Oxford. Organized by student volunteer and faculty leaders. Details TBA.

COURSE ITINERARY

Date	Location/Activities
Wednesday 5-26	Leave O'Hare Airport. AA Flight 46—meet O'Hare, Terminal 3, no later than 6:15 pm
London	
Thursday 5-27	• Arrive in London. Settle into hotel. • Tour of Westminster Abbey, Big Ben, Buckingham Palace. • Begin learning log (to be kept daily). OBJ: 1, 2, 3
Friday 5-28	• Tour of Tower of London. • St. Paul's Cathedral—discussion of Christopher Wren and ties to Oxford. • Group session focused on initial impressions of foreign travel, British culture, London. OBJ: 1, 2, 3, 4
Saturday 5-29	• Tour Covent Garden, Theatre District, etc.; 12:30 Globe backstage tour; London theatre performance: *Macbeth* 7:30. OBJ: 1, 2, 3

Sunday 5-30	• Travel to Oxford, get settled at CMRS. • Orientation by CMRS staff. • Lecture: Dr. Ted Lerud, "Introduction to Oxford." • Walkabout in City Centre. **1st Researched Site Session—St. Frideswide;** Drs. Lerud and Mulvaney <div align="right">OBJ: 1, 2, 4</div>
Oxford	
Monday 5-31	• A.M. 10:00—Lecture: CMRS professor, Dr. Nicholas Crowe, "Medieval, Renaissance, and Beyond: The Ascent of Oxford in English Culture." • Following lecture—Johnson and Lewis/Inklings teams' interviews with Dr. Crowe. • A.M./early P.M. Time for initial site research • P.M. 3:00—Tour Bodleian Library. • Group session focused on "initial impressions of Oxford." • Small group presentation of literary work over dinner—(Book Team 1). <div align="right">OBJ: 4, 5, 6</div>
Wednesday 6-2	• A.M. 10:00—Lecture: CMRS professor, Dr. Nicholas Crowe, "The Literary Legacy: Poetry in Oxford and Oxford in Poetry." • Student Research Group A—onsite lecture of researched figure. • Lecture: Dr. Ted Lerud, "Shakespearean Theatre." • Discussion of Shakespeare's *Antony and Cleopatra* (play to be attended on 6-3 in Stratford-Upon-Avon) <div align="right">OBJ: 4, 5, 6</div>

Thursday 6-3	• Excursion to Stratford-Upon-Avon (07:36 departure on train) • Tour Shakespeare's birthplace, burial site, Anne Hathaway's home. • P.M. 1:00 Attend scheduled play—the Courtyard Theatre matinee of *Antony and Cleopatra*. • Return (5:40) for dinner on own in Oxford <div align="right">OBJ: 1, 2, 3, 6</div>
Friday 6-4	• A.M. 9:30—Lecture: CMRS professor, Dr. Mark Philpott on Oxfordian history. • 11:00—Tour of the Oxford Castle. • Student Research Group B—onsite lecture of researched figure. • P.M. 4:00 Scavenger hunt for obscure Oxford sites led by CMRS professor, Dr. Nicholas Crowe. • Small group presentation of literary work over dinner—(Book Group 3). <div align="right">OBJ: 3, 4, 5</div>
Saturday 6-5	• A.M.—Student Research Group C—onsite lecture of researched figure. • P.M.—Student Research Group D—onsite lecture of researched figure. • Community-focused experience in Oxford. <div align="right">OBJ: 1, 3, 4</div>

Sunday 6-6	• Early A.M.—Church services (optional). • 11:30 a.m.–1:00 p.m.: Cowley Road area and beyond; diverse area of immigrant population. Discussion: Dr. Mary Kay Mulvaney, "Intercultural Evolution in Oxford." • 1:00 p.m.–4:00 p.m.: Free time for final explorations such as Oxford Museums, Ashmolean, Pitts-River • 5:00 p.m.–6:00 p.m.: Reflections/debriefing session OBJ: 1,4
Monday 6-7	Depart Oxford for London—Heathrow to Chicago, AA #47, 12:50; completion of learning log on plane.
Tuesday 6-15	Integrative Essay Due—submit by email to Drs. Lerud and Mulvaney.

CHAPTER 4

Learning as Salon:
Honors International Collaboration

MISCHA DEKKER, JUSTIN VAN DIJK, AND
MARCA WOLFENSBERGER
UTRECHT UNIVERSITY, THE NETHERLANDS

CHRISTINE HAIT, CHANTEL LUCAS, CORINNE MANN, AND
JOHN ZUBIZARRETA
COLUMBIA COLLEGE

INTRODUCTION

In May 2011, Dutch students from the honors program in geo-sciences of Utrecht University, led by Professor Marca Wolfensberger, engaged in an experimental-learning project in Paris, France, with a group of American students from the honors program of Columbia College, South Carolina, led by Professors Christine Hait, Corinne Mann, and John Zubizarreta. Literally and figuratively, the city of Paris served as a salon for the project: a place where rational discussion, cross-cultural dialog, collaborative

75

learning, and culminating critical reflection about the uniqueness and value of the learning process itself were stimulated by the informal setting of a vibrant international city that provided the context for the two groups of students to explore the topics of expatriate artist culture and film history in Paris, especially during the late nineteenth and early twentieth centuries.

One of the guiding principles of the international venture is the recognition that "learning as salon" is an enrichment of the successful, NCHC-trademarked City as Text™ pedagogical model that is well known in American honors circles. In such an approach to teaching and learning, the material landscape gains special meaning as active learners incorporate place-specific and other applicable content in discussions that occur on location. By detailing our extraordinary experiences in Paris and locating our activities within the larger framework of what makes such active, honors-level learning so powerful, especially when enriched by international collaboration, we will examine the possibilities of the salon concept in honors education. Our hope is that the cross-cultural salon concept extends beyond our own situation and will stimulate honors programs in the United States, the Netherlands, and other countries to collaborate across international borders in designing experiential-learning opportunities like this Paris salon venture.

CONTEXT

In fall 2010, Dr. John Zubizarreta led a number of invited workshops on honors education at several institutions in the Netherlands. During the visit, he discussed a plan to offer a study-travel trip to Paris with a small number of honors students scheduled to enroll in a required spring-semester senior seminar with an optional trip after the course. Taught primarily by an American literature scholar, with the help of a French professor and support from the college's honors program, the course, "Paris in Film and Literature," offered students a chance to explore Paris's unique culture of multi-national expatriates and its galvanizing role in the influential French New Wave film movement. Course discussions revolved around the amazing phenomenon of how many great artists of diverse genres and countries migrated to Paris during the modernist period, making the city a cultural magnet for many avant-garde innovations in art, music, dance, literature, and film. An optional study-travel excursion to Paris would transform students' classroom knowledge into deep, active learning, the kind of intellectual growth that, when combined with practical applications and opportunities to make interdisciplinary and personal connections, characterizes City as Text™ pedagogical strategies. Their learning would be materialized in real life.

As a model of one of many strategies that distinguish honors education, the Paris journey underscored the power of City as Text™ approaches to study-travel, shifting students' attitudes from being simple tourists and superficial consumers of another culture to being critical observers and active learners, to making study-travel a collaborative, reflective, intellectual endeavor. The effectiveness of such methodology is well documented in the vast research on experiential learning. John Dewey, David Kolb, Benjamin S. Bloom, and other educational theorists underscore the value of doing or application and connecting or synthesis in deep learning, and the Association for Experiential Education <http://www.aee.org> is one example of the many online resources available on the subject. The honors domain benefits from the valuable work of Bernice Braid, Ada Long, Joan Digby, and Peter Machonis, whose NCHC monographs on the benefits of experiential learning reinforce the message that accumulation of knowledge, traditional classroom work, and concentration on recall are not sufficient in moving students from surface acquisition of subject matter to significant, lasting, transformative learning. The lesson was eminently clear in the Paris salon idea that Zubizarreta shared with interested Dutch instructors and honors students.

Honors colleague Marca Wolfensberger of Holland's Utrecht University responded enthusiastically to the suggestion that such pedagogy could be enhanced by crossing cultural boundaries and bringing together honors students from different countries in a specific place. Such an enterprise would also facilitate the expansion of honors, in general, and NCHC's influence, in particular, into international arenas. The idea of an experimental international collaboration between students of American and Dutch honors programs took hold, and the salon concept, so prevalent in Parisian cultural history, became the framing metaphor of the project because of the French salon's emphasis on intimate gatherings, animated discussions, critical reflection, interdisciplinarity, intellectual rigor, and inclusive diversity of voices—all complementary facets of honors teaching and learning. And so we planned an experiential salon in Paris for the following spring.

PARISIAN SALONS

The Parisian Salon has undergone significant change since its inception in the sixteenth century when French kings imported it from their Italian neighbors. Upon arrival in France, the salon initially found its place, as literary circles, in the homes of the middle- and lower-ranking nobility. By the seventeenth century, although remaining open to the diversity of classes and disciplines, the salon incorporated one important restriction, accepting only those of so-called polite society. In the eighteenth century, the salon tradition took on one of its most important societal roles in becoming the inarguably revered haven for the exchange of ideas related to the very real possibility of social change. During this historic period, the Enlightenment ruled in Parisian salons. In the private homes of the salon keepers, most of whom were enlightened, upper-class women, the *philosophes* would gather to discuss, among other topics, the ideals underlying the questions of liberty and equality that would eventually lead to the French Revolution. Interestingly, as the French Revolution began, a marked decline occurred in such intellectual gatherings as the revolutionaries—sons of the salons, themselves—"suppressed" such "private gatherings" precisely because of their strong influence on public opinion. Indeed, after the French Revolution, the salon genuinely became a marginalized social happening (Spayde and Sandra 11).

One of these marginalized groups, which makes its appearance in the years just preceding World War I, was led by Gertrude Stein, a salonist of great renown. The gatherings at her home at 27 rue de

Fleurtus attracted salon enthusiasts from all walks of life, from a diversity of professional backgrounds, and from across the world. Stein's salon not only embraced the characteristics of the traditional Parisian salon but was also quite cross-cultural.

Although the Parisian salon declined around the time of the French Revolution, the ideals of the Parisian salon as an informal public space, inviting intellectual exchange among a group of diverse participants in terms of disciplinary orientation and class-rank, manifested themselves in the daily lives of Parisians in the form of café culture. In fact, a hybridization of the salon-café traditions occurred during the eighteenth century when the *philosophes* migrated from conversing at one of the recognized Parisian salons—be it Baron d'Holbach's (one of the few men who held a salon) or Madame Geoffrin's—to gathering at favored spots such as the *Procope*, one of the oldest Parisian cafés found in the heart of the 6th arrondissement, home of the *École des Beaux-Arts*, the *Académie français*, and the French intelligentsia in general.

The movement from the structured setting of the private home to the genuinely public space of the café, found at the heart of the Parisian district and intimately linked to the city's intellectual pulse, is but a step. Indeed, these encounters are today most known and embraced by those, such as our international honors group, interested in replicating the Parisian intellectual gatherings. The French cafés have long been the daily hang-outs of world-famous artists and intellectuals. *Les Deux Magots* was the favoured retreat of Jean-Paul Sartre and Simone de Beauvoir but also regularly visited by figures such as Pablo Picasso and Marcel Proust. Jean Cocteau's café, *Le Boeuf sur le Toit*, witnessed various discussions at different times, involving Igor Stravinsky, Wassily Kandinsky, Paul Gauguin, Sinclair Lewis, Vladimir Lenin, and Ernest Hemingway. Many films feature establishments such as *Maxim's*, which was in Jean Renoir's *La Grande Illusion* and was the favorite café of Maurice Chevalier's character in *Gigi*.

Through its heritage and its concrete manifestations, the salon, then, came to stand for an ideal. For authors such as German philosopher Jürgen Habermas, the term *salon* became synonymous with the abstract ideal of a place where intellectualism and sociability mix. According to Habermas, in the eighteenth century different countries in Europe saw the emergence of a bourgeois public sphere, where there was room for what he calls "rational-critical debate," an open communication space where people can engage in public discourse, exchanging and critiquing ideas (160). He draws connections among the urbane, intellectual traditions that developed in British coffee houses, Germany's eclectic dining clutches or *Tischgesellschaften*, and Parisian salons; more than just physical places for gathering over food or drink, these venues provided sophisticated, spirited occasions where intellectuals and artists met to discuss political movements and ideologies, art, science, and fashion (30–43). In salon culture, people from different occupations and nationalities gathered to partake in critical discussion about the important issues of their time. The discussions in such salons are never fixed, but they depend upon the contingent social and historical backgrounds of those engaged in the exchanges. The freedom of such collaborative discourse, the reliance on what each participant can bring to the conversation from his or her disciplinary expertise and personal connections, and the emphasis on utilizing the resources and influence of a unique gathering place play important roles in making the salon model an ideal structure for authentic collaborative learning in honors.

LEARNING AS SALON

Our collaborative Paris project was an experimental effort to see if the ideal of learning as salon would work as an enrichment to the City as Text™ model. City as Text™ stresses how the urban landscape reflects the *zeitgeist* of a place; likewise, learning as salon underscores how a specific geographical location or ambience influences and materially shapes not only *what* but also *how* people learn. Paris, of course, offers myriad opportunities for exploration, but to gather in salon fashion focuses attention on how the special history and contours of the city's salon culture foster the collaborative and inclusive critical discourse conducive to discussion of a particular subject in a particular place. In other words, our salon conversations about international expatriate art and avant-garde film in Paris mirrored the very content of our study: the participants did not just read and write about the burgeoning Parisian salon culture of international expatriate artists during a specific number of decades and then explore the city to find evidence to support our learning; rather, we replicated the features of the salon to enrich the already considerable benefits of experiential learning. Salon blurred the boundary between learning and experience.

Learning as salon worked out extraordinarily well for this project. The group visited many historically significant sites, with a focus on the extraordinary convergence of international expatriate artists and innovative French filmmakers in Paris at the beginning of the twentieth century. A large part of the time was spent onsite in salon-inspired discussions across the disciplinary concentrations of the students involved in this international collaboration. For these discussions we picked places that were especially suitable; for instance, the *Jardin du Luxembourg* has often been a gathering place for political dissidents but also for the display of political power. Here, the participants discussed Dutch, French, and American politics and political theory, linking the topics to different historical developments that have taken place in these countries and that can perhaps explain the differences. In the stimulating fashion of salon, the discussions ranged freely over wide intellectual territory, moving swiftly from social, political, philosophical, and artistic considerations to meta-level analysis of how learning as salon—situated in particular places where the Parisian salon itself thrived—provided the honors enhancement we envisioned for our international experiment. One of the students' written reflections captures the impact on her honors learning:

> My favorite part of being in Paris was seeing the topics we covered in class—in the form of pictures, reports and student papers—materialize right in front of me. I completed a mini-report on the *Jardin du Luxembourg* and then to have a casual, Parisian lunch, complete with baguettes and brie, on the Luxembourg lawn was surreal. We were immersed in the city—literally on the doorsteps of the Latin

Quarter—and interacting with Parisians and other Europeans is the experience I value most now that I have returned home. We were able to wander through the *Louvre*, contemplating Mona Lisa's countenance, and then walk past the iconic glass pyramid to bustling Parisian streets to order food at a local vendor. In essence, we experienced both worlds of Paris by seeing renowned landmarks, such as *Musée de Orsay* and *Père Lachaise Cemetery*, while stopping [at] less prominent sites to drink a café and critically reflect on the meaning of the journey as not just a trip but a profound honors international learning experience.

The salon discussions constituted a means to visit a place and understand it. Location became a starting point for engaged conversations not only about the meaning of place or about any related content information but also about how place and pedagogy become one: learning as salon. The students used place to progress intellectually, to connect knowledge across disciplines and international experiences, and to realize the power of critical reflection; they understood how place and a specialized approach to teaching and learning are linked.

INTERNATIONAL EXCHANGE AND INTERDISCIPLINARITY

Composed of students not only from different continents but also from different disciplinary fields of study, such as political science, history, geography, business, literature, art, and dance, the Paris group shared diverse points of view in the discussions, thereby reinforcing the quality of discourse and heightening expectations and standards for honors-level learning. These features of the collaboration brought the visit to Paris very close to the ideal of an authentic salon, a happening wherein artists and other intellectuals from different backgrounds meet in inspiring places to stimulate the growth of original ideas and the sharing of knowledge. Going beyond disciplinary borders, the group discussed historical, ideological, artistic, and social developments in Paris and compared these developments in our own countries. As such, both international exchange and interdisciplinarity formed the essential core of their model of learning as salon.

CONCLUSION

During their international collaboration in May 2011, the participants designed their own contemporary salon in Paris. Prior to coming together onsite, the students focused their learning on varied disciplinary content that could be synthesized in salon discussions situated in especially appropriate locations. Many of their conversations revolved around the material studied back home, to be sure, but also around how the group excursions, in City as Text™ mode, complemented individual study. But perhaps more significantly, especially in culminating reflections, the discussions also prompted the critically reflective insights gained while pondering how place and pedagogy, how learning as salon, provided an optimal occasion for higher-order learning and an honors approach to study-travel.

After departing from the City of Light, the students have stayed in touch quite extensively, an associated outcome of the intellectual and social camaraderie that is characteristic of salon culture. Thinking of learning as salon emphasizes the historically embedded and place-bound character of knowledge and provides a lively and inspiring method to study and share content among honors students from different cultural backgrounds and disciplinary fields. But for the implemented concept of salon to hold authentically and make the most difference in deepening and extending student learning, other essential elements include allowing students the authority to come up with ideas of their own, to challenge each other while constructing shared knowledge from diverse content areas, and to make the crucial connections between the particular character of place and the immersive process of teaching and learning in context. They can do so through the quality of discussions that occur in learning as salon. Coming together in Paris from honors programs in the Netherlands and the United States, the participants made this exciting experimental and experiential honors undertaking of learning as salon a great success, one that perhaps other honors programs within and outside the United States will adapt to further the innovative pedagogies and characteristics that programs worldwide cite when defining, realizing, and transforming what we mean by honors.

WORKS CITED

Association for Experiential Education. Web. 28 May 2013.

Bloom, Benjamin S. *Taxonomy of Educational Objectives.* New York: Longman, 1956. Print.

Braid, Bernice, and Ada Long, eds. *Place as Text: Approaches to Active Learning.* 2nd ed. Lincoln: National Collegiate Honors Council, 2010. NCHC Monograph Series. Print.

Dewey, John. *Experience and Education.* 1938. West Lafayette: Kappa Delta Pi, 1998. Print.

Digby, Joan. *Partners in the Parks: Field Guide to an Experiential Program in the National Parks.* Lincoln: National Collegiate Honors Council, 2010. NCHC Monograph Series. Print.

Habermas, Jürgen. *The Structural Transformation of the Public Sphere: An Inquiry into a Category of Bourgeois Society.* Trans. Thomas Burger and Frederick Lawrence. Cambridge: MIT P, 1989. Print.

Kolb, David A. *Experiential Learning: Experience as the Source of Learning and Development.* Englewood Cliffs, NJ: Prentice Hall, 1984. Print.

Machonis, Peter A., ed. *Shatter the Glassy Stare: Implementing Experiential Learning in Higher Education.* Lincoln: National Collegiate Honors Council, 2008. NCHC Monograph Series. Print.

Spayde, Jon, and Jaida N'ha Sandra. *Salons: The Joy of Conversation.* Gabriola Island, BC: New Society, 2001. Print.

CHAPTER 5

Lessons from Ten Years of a Faculty-Led International Service-Learning Program: Planning, Implementation, and Benefits for First-Year Honors Students

PHAME CAMARENA AND HELEN COLLINS

CENTRAL MICHIGAN UNIVERSITY

The central role of international perspectives and experiences in honors education has a long-documented history beginning with the language study of the classic liberal arts program but increasingly focused on global citizenship and study abroad experiences.[1] Although these standards may have evolved over time with a wide range of requirements now more common across honors curricula, a gold standard for international education, more generally, still exists and includes features such as the use of a second language, home stays or residence with natives in the host country, and full semester or longer cultural immersion experiences. The real value of a study abroad experience for honors students must, however, be measured in terms of the goals and needs of a particular program within the context of its own institution of higher education. In that vein, especially for students in public universities without deep traditions of required language study and significant numbers of students studying abroad, faculty-led international programs developed to meet the specific needs and goals of the students and program may represent an especially valuable mechanism for internationalizing the curriculum.[2]

Drawing from the often-painful lessons learned during the past ten years in developing and refining a three-week, faculty-led international service-learning project to work in children's shelters in Oaxaca, Mexico, this paper will provide a brief overview of the program, highlight key features of program planning and implementation that have contributed to its success, and describe the special meaning this project has for the intentional recruitment of first-year honors students into international experiences. Although the structure and focus of this project may not directly match the needs of other honors programs, at least some of the general principles and strategies should be relevant to other educators wishing to initiate or refine faculty-led programs of their own.

OVERVIEW OF LOS NIÑOS DE OAXACA

Los Niños de Oaxaca began formally in 2002 as a special topics, faculty-led, three-week, study abroad course co-sponsored by the Department of Human Development and Family Studies and University Honors Program of Central Michigan University (CMU). The first program included eighteen students with half drawn from the honors program and the other half drawn from across campus through the co-sponsoring academic department. The most recent Tenth Anniversary class enrolled a total of sixteen students, including ten honors students. This excursion was co-led by two Human Development and Family Studies faculty members who also have appointments as honors faculty, and one was Director of Honors when the Oaxaca program was first developed. Fees for the program this year were set at $1,650 and covered lodging; some meals, including a fiesta/Guelaguetza on the final night dinner; multiple excursions; supplies for service activities; in-country transportation; health insurance; and administrative fees. Although students must also pay for tuition and airfare, the faculty leaders arrange the air reservations, and the honors program subsidizes at least half of the airfare for all honors student participants.

All of the classes have included academic content about Oaxaca, but the learning goals are more narrowly focused on the ways culture matters for understanding and serving the needs of disadvantaged children and youth in Oaxaca. Additional readings on poverty and resilience in children add to the intellectual framework from which students are encouraged to make sense of their service experience. An essential feature of the program is that approximately half of each weekday is spent in direct service to children and youth who live in an *albergue*, a children's shelter for the orphaned, abandoned, or otherwise disadvantaged, or youth who receive support from some other service center meeting the needs of this population. Although the specific focus of the service changes each year depending on the needs and requests by the local partners, activities have generally focused on developing educational enrichment activities; providing one-on-one care for children who would otherwise not receive as much personal attention, such as children with physical or cognitive needs or infants in group care; and teaching conversational English to children who would benefit from language skills. Additional readings, cultural excursions, journaling, and supervised activity round out student classroom time while in Oaxaca. Students also enjoy considerable free time to explore the central historic section of the city during the evenings and weekends. Post-program activities depend on individual learning contracts but always minimally include written reflections on learning experiences tied to both the culture and service themes of the class.

KEY PROGRAM PLANNING AND IMPLEMENTATION ISSUES

From the beginning, the founders of this international project intended to create a course and experience that could successfully run for multiple years and advance both the service and global citizen mission of the CMU University Honors Program. The planning began with a formal year-long needs assessment that involved meetings with the study abroad office staff, faculty from across campus departments, and university administrators and focus-group discussions with students in both honors and regular departmental classes. Although other countries were considered, Mexico was chosen as the destination for the development of the program because of the faculty leader's familiarity with the country, the percentage of honors students who had taken at least some Spanish-language training in high school, and the relative low cost of both transportation and in-country expenses.

The summer after the on-campus needs assessment work was completed, a faculty member and three honors students made an exploratory trip to Central and Southern Mexico to visit a variety of sites and potential partner institutions. They selected exploration sites with the assistance of campus staff and faculty who already had established relationships with colleagues in Mexico and had been alerted to the goals of the program. Onsite visits gave the team the opportunity to assess the potential for meaningful service activities, access to significant cultural experiences outside of the service work, practical issues including the cost of housing and safety of the community, and the availability of a strong onsite advocate. The lessons from both the early assessments and the site visits led to the formalization of a first-year plan for the study abroad experience in Oaxaca, Mexico. Although the program has been substantially enhanced in the ten years that have followed, a core set of identifying features has contributed to the long-term success of the program.

Curricular Mapping

Comments from all of the CMU stakeholders immediately confirmed that the ability to recruit students to a faculty-led study abroad course was largely dependent on how the course would map onto students' academic requirements and fit within their academic schedules. Therefore, the course was developed to run the first three weeks immediately after the end of the spring term so that students could return from the excursion and still be available

LESSONS FROM TEN YEARS

for summer jobs and other on-campus academic experiences such as summer classes or research positions. To maximize the usefulness of the credits, the class was structured with variable credit (3–6 credits) and approved through both the general education committee and honors advisory council to ensure that credits earned could be used in multiple ways to fulfill students' academic requirements. The class can now be used to meet at least four separate sets of requirements, including the General Education Global Cultures requirement, major/minor diversity requirements, advanced honors credits, and honors international credits that replace the foreign language requirement.

Departmental Collaboration

Although the course was developed with a specific focus on the curricular needs of honors students, concerns about recruiting an adequate pool of students each year led to a formal collaboration between an academic department and the CMU University Honors Program. In addition to numerical strength, this strategy also enhanced the recruitment of students with a wide range of skill sets to make the project a success. For example, many honors students have stronger Spanish-language skills than students from the Human Development and Family Studies Program, but relatively few honors students have taken coursework in child behavior management or activity planning. Records verify that honors student participants have come from every college in the university and are as likely to be from business and science as education and human services. Relatively few honors students have come from the co-sponsoring department although some honors students have added a major or minor from that department after their time in Oaxaca.

If this class had been proposed for honors students alone, it would have been approved because of its emphasis on promoting global citizenship and service for the greater good, which are core values of the honors program. The partnership, however, ensures that the enrollment is always adequate so that students can count on the program running each summer. To ensure that the class meets the standards for honors offerings, however, the honors program lists a separate honors section of the class in the schedule. Consistent with expectations for honors sections, although honors students meet all of the core requirements of the regular class, they also take on some additional responsibility for the learning experience and typically work more closely with faculty members in both preparation and follow-up after the summer program. The nature of these activities is modified each year, depending on the faculty leaders and number of honors students, but they have included leading a special renovation project at a site, developing recruitment materials for the following year, identifying readings for the group, and leading discussions about how ideas in the readings are reflected in the experiences of students. Because honors students may have different needs and reasons for participating in the program, faculty members are generally willing and able to develop a special project for honors students. These projects have included special excursions to the hospital for pre-med students and visits to local preschools and elementary schools for students preparing for teacher certification. In the end, as honors students return, complete final reflections, and present to their peers back on campus, faculty also encourage them to connect their learning experience to the service and global citizenship goals of the honors program.

A Service Emphasis

A service focus was an explicit goal of the program from the beginning because it matched the values and objectives of both the academic department and the honors program. The value of this emphasis was clearly reaffirmed in the focus-group discussions with honors students who reported that the ability to directly serve and work with children would be a deciding factor in choosing this class over other options. Students also noted that this emphasis would elicit greater parental support. The challenge, therefore, became finding a service opportunity that would allow a group of students with inconsistent or limited language skills to meet the needs of the site and the children. The strategy developed during the first visit was to ensure that at least some of the children in shelters or centers were so young that language skills became less essential for basic care and enrichment. In the first two years, it became clear that if students worked in teams and had at least one moderately proficient Spanish-language speaker, the team could be effective in leading activities and interacting with the children. Most of the students have at least two years of high school Spanish, and many of the older youth at the centers are also learning English. Thus rich interactions were possible. Although part of the service students provided in each site included some manual labor, such as painting or cleaning, all students are promised during recruitment that they will spend at least some time during most days working directly with children.

Effective International Partnership

From the first meetings over ten years ago to the current inter-actions, the success of this program has been substantially enhanced by the efforts of an explicit partnership formed with an institu-tion and a specific contact person at that partner institution to work with the visiting class. This close connection facilitates better navigation of changes at the sites or in the political environment, like the annual teacher strikes that close down the city each year. Although the basic format of the program has remained consistent, faculty and students have completed projects in multiple sites, and adjustments have been made even after the group has arrived in Oaxaca because of political upheaval and changes in center staff-ing. Having a well-known local professional to smooth relation-ships and address the last-minute crises that arise every year is essential when traveling and housing a group of this size. A further benefit of these long-term relationships is that lessons learned one year about what works can be transferred to decisions made for the following year so that even as sites and faculty leadership of the program change, the historical memory of the project endures intact and is translated to the next group. Thus, when the annual review of sites is conducted in advance of the summer program, the international partner is able to meet with site administrators well in advance to complete a needs assessment based on a clear understanding of what is appropriate and possible for the group set to visit. Of course, any partnership must be mutually beneficial, and this factor means that the project leaders must be sensitive to what the host needs to continue the collaboration, such as remuneration or an exchange agreement to host visitors in the U.S.

Housing and the Balance of Immersion and Retreat

Although the instructors considered home-stays on the initial planning trip, the need for working time to prepare for service activities led to the decision to seek group housing that could also provide space for both formal and informal meetings between students and faculty leaders. Because of the size of the group and the desire to provide students with freedom to explore on their own, a modest hotel with a small courtyard near the historical city center was selected as the home for the group each year. Although this hotel is usually some distance from the service sites, having students learn to navigate the bus system or to hail a cab when needed quickly became part of the cultural immersion experience for students. After a first-day walking tour and orientation to life in the neighborhood surrounding the hotel, students have permission to explore the city center during their free time. What begins with tentative explorations around the block ends with a sense of belonging in the community as students identify favorite locations for coffee, Internet use, and salsa dancing with new friends. Students report that the combination of immersing in the culture at the work site for the day but being able to retreat to the hotel with peers and faculty leaders in the evening eases the rapid cultural adjustment required for this kind of project.

Structured Class Assignments, Activities, and Discussion

Although service is the core feature of this international program, experience over time has reaffirmed the importance of providing clear academic structure and expectations through class assignments, activities, and discussions. Formulating this structure begins in the semester prior to the trip with at least one large-group mandatory orientation meeting to ensure that everyone is clear on everything from what to pack to the academic requirements of the course. Because the majority of the students recruited for this program have little or no previous international experience, a meeting for parents addressed their concerns. Although journaling remains an important fixture of the program, faculty leaders have added additional structure to the journaling process to help identify the problems as they are emerging and to provide some guidance for students to make more effective meaning of the challenges they are facing in managing issues ranging from language deficiencies and cultural adjustments to new ideas about the nature of poverty and need in the new environment. Given the necessity of preparing for activities each day and making sure that everyone is accounted for, faculty members arrange for at least one daily group meal that also serves as a debriefing time for the entire group. There, small-group work and individual assignments can be clarified. Additional course meeting times are also clearly announced, and attendance is verified in each setting to ensure that everyone is accounted for and on task. Interestingly, although significant cultural activities are also scheduled as part of the class and are required for approval of global cultures credit, and excursions to the impressive ruins or the mountain village to meet indigenous craft workers are reported as memorable, student journals and final reflections reveal that, without a doubt, the daily service with children and the everyday navigation of the city have the largest impact on cultural understanding and appreciation.

Co-Leadership and Ownership

A unique feature of this program is that from the first year of full operation, the class has been co-taught by two faculty members with one taking primary leadership and the other serving in an assistant capacity. After the early success of the class and the positive word-of-mouth advertising from students who had participated, the architects of the program realized it could continue to succeed and be refined if they could identify new leaders. To that end, a formal process emerged; after serving for a year or two as an assistant, that faculty member became the leader and recruited a new assistant. Often, prospective faculty assistants might visit the program to observe its operation. This experience would excite them about the potential of the project and reassure them that many of the operational details had already been developed, making their role easier when their turn to take over arrives. Conversely, although many of the operational procedures can still be traced to the first trip, each leader has ownership of the project and is free to make adjustments to accommodate the needs of the group and the changing options and issues of the sites being served. In addition to providing a stable learning opportunity for students, this program has also become an international faculty development opportunity for those who would otherwise never have considered leading an international program. Finally, each of the six leaders who have taken responsibility for this program over the years agrees that having a colleague on the ground in the country is essential because of the potential for crisis and the need for flexibility.[3]

SPECIAL SIGNIFICANCE OF FIRST-YEAR EMPHASIS

Although less essential to the core success of the program, one additional feature of the program that deserves further discussion is the explicit focus on recruiting first-year honors students into the program. Early focus-group discussions clearly revealed that despite honors students being encouraged to complete a semester study abroad program, many students lacked both a basic competence and confidence about functioning in an international setting because they had no international experience prior to college. For them, leaving family and school to travel to another country for a semester as a junior seemed overwhelming. Advertising the Oaxaca project as a way to meet an honors requirement, while also assuring the safety of a group and providing faculty whom students could meet in advance, set the stage for successfully recruiting first-year students during the initial years of the project. The success of these students on the trip and the enthusiasm they demonstrated upon return reinforced the value of this strategy and made first-year honors student recruitment a priority each year. Through the years, a little over 50 percent of all of the honors students who have participated in the Los Niños de Oaxaca program have been first-year students. During the most recent trip, seven of the ten honors students participating in the class were completing their first year of college.

First-Year Student Reports

To evaluate some of the perceptions about the program's significance for first-year honors students, the faculty leaders conducted a formal assessment of the students by collecting data from interviews that addressed students' motivations for participating in the project, their experiences during the study abroad class, and their perceptions of the impact of this experience on their development. (See the Appendix.) They also recruited participants from all previous cohorts of the project via Facebook and email contacts maintained in both current records and the honors alumni database. All fifteen of the twenty-two first-year honors students who were located agreed to participate in the interviews. Two-thirds of the interviews were completed with alumni over the phone; the other third was completed in person because the students were still in residence at the university. Major themes and core constructs from these interviews were identified using a grounded narrative analysis method consistent with the work of Anselm L. Straus and Juliet Corbin.[4] The results from this analysis reinforce many of the responses found in the end-of-program final reflections used for assessment of all students but also highlight the special impact of this project on these students because of their first-year participation.

Similar to the other students participating in the program, a majority of the first-year honors students described growing up in small towns or sheltered suburban neighborhoods where they had limited international experience or exposure. Most described themselves as being "shy," "naïve," and "nervous" about the prospects of leaving home for Mexico for even their brief three-week trip. These students commented that the potential to serve the children in another country was a strong motivation, but that fears of confronting poverty and cultural differences were holding them back. In the end, knowing that it was a faculty-led trip and that they would be with peers eased their anxieties and gave the students the confidence to enroll.

Descriptions of the experiences in Mexico focused largely on the challenges and joys of serving the children, and remarkably few students focused on culture shock in the initial transition to Mexico and the service sites. Students attributed success in the adjustment to the pre-trip preparation and the group support from faculty and peers. Having to confront poverty and seeing children every day on the street, struggling to survive, were consistently noted as "eye opening" and as "something never seen before." These observations, however, were balanced by descriptions of the "resilience of the children" and a "new perspective" on the children's appreciation of the little that they did have and their willingness to share with each other. Rather than judging Mexico ethnocentrically, these students consistently noted the efforts of the caregivers and the gratitude of the children and caregivers for their efforts during their relatively short time at the sites. Almost all of the students had a personal story about a particular experience with a child in a shelter who touched their lives, such as trying to soothe a crying child who was both deaf and blind or observing an act of unselfish sharing between children. More of the students interviewed described significant cultural readjustment challenges upon returning to the United States compared to their adjustment to Mexico. Because of the service nature of the cultural immersion experience, students expressed "frustration" and "sadness" that friends and family members could not understand what they had experienced either in terms of cultural differences or in terms of the service's impact on perceptions of meaning and value. The Mexico they knew was not the same as that experienced by people who had been there only for spring breaks and cruise stops.

Most importantly, when asked to explain in follow-up questions the impact of their experiences and to examine whether these outcomes might be the same had they participated in the same project during their junior year, all of these students resoundingly affirmed that participation in the project had demonstrable short- and long-term effects, and all but one believed that the timing of the project was essential in shaping these outcomes. In addition, they reported new "insights" and "perspective" about an ethic of service and cultural appreciation. Most students described changes in their activity during the semester after they returned. These included visiting the volunteer center to seek new service opportunities; getting more engaged with the international community on campus, perhaps by volunteering to be a conversation partner for a visiting international student; and changing course schedules to explore new academic and career interests spurred by the program. The effect of these choices compounded over time so that over half of the students reported that what began as a class turned into a new major, a commitment to further study abroad, or a new career path or emphasis. For at least a handful of students, this first-year program triggered a series of choices and follow-up experiences so that service and international experience have become the defining focus of their new career paths. For example, one student changed majors after participating in the program and then returned to one of the sites to complete a needs assessment as part of her senior honors project. This commitment led to her finding a PhD program in international service. Similarly, another student found the experience so meaningful that she changed majors, found additional study abroad opportunities, and is now preparing for a career in the Foreign Service.

As the students explained, because this program took place early in their academic careers, they still had flexibility in their academic schedules and the opportunity to make significant adjustments to their academic and career plans. Four of the students reported that the structure of their majors would not have permitted them to participate in an international program had they not traveled during the first year. Even if they did not change their major, the Mexico trip did change the rest of the student's undergraduate experience by producing a greater willingness to take appropriate risks, seek international experiences, and redefine life priorities with a commitment to serving the greater good.

SUMMARY LESSONS

Although the Los Niños de Oaxaca Project varies considerably from the traditional semester study abroad experience described in the international education literature, the planning and structure of this specialized project have ensured continued success consistent with the goals and mission of the university honors program for which it was designed. This approach reaffirms the conclusion drawn by Rosalie C. Otero in her discussion of faculty-led honors international programs where she notes that a strength of these kinds of programs is the degree to which they can be "customized both to the students and the honors program" (41). For the students in the Central Michigan University Honors Program, this customization focused primarily on creating a program that matched curricular requirements or emphasized service, a core value of the CMU Honors Program, and eased anxiety for groups of students with little or no previous international experience. The additional emphasis on recruiting first-year honors students emerged out of these goals but was made possible by the academic collaboration that ensured students from other areas of the university would bring complementary skills to ensure the success of the service activities. Although someone considering the development of a faculty-led international project might draw any number of different lessons from what has been shared, three specific themes deserve special attention because they are unusual in the study abroad field more generally.

The Special Challenges and Opportunities of Service-Learning Projects

In order for the most substantial intercultural learning to occur, according to Carolyn Haynes, students must actively and "meaningfully engage with members of the host country" (21). As the reflections from students participating in this project reveal, the daily work and activities required to serve in the host country provided both sustained and meaningful engagement in ways that many semester study abroad programs do not. Both in the direct service to the children and in the work required to complete the service activities, such as planning a culturally sensitive art activity for a small group of children and then going to the paper store to buy the supplies, CMU honors students are engaged in situations that transform their identities into something much more than those of tourists. They may be outsiders, but they quickly realize the need to adapt to the norms of the culture and to respectfully support the efforts of the service site hosts who have devoted their lives to the care of the children the students soon come to love.

In this vein, faculty leaders of any kind of intercultural service project have extra responsibility to ensure that students are prepared to resist imposing U.S. cultural norms in the service activities.[5] A service-learning emphasis also requires substantially greater adaptability on the part of the faculty leaders because much of what happens on a daily basis at the service site is beyond the control of the leaders. In the end, though, as noted in the feedback from end-of-program evaluations and the narratives of the first-year students, the service activities enhanced both intercultural appreciation and heightened students' commitment to global service and civic engagement back home, suggesting that the outcomes from this kind of project may be multi-pronged in ways that other international programs are not. Further, the depth of learning and outcomes are more directly tied to the service experience than to any other aspect of the course or trip. The intense immersion in and engagement with the culture that come from these experiences are consistent with Mary M. Dwyer's research that shows that a well-designed summer faculty-led program can have as much impact on at least some dimensions of student learning as a full-term or academic-year program (161).

Collaboration Matters

The efforts required to successfully develop and implement a faculty-led international project are substantial, and the addition of a service component only complicates the relationships that must be maintained over time both on campus and with the international hosts. For this project, being able to recruit multiple faculty members who are engaged, flexible, cooperative, and comfortable with cultural ambiguity, even if not experts in the culture, has made the continuation of the project beyond its original three-year plan possible. Shared ownership between an academic department and the Central Michigan University Honors Program has ensured strong enrollments and extra opportunities for both students and faculty that might not have otherwise endured. Respect for the wisdom and support of a stable international partner and the quality of the transitional leadership process that has developed over time have also ensured that even as the leadership of the program changes, lessons learned about service issues and the course continue to be infused to improve the project each year. Compared to the expenditure of time and money required to develop a new international program, efforts to build strong collaborations and shared ownership from the beginning have paid off and helped to create a self-perpetuating program as each cohort of faculty and students returns energized by the transformative experience and ready to recruit the next group of leaders and participants.

First-Year Focus

Finally, scholars like Robert Selby have emphasized the potential power of international education to transform students and contribute to the growth of informed global citizens. As the work from this project has demonstrated, however, efforts to target and recruit first-year honors students may have special significance for intensifying the transformative potential of these experiences. An early meaningful international experience empowered these first-year students and encouraged their continued action as global citizens beyond what would have happened had their first study abroad experience occurred during the more traditional junior year. Consistent with the findings of Joshua S. McKeown and Duarte Morais and Anthony Ogden, this study found that a short-term, faculty-led study abroad experience may be the catalyst for creating the kind of life-altering outcomes that honors hopes to facilitate. As is true for this program, the potential value of this kind of faculty-led class is further heightened when most students have limited prior international experience or have matriculated at a university where full-term study abroad programs are not normative for the student population.

CONCLUSION

The major lessons and themes in the planning and review of the Los Niños Project were chosen primarily because of the potential for these lessons to translate to other honors faculty and staff who are considering the development of new international programs and activities. What is not noted here, therefore, is the myriad number of decisions that can directly influence the program outcomes, such as alcohol policy, formal curfew, minimum language requirement, structure of academic projects, and specific dates for the program, that faculty leaders must make each year for all study abroad programs. One thing that should be clear from the themes and lessons that have been shared is that leading a group of students on an international service-learning project is not for the inflexible or faint of heart because the experience is among the most stressful teaching experiences that faculty leaders report across their academic careers. At the same time, the faculty leaders acknowledge that running Los Niños de Oaxaca is also one of the most meaningful and memorable teaching experiences of their careers. In the end, both the anecdotal observations and more formal reflections from the students confirm that while this program cannot save the children of Oaxaca, nor should it be expecting to, it can certainly provide experiences that transform the lives of the students who participate. As students from the very first cohort noted in their thank you card to the service host on the last day of the trip, "*Vinimos a ayudar a los niños de Oaxaca. Al final, nosotros fuimos los que mas cambiamos.*"[6]

ACKNOWLEDGMENTS

Faculty leaders of Los Niños de Oaxaca have included: Phame Camarena, Helen Hagens, Phyllis Heath, Tara Saathoff-Wells, Edgar Long, and Jeff Angera. All have made significant contributions to the development of this program. Funding for the development of Los Niños de Oaxaca was provided by the CMU Offices of International Education and the University Honors Program.

NOTES

[1]Both Haynes and Shoemaker provide useful background context for the role of international programs in honors education.

[2]Morais and Ogden; Otero; and Sachau, Brasher, and Fee offer recommendations on ways to ensure that short-term study abroad programs are meaningful and connected to the goals and missions of institutions.

[3]During the ten years of the project, multiple students have required medical attention, service sites have been altered after arrival in the city, and faculty leaders themselves have been ill. In each case, having a second faculty member onsite ensured smooth continuation of the program activities.

[4]The Straus and Corbin method uses a grounded, constant-comparative strategy to identify the themes and constructs that emerge from within the voices of the participants themselves rather than to test for a particular finding or pattern of results.

[5]Gammonley, Rotabi, and Gamble as well as Hartman provide important cautions about the potential for ethnocentric biases in international service projects that harm the effectiveness of the service and diminish the value of the learning.

[6]We came to help the children of Oaxaca. In the end, we were the ones who were changed the most.

WORKS CITED

Dwyer, Mary M. "More is Better: The Impact of Study Abroad Program Duration." *Frontiers: The Interdisciplinary Journal of Study Abroad* 10 (2004): 151–63. Print.

Gammonley, Denise, Karen Rotabi, and Dorothy N. Gamble. "Enhancing Global Understanding with Study Abroad: Ethically Grounded Approaches to International Learning." *Journal of Teaching in Social Work* 27 (2007): 115–35. Print.

Hartman, Eric. "Balancing Risk and Reward in Service Abroad." *International Educator* 20.4 (2011): 48–51. Print.

Haynes, Carolyn. "Overcoming the Study Abroad Hype." *Journal of the National Collegiate Honors Council* 12.1 (2011): 17–24. Print.

McKeown, Joshua S. *The First Time Effect: The Impact of Study Abroad on College Student Intellectual Development.* Albany: State U of New York P, 2009. Print.

Morais, Duarte, and Anthony Ogden. "Embedded Education Abroad and Unacknowledged Populations." The Forum on Education Abroad Annual Conference, Charlotte, NC, March 24–26, 2010. Web. 26 July 2011.

Otero, Rosalie C. "Faculty-Led International Honors Programs." *Journal of the National Collegiate Honors Council* 12.1 (2011): 41–45. Print.

Sachau, Daniel, Niel Brasher, and Scott Fee. "Three Models for Short-Term Study Abroad." *Journal of Management Education* 34.5 (2010): 645–70. Print.

Selby, Robert. "Designing Transformation in International Education." *Developing Intercultural Competence and Transformation: Theory, Research, and Application in International Education* Ed. Victor Savicki. Sterling, VA: Stylus, 2008. 1–10. Print.

Shoemaker, Mel. "New Paradigm of Honors Education." *National Honors Report* 12.4 (2002): 6–8. Print.

Strauss, Anselm L., and Juliet Corbin. *Basics of Qualitative Research: Grounded Theory Procedures and Techniques.* Thousand Oaks, CA: Sage, 1990. Print.

APPENDIX

Interview Protocol

As you know, my job is to get your story and thoughts about experiences with the Los Niños de Oaxaca project as a first-year honors student. To do this, I am going to ask you a series of open-ended questions starting back from when you first started at CMU and learned about the project all the way up to now and what meaning you think your experience wound up having in your life overall.

1. To start, first, tell me a little about yourself when you first came to CMU as a first-year honors student. If I would have met you as a first-semester student, how would you have described who you were—where were you from, how did you feel about coming to college, what was your academic plan, or anything else you think was important to understanding who you were at that time?

2. How did you first hear about the Oaxaca program and what was your immediate reaction to the project?

3. Why did you finally decide to go to Oaxaca? What influenced your decision to participate?

4. As you were preparing for the trip, what were your impressions, concerns, and thoughts?

5. Tell me about when it was time to travel and you finally left for Mexico. What was the transition to Oaxaca like for you?

6. Looking back know, what other experiences from your three weeks in Oaxaca most stand out to you as being meaningful and important? (probe: any other experiences that you think were important for you to add?)

CHAPTER 6

An Interpersonal Engagement Approach to International Study:
Lessons in Leadership and Service Learning from South Africa

Kevin W. Dean and Michael B. Jendzurski
West Chester University of Pennsylvania

In May 2011, the Honors College at West Chester University of Pennsylvania (WCU) celebrated a decade of student and faculty research and service in South Africa. In its curricular and co-curricular offerings, honors education at WCU focuses on leadership development for the purpose of community engagement. To that end, our relationship with South Africa serves as a hallmark of our honors college and links to its mission: to be honorable is to serve. Through sustained involvement in South Africa, WCU students have strengthened their research skills, leadership skills, global awareness, and commitment to community service.

Through our experience in South Africa, we have learned that international travel itself does not accomplish these goals; indeed, in a global society students often have multiple opportunities for international travel. The key contributor to the outcomes mentioned above has been interpersonal engagement. Communication theorists Stephen W. Littlejohn and Karen A. Foss suggest "interpersonal" involves direct and personal connections between at least two individuals who create understanding and meaning through dialog in a particular context (229–62). Carolyn Haynes identifies "engagement" as a key indicator of meaningful international experiences (21). In this context, engagement denotes active participation rather than passive observation. As the program in South Africa expanded over the past decade, it not only provided opportunities for international travel but also intentionally deepened student experiences of interpersonal engagement with those living in the communities they visited. Two key strategies frame the approach to interpersonal engagement: dialog with cultural others and service-based research. These approaches are literally transformative for the participants, as evidenced through a deep sensitivity to global inequities, a recognition of themselves as change agents, and an articulated commitment to service.

SOUTH AFRICA: TWO WORLDS

It does not take long to be awed by the natural beauty of South Africa, particularly the Cape Town region. Pristine beaches and deep-blue water share the dual horizons of infinity and breathtaking landscapes of lush mountains. Protected by the iconic Table Mountain, high-quality artisan craft shops intermingled with exclusive boutiques and fine-dining establishments dot the inner harbor area. State-of-the-art transportation and communication systems, coupled with an almost universal use of the English language, make South Africa an attractive tourist destination. This positive image gained further acclaim when South Africa hosted soccer's 2010 World Cup and showed the global audience a vibrant, dynamic country.

At the same time, South Africa's wealth and natural beauty stand in stark juxtaposition to the developing-world realities experienced by the majority of the country's people. Approximately thirty minutes from downtown Cape Town lie Gugulethu and Khayelitsha Townships. These densely populated areas are aptly described by acclaimed Yale historian Leonard Thompson. He vividly depicts township life where multiple family and often non-family members share one- or two-room informal dwellings made of cardboard, corrugated aluminum, and scrap metal panels. Most lack running water, electricity, and indoor toilet facilities. Poverty and its persistent companions, disease and hunger, abound as daily reminders of the tyrannical system of apartheid (187–297). The promises of the Mandela government and the New Constitution of 1994, while providing great hope and inspiration, remain largely unrealized by millions.

The abolition of apartheid in 1994 provided the pivotal reason for selecting South Africa as a laboratory for investigating issues of community building, democracy, and leadership that are central concerns for the WCU honors curriculum. The South African context further enhances the curriculum by affording students interpersonal engagement opportunities with two unique populations of social activists.

The first group became engaged at the same age level as the WCU students. Thompson emphasized how South African teenagers dramatically focused world attention on apartheid's injustices in 1976. In Soweto Township, high school students took to the streets to protest studying in Afrikaans and advocated instruction in English. When government troops fired upon the youth, images of the "Soweto Uprising" flooded the world media (212). This flash point helped to usher in a wave of international sanctions and boycotts against the South African government that eventually forced its capitulation. WCU students experience both inspiration and humility concerning their own roles as community change agents upon discovering that students of their own age catalyzed the movement ending apartheid.

A second important group of activists who engaged the students are jurists, who shared personal experiences with the Truth and Reconciliation Commission (TRC), the iconic model for enacting social justice. Award-winning documentary directors Frances Reid and Debra Hoffman captured the essence of the proceedings:

> Under the leadership of Archbishop Desmond Tutu, jurists conducted hearings nationally, affording victims of apartheid opportunities to share their stories and for perpetrators to come forward into the glaring lights of the media, tell the truth of what happened, and seek forgiveness.[1]

Unlike the Nuremburg Trials after World War II, which sought retributive justice, the TRC aimed for restorative justice. Put simply, if individuals acting under the orders of the government committed a violent crime of torture, rape, or murder and came before the TRC with a full and truthful account of the case, they received absolution for the crime.

By 2001, the first year of WCU's group program, South Africans who had been teenagers during the Soweto Uprising had grown into men and women in their 30s to early 40s. Many of the jurors of the TRC were now in their mid-to-late 50s, and representatives from both groups graciously offered the students opportunities for dialog. Interacting with such living history enabled students to understand that just one voice can make a difference and challenged them to create their own leadership journeys.

BEGINNINGS

In 1996, a three-year grant from the Kellogg National Fellowship Program (KNFP) launched the program in South Africa. With its focus on leadership training and global development, the KNFP grant provided the opportunity for the WCU honors director to travel to South Africa in 1997. The KNFP project involved conducting interviews with university presidents to discern best practices in leadership; one interview was arranged with the president of Huguenot College in Wellington, South Africa. Interactions with Deon Kitching, then professor of Youth Ministry and Culture at Huguenot, resulted in Kitching's offer to facilitate international study and a service project in South Africa. Kitching's passion for education, vast personal connections, and commitment to onsite support provided critical elements for initiating a long-term partnership.

A major grant from the Pennsylvania State System of Higher Education (PASSHE) cleared the financial hurdle for the initial international program. Key elements of the curricular program development—both stateside and in South Africa—and the international experience follow-up that were devised for this initial experience remain foundational programmatic elements of WCU's current global education initiatives.

The grant provided two thirds of the funding, with WCU supplying the balance, for twenty-eight honors students (two from each of the PASSHE Universities) and seven WCU faculty to engage in an intensive week's training at WCU, followed by a two-week international immersion.[2] During the week at WCU, students explored approaches to the study of leadership and the political, social, and cultural realities of pre- and post-apartheid South Africa, focusing on the TRC and its support for nation building. Participants were also introduced to the devastation of HIV-AIDS and trained in ethnographic research. During their two weeks in South Africa, students spent time with HIV-AIDS victims served by the J. L. Zwane Center, and they explored educational outreach provided by social work faculty at Huguenot College and health care providers at Sparrow Village, an HIV-AIDS children's hospice. Students met with their peers at Huguenot College to discuss cross-cultural perspectives of college life and how post-apartheid youth viewed their social and political culture. More formal dialogs were held with community change agents: professionals from a variety of vocations including health care, education, law, media, business, and religion. None of these individuals held any substantial power through wealth or title; they represented ordinary citizens who became agents of change through conviction to social justice and contributed to the transition from apartheid to democracy.

While in South Africa, the group traveled to Robben Island for a personal tour by a former inmate, the Cape of Good Hope, a wine estate, Table Mountain, and the District Six Museum. The group also participated in two service projects: delivering nearly one ton of school supplies that they had collected to an elementary school and spending a day preparing and delivering soup to three elementary schools. The program concluded with three nights in a game park, where students saw a vast array of wildlife and discussed eco-tourism with guest speakers.

Upon returning to WCU, the group met for a two-hour debriefing session before students left for home. Each student and faculty member shared a memory from the experience. Almost to a person, the students recounted personal conversations and specific relationships forged as the memories that most powerfully shaped them: a child at one of the elementary schools who had no shoes, a person afflicted with HIV-AIDS who expressed deep appreciation that a stranger came to listen, the admonishment of TRC jurors who challenged students to consider forgiveness over retribution for those who offend them. Beyond reflection, delegation members were invited to identify a way to give back to their local communities through engaging in a specific act of community service. Students and faculty wrote personal commitments on newsprint and then reported outcomes of their local investment at a reunion event held in October. Students' application of lessons learned globally inspired faculty and administration.

Very quickly, the faculty and the two WCU students on the trip experienced what might be termed "survivor's guilt." How had they been so fortunate in receiving this trip of a lifetime? What could they do to allow a wider campus audience to hear the stories and learn the lessons of leadership that they had been privileged to experience firsthand? Drawing from the summer curriculum, the faculty members developed a new course, Personal Leadership Development: Lessons from South Africa, for the fall 2001 term. Within two weeks of advertising the course, it filled to capacity. Initially proposed as a one-time offering, the course garnered such student enthusiasm that it justified a second run in fall 2002. Enrollment for that course reached maximum capacity within twenty-four hours, and students advocated for an international travel/service opportunity linked to the class. Because PASSHE funds were not available for a return program, students recognized the need for independent fundraising; by fall 2003, a core of twenty students committed to raise $3,500 each towards an all-inclusive twelve-day international experience in South Africa. The international project would function as a capstone experience to a spring 2004 honors seminar, and thus, the next phase of the South Africa partnership began. Since 2004, the WCU Honors College has sponsored research and service-learning programs in South Africa in even-numbered years. Financial considerations drive the even-year cycle because most students require two years to generate needed funds.

2004 AND BEYOND

The program begins on campus during the spring semester when students enroll in an honors course focusing on South Africa's unfolding story of nation-building in the post-apartheid era. Students learn ethnographic research methodology, which serves as the basis of their research and service projects. The course culminates with a two-week immersion experience in South Africa, where students, facilitated by honors faculty, conduct community needs-assessment research.

Building upon the mission statement of the WCU Honors College, "To be honorable is to serve," a research-based, service-learning project functions as the foundation of each international experience. While students engage in physical service during the program such as distributing school supplies and shoes or preparing and delivering soup, the principle service-learning experience requires research-based service through ethnographic interviews. These interviews require students to research and develop solutions to community issues. The specific topics are developed through a dialog between the South African partners and WCU faculty, who specialize in community needs-assessment research.

Rev. Spiwo Xapile, a Presbyterian pastor and CEO of the J. L. Zwane Center (JLZC), served as the primary partner for our

2004, 2006, and 2008 research programs in South Africa. Located in Gugulethu Township, the JLZC provides support for victims of HIV-AIDS and their caregivers. Urged to focus on caregivers, who are the forgotten victims of AIDS, WCU faculty and students researched the needs of three care-provider populations: (1) grandmothers responsible for grandchildren because of their own children's deaths from AIDS (2004); 2) orphaned teens serving as heads of households and providing for younger siblings because of their parents' deaths (2006); and 3) non-relatives who open their homes to HIV-AIDS orphans (2008).

Paired into interview teams, WCU students conduct ninety-minute interviews with caregivers. All interviews are audio-taped (and, from 2008 onward, video-recorded) and transcribed. Each project involves the completion of thirty to forty interviews. The students analyze the interview transcripts for repeating themes in terms of the caregivers' needs. The students write a final report for the JLZC, identifying needs and the strategies to address them. In 2004, for example, a prevalent concern articulated by the grandmothers centered on a lack of available transportation to take their sick grandchildren, many of whom were HIV-positive, to a clinic. This finding surprised everyone at the JLZC. Equipped with the data, the JLZC staff drafted a successful grant request for a mini-van to address the transportation inadequacy.

Another critical component of WCU's program involves incorporating regular debriefing sessions, both during and immediately after the program. Such sessions help students to codify what honors educators Bernice Braid and Gladys Palma de Schrynemakers identify as central to effective programs: the examination of connections between coursework and experience (26). In such gatherings, faculty serve as culture brokers who help students interpret cultural differences. These sessions also reinforce the communication patterns appropriate in a cross-cultural context. As communication scholar Kevin W. Dean notes, international education mandates "rhetorical sensitivity"; students and faculty must recognize their primary role as guests and not social reformers (1329). Students and faculty may be tempted to fix and critique perceived problems. This feeling is particularly strong during the days of interviews when the narrative accounts of hunger, abuse, disease, and death become a face seen, a voice heard, a touch felt, a full person realized. Contact with human pain and suffering trigger emotional challenges for participants. In small group discussions, asserts community builder Peter Block, students "discover that individual concerns are more universal than imagined . . . [that] we are not alone" (95). Despite their anxieties, as invited guests in the presence of hosts whose culture, values, beliefs, and practices the participants do not fully understand, they are not in a position to voice their perceptions of social injustice in a public arena. As honors educators Leena Karsan et al. caution, "the service component of our trip [is] not necessarily to help 'solve' the problem but rather provide 'human capital' that works in implementing action steps under the guidance of a host country's non-profit leaders" (34). More bluntly, Block advises that "we leave our self-interest at the door and show up to learn rather than to advocate" (76). Internalized frustration can cripple without a healthy outlet; thus, students and faculty alike need safe and ample time for processing all the powerful stimuli of each day.

When the group returns to the U.S., they gather for a final debriefing session. This session provides time for each student to articulate a concrete story that captures the essence of his or her experience. The typical questions students face from family and friends include: "Well, how was it?" or "Did you have a nice time?" Riveting images of human suffering often challenge students to find the right word or phrase to capture a memorable event or image. Allowing students to articulate such images in a safe space eases their transition back into American society.

Michael Jendzurski faced such a challenge during his freshman year with a boy of ten at Nkosi's Haven, an HIV-AIDS hospice outside of Johannesburg. Michael sports ball caps and noticed this particular boy wore one as well; through the hats they connected. As we left the two posed for a picture. The boy became transfixed by the camera screen because he had never seen an image of himself. Without hesitation Michael promised to return one day and give the boy a copy of the picture. Michael soon realized the risk his promise represented: he did not know the boy's HIV status nor had he been able to get the boy's name. The following spring, Michael had an unexpected opportunity to return to Nkosi's Haven. At the center, Michael waited for over thirty minutes, wondering if the boy would remember him, wondering if the boy was still alive. Suddenly the young boy bolted around the corner and broke into a wide grin at the sight of Michael. After an embrace the two posed for a picture with the picture that Michael brought. The young boy, Samkelo, and Michael have shared subsequent conversations.

ASSESSMENT OF PROGRAM OUTCOMES

From 2003 to 2011, seventy-eight WCU students participated in research and service-learning projects in South Africa. To measure the impact of these international experiences on the students, the honors college conducted a survey of program alumni in 2011. (See the Appendix.) The first section of the survey asked program alumni to reflect on the impact of their South Africa experience on their research skills, leadership knowledge and skills, and community involvement. In each area, respondents were asked to compare this program's impact with that of other curricular programs with which they had been involved. The second section of the survey was composed of open-ended questions that afforded respondents the opportunity to share personal narrative accounts. Fifty-two of the seventy-eight program alumni participated in the survey. (One problem with the methodology is that no pre-travel student perceptions were gathered, so the assessment is based exclusively on participants' post-travel reflections.)

Demographics

That females composed 57.7% of the respondents and males 42.3% reflects the predominance of women in study abroad programs noted by the Institute of International Education ("Open Door"). Although still in the minority, the male participation is, however, quite strong, especially when considering that the WCU Honors College student body is seventy percent female and thirty percent male. In terms of major, respondents represented seventeen academic disciplines. The greatest representation (38%) came from the sciences, which is counter, according to Mark Salisbury et al., to generally lower participation in study abroad programs of students majoring in STEM fields (ctd. in Haynes 19). The higher representation of students in the sciences suggests that the program's focus on HIV-AIDS exposure in at-risk populations is particularly relevant to those in scientific and health-care fields. Students of all class levels participated in the program, but it is notable that a majority (55.5%) were first- or second-year students. This factor contributed to program sustainability because the best recruitment tool for international study comes from student participants who share the value of their experiences with their peers. Students also returned energized to assume leadership and service roles within their communities. (See Tables 2 and 4.) Travel early in the college experience affords students time for greater campus and community involvement as well as the possibility of further international study during their undergraduate careers

An additional demographic item suggests another valuable recruiting technique. Eighty-six percent of respondents completed an academic course, Honors 352: Personal Leadership Development: Lessons from South Africa, before enrolling in the honors course that directly involved international travel. Of that number, 95% indicated the course influenced or strongly influenced their decision to participate in international study. Haynes advocates infusing lessons learned through international travel with academic coursework prior to any international travel (21). Enrollment in Honors 352 achieved the dual goals of providing academic preparation and inspiring participation in the subsequent international travel course.

Across all demographic categories, respondents reported that participation in the South African projects had and continue to have a transformational impact. A majority of respondents confirmed that the international service-learning projects provided significant opportunities to enhance their development in five noteworthy areas: (1) research skills; (2) knowledge of leadership theory and practice; (3) leadership skills; (4) global awareness; and (5) commitment to service. The survey findings are summarized below.

In the first part of the survey, students were asked to reflect on the impact of their participation in the South Africa project on their social science research skills. A significant majority of respondents (95.7%) agreed that participation in the South Africa project significantly enhanced their ethnographic research skills, including training in interviewing, videotaping, and transcribing oral interviews. More than four-fifths of respondents (82.2%) emphasized that the South Africa project had also significantly strengthened their survey-construction skills.

Table 1 presents students' perceptions of the impact of their South Africa experience on their understanding of leadership theory and practice. As a result of their participation in the South Africa project, 95% of respondents noted that they gained a greater understanding of leadership theory and practice. Gaining more than theoretical knowledge of leadership, students also broadened their self-knowledge of their leadership skills. Importantly, 87.3% recognized that leadership can emerge without a formal title, and nearly all gained a greater awareness of their personal strengths and limitations as leaders. This enhanced self-knowledge is reflected in one student's comment: "People with little means could make a great impact . . . [so] stop using the excuse of, 'I'll do it when I have more money,' or 'I'll begin working in a non-profit after I'm done with college.'" The local leaders who effect change in the face of staggering odds in South African townships provide students with inspirational role models. One student commented on the actions of Rev. Cecil Begbie, President and CEO of H.E.L.P. Ministries, which feeds some 5,000 people daily: "Watching Cecil Begbie interact with the unemployed community members was something I will never forget. They seemed so disheartened and beaten as they stood in line, waiting for their cup of soup and slice of bread. But when Rev. Cecil Begbie spoke with them and asked them about their families and lives, they changed immensely: they smiled. Rev. Begbie did more than fill their stomachs: he fed their souls." Begbie's leadership and interpersonal engagement demonstrate how

TABLE 1: IMPACT ON LEADERSHIP THEORY, PRACTICE, AND SELF-KNOWLEDGE

Element of Leadership	Much More	More	Some	Less	Much Less
Understanding of multiple theories of leadership development and practice	42.60%	42.60%	8.45%	6.35%	0.00%
Understanding that leadership can emerge without a title (expert power)	36.15%	51.10%	12.75%	0.00%	0.00%
Knowledge of personal strengths as a leader	42.60%	42.60%	8.45%	6.35%	0.00%
Knowledge of personal limitations as a leader	48.90%	29.80%	17.00%	4.30%	0.00%
Knowledge of historical and contemporary international leaders in community change	59.60%	40.40%	0.00%	0.00%	0.00%

one person can make a positive difference, even against an enemy as powerful as hunger.

As a final observation, all participants indicated that this experience provided greater knowledge of international models of community change than any other curricular experience. Familiarity with leaders outside the American context benefits students coming of age in a global society, and this finding clearly advocates student engagement in research and service-based international programming.

Table 2 focuses on the application of leadership concepts. Students articulated the impact of the project on the development of the practical skill sets or tools that leaders use as they interact with others. As a result of their South Africa experience, the students perceived a greatly improved ability to discern the leadership gifts of others (87.0%) and understand the value of building teams of gifted leaders (78.8%). Nearly 90% also noted improved team-building skills. Several respondents saw these skills exemplified in the work of the staff members at Sparrow Village, an HIV-AIDS orphanage southwest of Johannesburg. One student recalled, "They each brought their own unique gifts and abilities to meet a need in the community. Some of them were blessed with ideas and entrepreneurship, while others were cooks, educators, and medical personnel." Others saw the implementation of multiple gifts and teamwork through those who fought against the injustices of apartheid: "None of them did it alone; leadership was team-based and people-centered. I learned that as a leader I am not an island, but rather there are other diversely gifted and talented leaders around me and we need each other to use as resources." These lessons are reflective of Harvard's Kennedy School of Government scholar Ronald Heifetz's notion of balcony leadership, in which effective leaders, entrusting operations to the giftedness of others, step back from the action, thus enabling them to have an opportunity to see the larger picture (ctd. in Heifetz and Linsky 51–74).

Respondents also recognized the importance of prioritizing personal health and well-being to sustain leadership in challenging situations. "It is really important," noted one respondent, "to stay strong for yourself so you can be strong for others." Such comprehension is particularly valuable for honors students who often feel they must be practically perfect in every way. Often defined since grammar school as "the smart kids," many honors students place

Table 2: Impact on Leadership Skills

Element of Leadership	Much More	More	Some	Less	Much Less
Skills in discerning the leadership gifts of others	43.5%	43.5%	8.7%	4.3%	0.0%
Understanding of value of collaborative teamwork	36.2%	42.6%	17.0%	2.1%	2.1%
Team-building skills	39.2%	47.9%	4.3%	6.5%	2.1%
Skills in self-awareness and self-care	45.7%	37.0%	15.2%	2.1%	0.0%

unrealistic expectations on themselves to excel at every task, which can lead to burn-out. South African community leaders modeled the firm commitment needed to lead others. Including rest and play, designated time for invigoration and regeneration proves essential for maintaining the energy and focus needed for leadership.

Table 3 summarizes the impact of participation in the South Africa project on students' global awareness. For nearly all respondents, the program provided a much keener understanding of their part in a global community. One student captured this sentiment:

> The most valuable lesson from my trips to South Africa is that of my place in the global world. I learned that I am privileged to have been born in the USA to an amazing family and the rights that go along with that. I have a responsibility to those people in my community and abroad to give them those same opportunities and blessings. It is inspiring when you learn to think in terms of others and to pass that way of thinking on to others.

TABLE 3: IMPACT ON GLOBAL AWARENESS

Global Awareness	Much More	More	Some	Less	Much Less
Understanding of membership in a global community	70.2%	23.4%	6.4%	0.0%	0.0%
Awareness of global needs	76.1%	21.7%	2.2%	0.0%	0.0%

Such insights bring a sense of hope to South African leaders who view Americans as isolationists. The students are fortunate to regularly interact with Reverend Peter Storey, former Bishop of the South African Methodist Church and frontline activist on the national level in the transformation from apartheid to democracy. He confronts students with the harsh observation that Americans live in a bubble where they are oblivious to pain and suffering in the world. The reaction of over 93% of the respondents, who provided testimony about their heightened personal awareness of the global community, demonstrates the potential influence international education has to move students out of the bubble of indifference.

All respondents also noted a heightened recognition of global needs. Block defines citizen as "one who is willing to be account-able for and committed to the well-being of the whole" (63). One approach to fulfilling this definition is recognizing human need, and international study offers that possibility. The initial images of South Africa that participants shared were ones of stark contrast: "Riding to the Cape of Good Hope, I clearly recall staring out the left window of the bus, watching the hiccup hills rise and set in front of the Indian Ocean. I was awed by the beauty. Yet, to my right, impoverished townships spread out to the horizon, seem-ingly more endless than the ocean." Upon seeing Gugulethu for the first time, one student shared, "All that ran through my mind was the question, 'Do people really live here?'" These preliminary views from the bus gave way to greater understanding and appreciation as students and faculty exited the bus and began forming relationships. Another respondent wrote:

> The woman providing care to HIV-afflicted children was only 19—I was also 19 at the time. Hearing her stories made me see how much hope she had despite the poverty and disease around her. After our interview, we sat with tea and talked about music—we realized we both liked a lot of the same artists. Despite our homes being on opposite ends of the world, we still shared connections.

In South Africa, many students confronted issues of white and middle-class privilege for the first time. This experience led to deep reflection and became a powerful mirror for students. One participant cautioned against passing judgment through the eyes of privilege: "We walk into their country and see need everywhere, and pain and struggle. South Africans look at their country and see a miracle." Such commentary demonstrates a high level of reflective thinking and provides students with an opportunity to reframe the way they might view the world. Rather than seeing a township in South Africa or a tenement in Philadelphia as a problem to solve, students now have a lens to view the context as an opportunity to learn. Embracing such a linguistic shift transforms hopelessness into possibility.

The open-ended responses to the survey also emphasized the increased development of intercultural competencies. As Block notes, international programs provide opportunities for students to "cross boundaries where they become connected to those they are not used to being in the room with" (75). For many respondents, recognition of the cross-cultural other comes through relational interactions that transform abstract notions of otherness into the reality of a distinctive human being. The primary relationships form through the ethnographic research students conduct; it affords students sustained time with one or two individuals in a setting that promotes self-disclosure. In 2004, when students interviewed grandmothers who care for HIV-AIDS-afflicted grandchildren, the first question on the survey was "how are you doing?" Many of the women interviewed began to weep and through tears replied, "no one has ever asked me that." Several proceed with comments such as "you are an angel to have come all the way here from America to ask me that question" and "you now have a Granny in South Africa." In follow-up interviews conducted with these women in 2006, the women broke into smiles and embraced the students when they entered the center, a powerful testimony to sustained partnerships.

Memorable encounters, like those with the grandmothers, were not limited to that particular population; in response to a question regarding their lasting memories from the program, 78% of the student participants recalled a relationship with a cultural other, while fewer than 10% noted physical locations and natural beauty. The majority who highlighted relationships reinforces the value of interpersonal engagement as a critical component of international programs and supports the claim that encounters with others produce powerful and lasting memories that can function as motivational forces for personal and global change.

Table 4 summarizes the program's impact on students' commitment to service. This information provides insight into actions the students took following their international experiences. Participation in the South Africa project led to a powerfully heightened commitment to service among program participants. The data demonstrate a level of commitment that is rather unusual in the millennial population. Sociologist Christian Smith conducted in-depth studies of the millennial demographic and concluded:

> The idea that today's emerging adults are, as a generation, leading a new wave of renewed civic-mindedness and political involvement is sheer fiction. The fact that anyone ever believed that idea simply tells us how flimsy the empirical evidence that so many journalistic media stories are based upon is and how unaccountable to empirical reality high-profile journalism can be. (qtd. in Smith et al. 224)

The respondents in this survey, however, embraced the notion of giving time and financial support to others. Similarly high numbers articulated a willingness to motivate others to serve. Additionally,

TABLE 4: IMPACT ON COMMITMENT TO SERVICE

Commitment to Service	Much More	More	Some	Less	Much Less
Increased motivation for giving your time to others	69.6%	23.9%	6.5%	0.0%	0.0%
Increased motivation for giving your financial resources to others	48.9%	33.3%	17.8%	0.0%	0.0%
Increased motivation for inspiring others to engage in serving others	58.7%	34.8%	6.5%	0.0%	0.0%
Commitment for sustaining the service you provided to South Africa after your return to the United States	47.8%	41.3%	8.7%	2.2%	0.0%
Recognizing the value your service brings to you	60.9%	34.8%	4.3%	0.0%	0.0%
Recognizing the value your service brings to others	60.9%	32.6%	6.5%	0.0%	0.0%
Understanding the principle of servant leadership	54.3%	39.2%	6.5%	0.0%	0.0%

89.1% indicated a commitment to ensuring that their service remained sustained after their personal connections to the given service project ended. As further support that these projects generate a philanthropic spirit, the participants strongly agreed that service benefits both those who give (95.7%) and those who receive (93.5%). One participant reflected: "The most valuable lesson learned through the project in South Africa is how beneficial service can be and not only that, but how rewarding. South Africa and the honors program have influenced me to have new experiences and [to] value serving the community." In preparation for international study, students gain familiarity with the writings of management scholar and founder of the Center for Applied Ethics, Robert K. Greenleaf. He articulates a vision of leadership where "the great leader is seen as a servant first" (7). Servant leaders, according to Greenleaf, become motivated for leadership when they take time to know the needs of those whom they serve and avoid presuming "to know more of what is in the best interest of the recipients than the recipients know for themselves" (168). Although students' motivation for service is often subject to skepticism, a vast majority (93.4%) articulated a perceived understanding of Greenleaf's principle of servant leadership. This perspective places the leader's focus constantly on the other rather than the self.

CONCLUSION

For over a decade, WCU's partnership in South Africa has benefited students by powerfully enhancing their research skills, leadership knowledge and skills, global awareness, and commitment to community engagement. As one respondent summarized: "Gaining firsthand experience of global poverty and the effects of the AIDS pandemic was very valuable. Reading articles and books is moving, but they do not have as great of an influence as actually interacting with people who live in poverty, are affected by HIV/AIDS, and hold hope for a better future."

While the transformative power of the South Africa partnership is evident for student participants, the impact extends beyond those who travel internationally. These ventures have spawned three regular curricular offerings: Personal Leadership Development: Lessons from South Africa; Video Production for Social Justice; and a Special Topics in Globalization and Leadership seminar, which is offered in the spring of even-numbered years in conjunction with the travel to South Africa. Since 2002, over 550 students, none of whom traveled to South Africa, have enrolled in one or more of these offerings. Another signature outgrowth, now in its eighth year, is "Aid to South Africa," an annual student-run event that raises funds for South African children who are infected with HIV-AIDS. Over 80% of the proceeds go directly to one of WCU's three service partners: H.E.L.P. Ministries, Sparrow Village, and Nkosi's Haven.

These outcomes are realized through the program's emphasis on interpersonal engagement, defined by sustained dialog with cultural others and research-based service learning. When international study affords students opportunities for interpersonal engagement through sustained dialog with others and the utilization of service-learning pedagogy, intellectually driven in both theory and practice, the results can be transformative. As one respondent shared:

> There is no substitute for seeing with your own eyes. When I came back to the states after the trip, I quickly realized that there was no way I could explain what I had seen. No matter how many times I tried, I never gave it justice. It feels unsatisfying and frustrating to not be able to explain an experience that affects you at your core. At the same time, this lesson motivates me to see and do more.

ACKNOWLEDGMENTS

The authors would like to thank the faculty and administrative leadership of the West Chester University Honors International Study Programs to South Africa for their work in shaping the curricular offerings and advocating international study focused on interpersonal engagement. They would also like to thank the student participants, particularly those who responded to the survey. Their devotion and service epitomize leadership in action.

NOTES

[1]Desmond Tutu provides an elaborate account of South Africa's Truth and Reconciliation process in his work, *No Future Without Forgiveness*.

[2]The following universities are members of the Pennsylvania State System of Higher Education (PASSHE): Bloomsburg, California, Cheyney, Clarion, East Stroudsburg, Edinboro, Indiana, Kutztown, Lock Haven, Mansfield, Millersville, Shippensburg, Slippery Rock, and West Chester.

WORKS CITED

Braid, Bernice, and Gladys Palma de Schrynemakers. "A Case Among Cases." *Journal of the National Collegiate Honors Council* 12.1 (2011): 25–32. Print.

Block, Peter. *Community*. San Francisco: Berrett-Koehler, 2009. Print.

Dean, Kevin W. "Rhetoric." *Encyclopedia of Leadership*. Ed. J. M. Burns et al., Vol. 3. Thousand Oaks, CA: Sage, 2004. 1327–34. Print.

Greenleaf, Robert K. *Servant Leadership: A Journey into the Nature of Legitimate Power and Greatness*. New York: Paulist P, 1977. Print.

Haynes, Carolyn. "Overcoming the Study Abroad Hype." *Journal of the National Collegiate Honors Council* 12.1 (2011): 17–24. Print.

Heifetz, Ronald A., and Marty Linsky. *Leadership on the Line: Staying Alive Through the Dangers of Leading*. Boston: Harvard Business School P, 2002. Print.

Karsan, Leena, et. al. "Honors in Ghana: How Study Abroad Enriches Students' Lives." *Journal of the National Collegiate Honors Council* 12.1 (2011): 33–36. Print.

Littlejohn, Stephen W., and Karen A. Foss. *Theories of Human Communication.* 10th ed. Long Grove, IL: Waveland, 2010. Print.

"Open Doors 2009: Americans Studying Abroad." Institute of International Education. 2009. Web. 4 May 2011.

Otero, Rosalie C. "Faculty-Led International Honors Programs." *Journal of the National Collegiate Honors Council* 12.1 (2011): 41–45. Print.

Reid, Frances, and Deborah Hoffman, dirs. *Long Night's Journey into Day.* California Newsreel, 2001. Film.

Smith, Christian, et. al. *Lost in Transition: The Dark Side of Emerging Adulthood.* New York: Oxford UP, 2011. Print.

Thompson, Leonard. *A History of South Africa.* 3rd ed. New Haven: Yale UP, 2001. Print.

Tutu, Desmond. *No Future Without Forgiveness.* New York: Doubleday, 1999. Print.

"U.S. Study Abroad: Student Profile, 2000/01–2010/11." Institute of International Education. 2012. Web. 20 July 2013.

APPENDIX

West Chester University Honors College

South Africa Delegation Survey

Part 1—Demographics

1. Please check your gender.
   ☐ Male

   ☐ Female

2. Check your participation with the Honors Program.
   ☐ Core

   ☐ Seminar

3. Did you hold a position of leadership within Honors?
   (Check all that apply.)
   ☐ HSA Executive Board

   ☐ HSA Committee Chair

   ☐ Aid to South Africa Executive Board

   ☐ Aid to South Africa Chair

4. Which year(s) did you participate in the WCU Honors South
   Africa International Project? (Check all that apply.)
   ☐ 2001

   ☐ 2004

   ☐ 2006

   ☐ 2008

   ☐ 2010

   ☐ 2011

   ☐ 2012

5. Of those years, please check what class you were in at West Chester University.
   ☐ Freshman

   ☐ Sophomore

   ☐ Junior

   ☐ Senior

   ☐ 5th Year+

   ☐ Faculty/Staff

6. Were you a student in HON352: Lessons from South Africa, taught by Dr. Kevin Dean, during your time at WCU?
   ☐ Yes

   ☐ No

7. If you answered YES, please respond to the following statement.

   The HON352 seminar class influenced my decision to participate in the international program to South Africa.
   ☐ Strongly Agree

   ☐ Agree

   ☐ Neutral

   ☐ Disagree

   ☐ Strongly Disagree

Part 2—Leadership & Service Applications

8. Leadership Knowledge
   The following prompts are related to how you believe the South Africa International Experience through the Honors College helped to develop your knowledge of leadership. To this end, please indicate whether your participation in the international project increased your knowledge and understanding in the following areas relative to your other curricular experiences at WCU: Much More, More, Some, Less, or Much Less.

- Understanding that leadership does not require a formal title (expert power).

- Understanding that you can make a difference by being a change agent in your community.

- Understanding that a team approach can yield better results than working as an individual.

- Understanding that gathering public opinion and practicing audience analysis are critical steps in enacting change.

- Understanding that you are a part of the global community.

- Understanding the value of celebration as part of the leader's role.

- Knowledge of multiple approaches/theories related to leadership development and practice.

- Knowledge that the environment plays a role in social change.

- Knowledge that ethical/moral reasoning are components of decision making.

- Knowledge of your personal strengths as a leader.

- Knowledge of your personal limitations as a leader.

- Knowledge of international historical and contemporary figures who were/are effective leaders in community change.

9. Leadership Skill

The following prompts are related to how you believe the South Africa International Experience through the Honors College helped to develop your skills and practices in leadership. To this end, please indicate whether your participation in the international project helped develop your skills as a leader in the following areas, relative to your other curricular experiences at WCU: Much More, More, Some, Less, or Much Less.

- Skills in oral communication/public speaking.

- Skills in written communication.

- Skills in team building.
- Skills in conflict resolution.
- Skills in giving and receiving constructive feedback.
- Skills in conducting ethnographic research (interviews, videos, transcriptions, etc.).
- Skills in discerning the leadership gifts of others.
- Skills in prioritizing multiple demands on your time.
- Skills in planning an event.
- Skills in constructing survey instruments.
- Practices in self-awareness and self-care.

10. Service

    The following prompts are related to how you believe the South Africa International Experience through the Honors College helped to develop your involvement with service. To this end, please indicate whether your participation in the international project enhanced your commitment to service in the following areas, relative to your other curricular experiences at WCU: Much More, More, Neutral, Less, or Much Less.

    - Understanding the principle of servant leadership.
    - Recognizing the value your service brings to others.
    - Recognizing the value your service brings to you.
    - Recognizing the value of intellectual service (in addition to physical service).
    - Heightened recognition of needs within the campus and/or local community.
    - Heightened recognition of global needs.
    - Increased motivation for giving your time to others.
    - Increased motivation for giving your financial resources to others.

- Increased motivation for inspiring others to engage in serving others.

- Commitment for sustaining the service you provided internationally once you return home/once the international travel component concludes.

- Increased volunteerism with HSA Community Service events while at WCU.

- Increased involvement with Aid to South Africa while at WCU (if applicable).

Part 3—Open Response

In your own words, please identify/describe the following with regard to your personal experiences in South Africa:

11. Two images from South Africa that remain with you.

12. A leadership lesson you learned from your experience.

13. What in South Africa inspired your commitment to community service? And how you have put this into action?

14. The most valuable lesson learned/experience gained through your participation in this project with South Africa.

15. Your participation in this project gives us incredibly valuable primary source data that are both quantitative and qualitative. While you may certainly keep your remarks confidential, if you provide your name with your returned survey, we intend to thank you by listing your name in the research credits.

Name: _____

Thank you for completing the Honors South Africa International Study Survey. Please know that your input is greatly appreciated, and we sincerely hope that you will keep in touch with our Honors College at WCU.

CHAPTER 7

Developing Global Community-Based Undergraduate Research Projects

MARY ANN STUDER

DEFIANCE COLLEGE

In *Community-Based Research and Higher Education*, the education researchers Kerry J. Strand and his coauthors identify three principles associated with community-based research. The first principle emphasizes collective and collaborative learning that challenges the hierarchy between faculty and students in a manner that allows students to gain insight into power struggles in other contexts. This practice fosters students' professional development and encourages them to apply their academic expertise in real-world settings (8–11). The second principle that Strand et al. associate with community-based research is the "demystification of conventional knowledge" (13). The final major tenet in community-based research pedagogy, according to Strand and his fellow researchers, is the emphasis on teaching for social change (13–15). This pedagogy challenges students to recognize the long-term impact of their research on communities so that they can understand how their research contributes to societal change. By participating in international community-based research projects, students, argue Strand et al., move from an extremely linear understanding of disciplinary knowledge gained in a conventional classroom setting to an interdisciplinary, practical knowledge base acquired by applying their academic expertise when they work as integral members of an interdisciplinary team both while preparing to travel to the site and while onsite (8–15).

Each of these Strand principles informs the pedagogy and the context for the undergraduate international initiatives at Defiance College, a small liberal arts college in northwestern Ohio. These initiatives are year-long, interdisciplinary learning communities developed within the college's McMaster School for Advancing Humanity. Collaborative learning is the essence of the research learning communities. These groups focus upon challenging conventional knowledge and applying that knowledge to community-based research. And finally, students develop their academic expertise while navigating a challenging research problem and then applying their expertise by working in partnership with community members and incorporating the community members' expertise into knowledge creation relative to the project. The aim of all of this is to effect social change.

Students participating in these research learning communities at Defiance soon realize that their individual and disciplinary specific research is tied to the context of the community and engulfs the other members of the learning community as they implement the project onsite. Students are also transformed as they struggle to understand complex, real-world issues in diverse cultural contexts as they work onsite to marry the knowledge of the local population with their academic research. Collectively, the students' transformation diminishes their ability to see themselves as separate from others. They become tied personally and professionally to a broader global citizenry, and they recognize their ability to contribute professionally to the greater good.

While the McMaster School for Advancing Humanity is open to all students on campus, the majority of McMaster Scholars are members of Defiance College's Carolyn M. Small Honors Program.

Since 2005 honors students have composed 54% of McMaster Scholars. This level of participation is not surprising because honors students thrive on the challenges presented by undertaking individual research and crossing cultures. In addition, the Defiance College Honors Program strategically engages students in discussions of current issues involving social justice and includes an annual short-term international academic initiative. Building a cohort of past McMaster Scholars in the program also inspires and supports other members of the honors program to apply to the McMaster School for Advancing Humanity.

DEMOGRAPHICS OF DEFIANCE COLLEGE AND THE McMASTER SCHOOL

Defiance College is a four-year institution affiliated with the United Church of Christ, and it serves a student population of just over 1000. Its mission statement emphasizes educating students for a much more diverse world than that found in its rural location in northwest Ohio. The mission reads, "We seek to inspire within our students a search for truth, a sensitivity to our world and the diverse cultures within it, the ability to lead in their chosen professions, and a spirit of service." This charge to educate beyond its boundaries has been integral to the institution throughout its over 150-year history. Most recently, opportunities to engage students in research with international community partners, research with true impact, has happened through Defiance College's McMaster School for Advancing Humanity. In 2002, Harold and Helen McMaster provided a generous endowment to establish the McMaster School for Advancing Humanity. The McMasters challenged faculty and students to apply their academic expertise and scholarship to improve the human condition. They also intended that through these efforts students would learn about the importance of individual liberties and the impact that these liberties have on the human condition around the world.

From the McMaster School's inception, Defiance saw the McMaster School as a mechanism to provide opportunities for faculty and students from all disciplines to engage in intentionally powerful research in diverse global communities. The McMaster School has evolved into a model that effectively supports academically rigorous research in the context of international interdisciplinary initiatives. The research is community driven and focuses on positive community impact. Students and faculty, through the McMaster School, are discovering how their professional expertise matters in the world in which they live, in countries that many of them never imagined they would be working in, and in conditions that are nothing short of challenging. The mission of the McMaster School clearly aligns with the mission of Defiance College, and it challenges faculty to accomplish the following goals:

1. educate students for responsible citizenship;

2. produce committed global citizens and leaders who understand the importance of individual liberties in improving the human condition worldwide; and

3. encourage graduates to take an active role in addressing these issues in whatever professions they may choose.

This mission comes to fruition through interdisciplinary learning communities wherein faculty and students work in partnerships with communities that have included Belize, Cambodia, Ghana, Guatemala, Israel, Jamaica, New Orleans, and Thailand. Some initiatives extend from one to several years; others, such as Belize and Cambodia, have been ongoing since 2005. These initiatives have developed into rich research opportunities for students and faculty and have had significant positive impacts for the in-country partners.

ALIGNMENT WITH ASSOCIATION OF AMERICAN COLLEGES AND UNIVERSITIES RECOMMENDATIONS

The McMaster-sponsored initiatives in both Belize and Cambodia, it is interesting to note, were influenced by the Association of American Colleges and Universities' 2002 publication, *Greater Expectations: A New Vision for Learning as a Nation Goes to College.*

This AAC&U national report lays out a vision of higher education for the twenty-first century that stresses the importance of an education that both "expands horizons while nourishing the mind" (10). The report argues that students must be not only academically challenged but also given opportunities to develop skills that provide self-efficacy and a positive world impact in order to enable both the individual and the global community to thrive. The mission of the McMaster School for Advancing Humanity is aligned with this AAC&U charge because it works to develop committed global citizens and encourages students to play an active role in improving the human condition through scholarship and professional preparation.

In addition, the Defiance College programs systematically align with the model included in George D. Kuh's 2008 AAC&U report: *High Impact Educational Practices*. The McMaster School also implements many of the high-impact practices defined by Kuh: common intellectual experiences, learning communities, writing-intensive courses, collaborative assignments and projects, undergraduate research, diversity/global learning, service-learning/community-based learning (9–10). Kuh clearly articulates that the benefits of student engagement through these high-impact practices "increase the odds that any student—educational and social background notwithstanding—will attain his or her educational and personal objectives, acquire the skills and competences demanded by the challenges of the twenty-first century and enjoy the intellectual and monetary gains associated with completion of the baccalaureate degree" (32). The McMaster Fellows and Scholars Program evidences the effectiveness of these high-impact practices in contributing to student learning and preparing students to function as global citizens in whatever profession they choose.

THE McMASTER FELLOWS AND SCHOLARS PROGRAM

The Fellows and Scholars Program operates on an annual cycle that begins in January. Faculty who are applying to be fellows submit a proposal outlining their intended research and their ability to support a multidisciplinary team of students who would travel during the following academic year. This proposal includes (1) the faculty's proposed research; (2) the context, location, and evidence of local community need; (3) the project's benefit to the community; and (4) the faculty member's commitment and ability to support a learning community of students from multiple disciplines. A selection committee, including the President of the College, the Vice President for Academic Affairs, and two additional Vice Presidents who are invited to participate by the Dean of the McMaster School, evaluate the proposals and name fellows in early February for the following academic year. The fellows receive a research stipend and a three-semester-hour course release to implement their initiative. Once the fellows have been chosen, recruiting of student scholars begins.

A large portion of Defiance College students, many of whom are first-generation college students, have never contemplated going abroad, and many have never even flown before. Students are recruited to participate through a series of events such as information sessions hosted by current and former fellows and scholars. In addition, the Carolyn M. Small Honors Program and Defiance College's Service Leadership Program implement programming that intentionally prepares students to take on the challenge of being McMaster Scholars. The honors program offers students the opportunity to participate in a short-term academic international trip to a developed nation to experience crossing cultures without the additional pressures of rough living conditions, limited sanitation, and impoverished communities. For many of the students, this transitional step is critical to their ability to cope and function within a developing nation. In preparing for this type of travel, the Defiance College Honors Program and Service Leadership Program conduct informational sessions and activities related to world concerns such as hunger, poverty, and health threats. These events connect students to the reality of the human condition beyond the geographic boundaries of the campus location and often stir their desire to participate. Although students are not required to be an honors student or a Service Leader, the majority of students participating in the McMaster Scholars program are, in fact, affiliated with these programs. For example, of the 2011–12 McMaster Scholars, nearly 70% were either honors program students or Service Leaders.

Students who wish to apply to be McMaster Scholars are limited to the locations that faculty fellows have been accepted to travel to during the following academic year. Unlike many research initiatives, students propose their own research projects and, if accepted, function as individual researchers, not as assistants in faculty-led research. That being said, the faculty fellows work with students individually as they write their proposals to ensure that they are addressing a clearly articulated community need and that the research can be accomplished with the allotted resources. In April, students submit scholar proposals for these individual onsite research projects at the various locations accepted for fellow-led travel. Each proposal includes (1) a rationale for the project; (2) a literature review that provides a disciplinary, locational, and community context for the project; (3) the project methodology; (4) a clearly defined anticipated outcome; (5) a statement describing the student's motivation for applying; and (6) three references, at least one from a faculty member within their major. The named fellows for each location rank the scholar applications, and an administrative committee finalizes the selection. The criteria for scholar selection are the quality of the proposal, the priority and logistical feasibility of the project, references submitted on the student's behalf, and budgetary parameters.

The McMaster learning communities are announced just prior to the close of the spring semester so that they can meet at least once before the summer break. Each learning community may also include associate fellows, who are faculty and staff serving in a support capacity by traveling with and participating in the learning communities for the entire initiative. While associate fellows are not required to engage in specific research, they often conduct exploratory research if they are faculty members to lay the groundwork for a fellow proposal for the subsequent year. Associate fellows submit applications and are selected at the same time as scholars.

In any given academic year, the McMaster endowment supports the cost of travel, food, lodging, and research equipment for approximately six to eight faculty and staff and thirty students in projects operating at three or four locations.

All projects accepted by the McMaster School clearly address the school's goals:

1. to examine the root causes of human suffering through community-based research that addresses systemic factors impeding human progress;

2. to give students the knowledge and capacities to be engaged world citizens;

3. to contribute actively through sponsored scholarship and service to the improvement of the human condition worldwide;

4. to exchange, create, and disseminate knowledge about successful models of active citizenship and public service; and

5. to create at Defiance College one of the nation's premier undergraduate educational programs with a focus on scholarship and service and a special emphasis on developing an innovative approach to teaching.

While each learning community functions with some autonomy because of the inherent differences in faculty leadership, clear program goals appear to be the impetus for uniformity across themes in regard to learning-community outcomes. Indeed, the learning outcomes of the two longest-running initiatives, which are in Cambodia and Belize and focus on developing students' capacity for international research and intercultural competence, are closely aligned.

INTERDISCIPLINARY LEARNING COMMUNITIES

Although formed during the late spring, interdisciplinary learning communities begin in earnest in the fall of the following academic year. They carry course credit under a McMaster School designation and can count as electives toward graduation. The learning communities vary in size but generally consist of two-to-three fellows, two associate fellows, and six-to-twelve scholars. Each learning community spans one year of on-campus study and includes a two-to-four-week, onsite field experience. On campus, the learning communities generally meet for two hours each week throughout two semesters, both to prepare for the onsite work and then to reflect post-trip and analyze the research conducted. Pre-trip sessions prepare the participants to travel, conduct the research proposed, and cross cultures effectively. These sessions also build context by facilitating the group's understanding of the project site's history, economics, politics, and social infrastructure, which are critical components to effectively understanding the issues the groups will address while onsite. Post-trip sessions include analysis of field data, focused reflection, assessment of learning outcomes, and preparation for project presentations.

At each learning community meeting, all participants must contribute to the material being explored, offer their disciplinary expertise, and cross-train the team. Each learning community functions a bit differently on the ground: some work as a single group while others break into small groups to complete their work. In Belize, for example, the group travels together for safety reasons; two vehicles moving through the jungle is better than one. After the group arrives together at a village, the work begins with some students teaching in the schools, others testing drinking water sources, and still others working with local farmers. These projects all happen in close proximity since the villages have populations of 100–200 people. Students help one another as they work on each specific initiative because the time that the group spends in Belize is limited.

Upon returning to Defiance, all participants must present at the McMaster Symposium, an annual spring event on campus. The theme varied in the first six years of the program, but it has remained the same for the last three years: *The Question of Individual Liberties as Critical to Improving the Human Condition*. This two-day symposium provides an opportunity for the community both on and off campus to attend presentations given by each learning community; hear speakers brought on campus to address various aspects of the theme; and engage in activities such as poster presentations, film screenings, and discussion groups. Some learning communities require that the students make off-campus presentations as well. In fact, most students do present off campus, even without the requirement, and the endowment supports this effort. Students have made presentations at local schools, Audubon chapters, alumni gatherings, and national conferences such as AAC&U's annual conference and the National Collegiate Honors Council's annual meeting as well as regional honors conferences.

Recognizing the value of interdisciplinary approaches in developing solutions to complex, real-world problems, the McMaster learning communities design, implement, and reflect on their individual research projects as an interdisciplinary team. Faculty and students working with their community partners onsite often explore nonlinear connections. For example, one scholar worked with teachers and students in a small village school in Belize to develop their soccer skills, which allowed the school team to participate in intermural games with nearby villages. The underlying goal of getting the students to this level of play, as articulated by the teachers, was to keep male teens enrolled in school because of their interest in soccer. The village women's group then capitalized on the games held in the village by selling food, thus increasing the limited income for those families. Both the village and the McMaster student scholar identified these connections post-implementation. Learning that effective analysis of acquired field data occurs in synergy with the interdisciplinary context of the world is a valuable outcome for the students, but more importantly, it is a critical component of planning effective action.

Incorporating the best practices of effective learning communities that Barbara Leigh Smith et al. identify in *Learning Communities: Reforming Undergraduate Education*, the group of fellows and scholars develop a diverse community that engages in integration, active learning, reflection, and assessment (22). Within these learning communities, students and faculty must develop collegial relationships and work constructively as they each pursue their individual research projects, receive input from each other about their evolving projects, and identify connections between the intended project outcomes and the impact on community partners. Smith et al. recognize that faculty and students, who are often accustomed to the authoritarian classroom model in which teachers and texts are the primary sources of expertise, experience new challenges in learning communities that require participants to engage in cooperative and collaborative learning to arrive at knowledge that is socially constructed and reconstructed by "negotiating with one another in [a community] of knowledgeable peers" (20). This collaboration results in a well-prepared research team or learning community that can complete projects effectively in the relatively short time that the group is on the ground because everyone involved has a clear understanding of each project. In fact, many times they have been cross-trained to aid with another scholar's or fellow's project implementation. As the learning community expands to include community partners on the ground, the students and faculty participants recognize that knowledge is not created solely within academia but rather through the critical inclusion of tacit local expertise.

Each learning community is diverse in terms of expertise, discipline, learning style, and identity. This diversity provides a foundation for students when they work on location with partners vastly different from themselves and contributes to their developing a global perspective. Through strategic preparation, the learning community can bridge the differences in ethnicity, socioeconomic background, expertise, need, and resource base. The preparation methodology varies for each learning community; however, L. Robert Kohls' *Survival Kit for Overseas Living* as well as the Peace Corps' World Wise Schools publication *Culture Matters: The Peace Corps Cross-Cultural Workbook* are typical resources that are utilized as the learning community learns to transition from isolation to appreciation for an individual's role in a global society. Most recently, scholar training has included the *CCAI Cross-Cultural Adaptability Inventory* developed by Colleen Kelley and Judith Meyers. This inventory allows the students to recognize their strengths and weaknesses relative to the qualities necessary to effectively cross cultures. Once they complete the inventory and rate themselves, they can utilize the descriptions of the qualities and suggestions to develop a personal action plan that will contribute to increased effectiveness on the ground. Working onsite gives students the opportunity to see themselves as professionals struggling in a difficult world where boundaries between disciplines are rarely clearly delineated.

McMaster Scholars have the opportunity to discover how their disciplinary knowledge can be applied in a real-world context, often with visible results. The process of striving to apply their disciplinary knowledge to new venues and unsolved problems provides a mechanism, as described by Noel Entwistle, for deep learning. Entwistle identifies conceptions of learning through transformation of "acquiring information—building knowledge—applying knowledge—making sense of the real world—[and finally] developing as person" (2). Education that becomes part of a person's evolving understanding of his or her discipline in a practical sense and that transforms the learner in some way is the deep learning desired. Deep learning flourishes in the safety of a community where students can take the risks necessary to relate past experiences to present challenges. By integrating traditional curricular knowledge with extreme challenges in the field, students move toward a more complex understanding of the world. For example, one McMaster scholar conducted a strengths, weaknesses, opportunities, threats (SWOT) inventory with the residents of a small village in order to bring the village together in terms of future developments and their movement toward sustainability. The results of the survey coalesced around a need for more income and the village's dream of starting a small restaurant. The student worked with the community to identify the material challenges to starting the restaurant as well as the impact, both positive and negative, that this project would have on village residents. In this process the student gained an understanding of the overlying economic cap on this agricultural village imposed by its location, lack of infrastructure, and limited employment opportunities and the lack of empowerment the women felt as they struggled to feed their children. The student was able to move beyond the initial SWOT analysis to develop a plan to support the village's efforts to open a restaurant. Within a year the restaurant was operational.

While the learning communities form a supportive cohort that shares the responsibility for the success of each project, the individuals working with local community partners still control the direction and implementation of their own research. The students, by working through intentional reflection and assessment exercises before the trip, develop a conscious connection between academic content and critical, creative application. The students' journey through disciplinary research toward a more specific and contextual application of their academic knowledge is facilitated by developing research questions that are reviewed by the entire learning community and by receiving feedback from the community as they formulate answers and direction. Throughout the experience, fellows and scholars examine what they know or assume and reflect upon their project-related learning as it evolves through participating in nightly discussions while onsite, responding to specific journal prompts, and presenting their results. In addition to the required McMaster Symposium presentations, some learning communities also assess student learning through final research papers, pre- and post-tests, and a series of videotaped interviews that are conducted pre-trip, onsite, and post-trip. The McMaster Fellows and Scholars Program challenges the participants to tap their knowledge, skills, and character so that they may effectively partner with people from another culture.

EXAMPLE INITIATIVE: BELIZE

Since 2005, the McMaster School has supported projects in Belize that focus collectively on a single goal: to empower small, isolated indigenous communities to develop sustainably while simultaneously supporting environmental conservation. To date, more than sixty completed research projects have been organized under an interdisciplinary framework developed by modifying the Integrated Natural Resource Management (INRM) schema as explained by Anne-Marie Izac and Pedro Sanchez in their work. INRM provides a framework for the projects' interdisciplinary goal of improving and developing sustainable communities in Belize. Each year's participants direct their efforts toward outcomes supported by the INRM framework: enhancing productivity, human well-being, and ecosystem functions. The coherent nature of this initiative facilitates clear and direct impact while allowing local community partners to provide direction for the research initiative and contribute to knowledge creation. Realistically, it enables students to see themselves and their projects as integral components of a process that produces significant results.

In Belize, the task is facilitated because the goals of sustainability and development are mutually reinforcing. People struggling to feed their families often place a low priority on environmental preservation. Yet as Jeffrey Sayer and Bruce Campbell assert, impoverished people often "depend upon the 'natural capital' that supports their lives just as much as they do on the more tangible assets of money and property" (8). Natural capital in the context of small agricultural communities in remote areas in the interior of Belize refers specifically to arable soil and water. Former rainforest soil becomes nutrient poor very quickly and with over fertilization can become degraded to the point that the soil cannot support optimal yield. Agricultural run-off, as well as inadequate sanitation management, can contaminate ground and surface drinking water sources. Degradation of soil and water resources can contribute to food and water insecurity. The work by students and faculty in Belize demonstrates that improved income levels, access to education, and more stable infrastructure do not have to come at the expense of the environment. Working with farmers to implement more sustainable agricultural practices such as no tillage, inter-row cropping, and application of manure, along with soil testing to regulate fertilizer application, has resulted in a reduction of macronutrient fertilizer input averaging 40% on the fields of the group's community partners. This reduction has lowered the farmers' expenses and minimized the probability that excess fertilizer will contaminate the surrounding environmental waterways or community's drinking water. This network of McMaster projects in Belize has empowered the community and improved productivity and profitability while considering the environmental impact.

While faculty and student participants change each year and the group's disciplinary perspectives consequently shift, my involvement as the faculty fellow to Belize has been constant since 2005. This continuity has facilitated the development of a viable long-term Belizean partnership. This initiative and the equally long-term McMaster initiative in Cambodia underscore the realization that sustainable partnerships are built on personal relationships, on developing trust between individuals over the long haul. The Belize initiative involves multiple partners: Programme for Belize, the non-governmental organization (NGO) that manages the Rio Bravo Conservation and Management Area, and the indigenous populations on the periphery of the Rio Bravo preserve who want and need to move beyond a subsistence level of living. The interdisciplinary infrastructure of this initiative engages in what educational theorists Julie Thompson Klein and William H. Newell describe as "a process of answering a question, solving a problem, or addressing a topic that is too broad or complex to be dealt with adequately by a single discipline or profession" (393–94). This process clearly happens when dealing with stakeholders who seem to have conflicting interests. For example, the goals of the Programme for Belize, a community partner whose mission is to preserve the environment, and the periphery agriculture communities, also a partner, who rely heavily on chemical supplements to grow food to feed their communities, were in conflict. When the McMaster Fellows and Scholars first started working in Belize, the animosity between the two was evident. Through environmental monitoring of both water and soil, agricultural education about soil health, drinking water quality monitoring, educational outreach programs between the conservation area and the community and alternative economic ventures, the McMaster learning communities have reduced that animosity.

Not surprisingly, since the McMaster School's founding, projects have evolved toward an increasingly interdisciplinary focus. The Belize initiative provides an example. The first team in spring 2005 consisted of two science fellows and three science scholars working on a single research project. By contrast, every subsequent team since December 2005 has consisted of multiple disciplines and individual research projects focused in each of those disciplines. This shift to a more engaged interdisciplinary team correlates to the growth of the Belizean partnerships in response to community challenges. This evolution has informed the movement of students beyond the narrow focus of their individual projects to a larger perspective in which they can develop an understanding of the big picture. This macro view challenges the students to examine not only the current issues but also to gain a sense of how the issues arose, how they are synergistically related, and how they can be remediated or solved.

As the students become fully engaged with their community partners and the learning community effectively supports developing both a context for the students' research and the skills necessary to conduct it, the students achieve important learning outcomes. Learning outcomes may vary because of the autonomy of each learning community, but all are aligned with the goals of the institutions that support them. The learning outcomes for the McMaster Belize Learning Community, outlined below, focus on four areas.

- Capacity for Research
    - Develop research skills.
    - Develop disciplinary knowledge and skills.
    - Develop an interdisciplinary perspective.
    - Learn to effectively disseminate knowledge.
- Contextual Framework
    - Develop an understanding of all aspects of the project site.
    - Develop an understanding of current conditions and quality of life at the project site.
    - Develop an understanding of the impact of individual liberties or lack thereof on the human condition at the project site.

- Cultural Competence

  - Gain a cultural understanding that allows one to develop in-country partnerships.

  - Gain a cultural understanding that enables one to understand and address real-world needs.

  - Gain a working knowledge for and an appreciation of cultural diversity.

- Connection with Community

  - Develop familiarity with the logistics of travel abroad.

  - Develop an understanding of the interconnectedness of the research, the experience, the project whole, the community, and the self.

  - Gain an understanding of working within a community and across communities through applied research.

In the McMaster Belize learning community, several mechanisms gauge students' development relative to the above outcomes. Students must submit a final research paper to Programme for Belize, the community partner. They also must submit a final product or analysis in an appropriate format for maximum usability to the local community partners whether it be an NGO such as Programme for Belize, an individual farmer, or a community group. This obligation requires a specific cultural understanding as well as contextual understanding of their disciplinary research, and this component often provides viable assessment material for some of the above learning outcomes. For example, one scholar's project was developing materials to support conservation efforts for the endangered Yellow-headed Parrot. She wrote and published a children's book in Spanish and English that carefully denounced poaching, mindful of the fact that many parents of the children reading the book probably poached parrot chicks and had done so for years. As one can imagine from the project description above, for students or fellows to assess or realize the outcome of their projects immediately is often difficult; however, over time, returning to the same locations allows the outcome of a project to be gauged even if causality cannot be directly identified. For example, in relation to the Yellow-headed Parrot project, Programme for Belize has now documented an increasing population of Yellow-headed Parrots in the region. Subsequent McMaster groups have seen the children reading the books the former scholar had distributed. Moreover, the student who originated the project has collaborated on a grant to support additional monitoring of the parrot populations in the Rio Bravo.

Being able to assess students' connections to the world community and the direct impact that their research had on the community they worked with is often difficult because indicators of these outcomes will most probably be evidenced years after the experience. Communication with students after graduation, however, often reveals that they are continuing to apply their professional skills to humanitarian efforts, an indicator of the ongoing impact of their experience as McMaster Scholars.

CONCLUSION

Since the McMaster School's inception in 2002, over ten percent of the student body has participated as McMaster Scholars, and nearly fifty percent of Defiance College's full-time faculty have participated as fellows or associate fellows. Other faculty members have assisted scholars in their research or have incorporated aspects of McMaster projects in their coursework, as in a general chemistry course that explores water-testing protocols or an educational methods class that develops lesson plans for use in teacher training. McMaster School projects have spanned every discipline on campus, and none of the currently supported locations focus on a single discipline.

In 2010 the faculty approved the McMaster Certificate Program for McMaster Scholars, allowing them to pursue additional coursework intentionally designed to expand students' perspectives on a specific area of the world. In addition to this certificate of recognition, the McMaster School has developed an annual workshop series that engages students across campus in the exploration of individual liberties, the U.S. Constitution, and the governments of other countries.

Defiance College's Honors Program now focuses annually on a theme driven by former McMaster Scholars' experiences abroad. These themes have included world hunger, fair trade, and conflicts between individual rights and liberties and public responsibility. This practice offers proof that the McMaster School's use of community-based research as an innovative teaching strategy has facilitated positive impact not only on its globally diverse community partners but on students as well.

The McMaster School's pervasive influence on campus has permeated every discipline. The President of Defiance College announced the Imagine Initiatives, a grouping of opportunities for students to become more academically and culturally engaged, stating that every student beginning with the incoming class in the fall 2011 would have the opportunity to travel internationally. This decision is due in no small part to the success of the McMaster School. Participants in the program have grown to a critical mass at Defiance College, creating a culture of awareness that disciplinary expertise can be applied in the global arena. Not only are these former McMaster Scholars able to identify their professional role in the twenty-first century, they understand a commitment to the betterment of humanity in a way that will allow them to thrive and to become significant global contributors.

WORKS CITED

Association of American Colleges and Universities. *Greater Expectations: A New Vision for Learning as a Nation Goes to College*. Washington, D.C.: Association of American Colleges and Universities, 2002. Print.

Culture Matters: The Peace Corps Cross-Cultural Workbook. Peace Corps World Wise Schools. Web. 18 May 2013.

de Becker, Gavin. *The Gift of Fear: Survival Signals that Protect Us From Violence*. New York: Little, Brown, 1997. Print.

Entwistle, Noel. "Promoting Deep Learning Through Teaching and Assessment." *Assessment to Promote Deep Learning: Insight from AAHE's 2000 and 1999 Assessment Conferences.* Ed. Linda Suskie. Washington, D.C.: American Association of Higher Education, 2001. Print.

Izac, Anne-Marie, and Pedro Sanchez. "Towards a Natural Resource Management Paradigm for International Agriculture: The Example of Agroforestry Research." *Agricultural Systems* 69 (2002): 5–25. Print.

Kelley, Colleen, and Judith Meyers. *CCAI Cross-Cultural Adaptability Inventory.* Chicago: Vagent, 1995. Print.

Klein, Julie Thompson, and William H. Newell. "Advancing Interdisciplinary Studies." *Handbook of the Undergraduate Curriculum: A Comprehensive Guide to Purposes, Structures, Practices, and Change.* Ed. Jerry G. Gaff and James L. Radcliff. San Francisco: Jossey-Bass, 1997. 393–415. Print.

Kohls, L. Robert. *Survival Kit for Overseas Living: For Americans Planning to Live and Work Abroad.* Boston: Nicholas Brealey, 1979. Print.

Kuh, George D. *High-Impact Educational Practices.* Washington D.C.: Association of American Colleges and Universities, 2008. Print.

Leki, Ray S. *Travel Wise: How to Be Safe, Savvy and Secure Abroad.* Boston: Intercultural P, 2008. Print.

Sayer, Jeffrey, and Bruce Campbell. *The Science of Sustainable Development: Local Livelihoods and the Global Environment.* Cambridge: Cambridge UP, 2004. Print.

Smith, Barbara Leigh, et al. *Learning Communities: Reforming Undergraduate Education.* San Francisco: Jossey-Bass, 2004. Print.

Strand, Kerry J., et al. *Community-Based Research and Higher Education.* San Francisco: John Wiley Sons, 2003. Print.

PREPARING TOMORROW'S GLOBAL LEADERS

Honors International Education

Promoting a Largeness of Mind: Preparing Faculty for Honors International Field Experiences

BERNICE BRAID

LONG ISLAND UNIVERSITY BROOKLYN

I am extended by everything I see, consume, amass. It is not a question of higher knowledge, it is more like sedimentation, an accretion of images, texts, of all the lasting impressions that come my way from the street, from television, conversations, newspapers. (Nooteboom 207)

Most faculty begin to think about travel in terms of place—that is, what actual in situ study provides that is missing from on-campus courses is a chance to BE somewhere that college courses can only talk about. For faculty, preparing students to move out of a classroom and into a world that will be simultaneously the framework and the content of investigation is integral to the actual travel project. For students, developing the skills to pay attention to their surroundings is probably their first step in an intricate way of moving through space that is not, for most, an already developed way of being in the world.

This sequence of considerations suggests that when faculty undertake to lead a study-abroad project, they need to think through their own pedagogy so as to utilize it differently from how they usually approach their campus-based courses. If abroad is to imply immersion, for instance, then the planning process must structure the expedition so that students will take careful notes, analyze, and then reflect on the complex and often contradictory cues of their direct experience. The requisite skills of mapping or finding one's way and of observing or acquiring information from one's senses that can be re-examined in the context of reflection/reading/lecture/discussion have to be honed. Faculty must prepare themselves by engaging in metaphoric and actual mapping exercises themselves before they imagine assignments and interchanges that will invite and stimulate a mode of learning unlike students' usual classroom habits of thinking and knowing.

Perhaps the most radical difference between site-specific learning and typical campus-based study is the expected outcome: finding out versus being told. An outstanding attribute of travel study is its potential for discovery and its capacity to generate in students an awareness of themselves as investigators. If these are among the objectives faculty aim for, then both the travel program—what students are asked to do beyond the reach of a professor's voice—and the mindset of the onsite faculty must be shaped to provoke student behavior that is itself apt to produce altered perspectives.

If faculty are going to initiate a re-configuration of their pedagogy to yield new ways for students to think and act, they must learn to be comfortable with structured but open-ended inquiry. Almost always they teach on-campus courses from the viewpoint that they are certain about what the correct answers to good questions should be. On the road, this attitude becomes a constraint that traps faculty and students behind blinders that stand between them and the new worlds they seek to explore. Re-fashioning the sensibility of faculty to assume the role of participant-observer is neither automatic nor easy, which is one reason that instructors who use City as Text™ modalities contrive multiple explorations of the same area. They assign small teams to traverse the same area and then write about it; they make sure that at least some of the observation assignments focus on interactions that students witness, interpret, analyze, then comment and reflect on; and they insert informal as well as formal debriefing sessions. In these discussions written accounts of the observed interactions are compared so as to bring out the anomalies in what students think they know. They can then identify what is uncomfortable about being a participant when they really thought of themselves as innocent bystanders, which is how they imagine observation normally works.

When instructors are preparing to travel with a group of students, usually they will be heading for a country they have already visited. In practice, this experience means they have a clear sense of the place that is the destination. They probably speak the country's dominant language and know its literature, arts, geography, history, and politics. They have drawn up a reading list in preparation and have held orientation sessions with their cohort in which they might well have lectured on what they themselves know and how they themselves see and understand the intended destination. In addition they no doubt assigned reading specifically about this country, its history, culture, and current affairs that they themselves have chosen as reflective of their own attitudes or past experiences of the country.

Leavening this material, which is really telling students what to expect and perhaps what to see when they arrive and not quite inviting them to see with new eyes, with theoretical work written from an ethnographic viewpoint, is important. Clifford Geertz, particularly in *Local Knowledge*, provides some useful terminology for those who want to figure out how to see and to sort through the contradictions between scholarly discourse about this place and what it feels like to live in it for a period of time. In particular his use of terms like blurred genres, translation, and thick description and his focus on interpretation—with his emphasis on insider/outsider interactions—are more than a useful framing device for analysis and discussion. They help students discover what a lens is, and how it works in actual practice (19–70).

Furthermore, Geertz's work provides brilliant examples of observation writing/interpretation/analysis, drawn from somewhat remote sites and times, that illustrate well the matter of viewpoint and perspective without telling students what they should see or how. Since Geertz's interest is in framing investigation, his argument is general enough to be applicable to many specific locales without packaging for students a ready-made set of images and metaphors that can actually control their initial glance and gaze once they have arrived at their immersion site. The quintessential task of what Geertz calls "constructing an account of the imaginative make-up of a society" is well served by a degree of consciousness about the role of frameworks, which can clarify a "sense of the dependence of what is seen upon where it is seen from and what it is seen with" (4).

The challenge for faculty is in preparing themselves first and then setting the students up to enter into new worlds with a capacity to "understand how it is we understand understanding not our own" (5). If instructors embrace what Geertz claims they are after when they enter into the lives of other peoples in other places, then they want to coach students to take in information in fresh ways: to use all their senses, to be conscious of what they are taking in, and to be aware that in order to make sense of all that they need for assembling details into patterns they need to note, to remember, and then to interpret and analyze.

What are the open-ended questions faculty have prepared for students? What assignments have they designed that require students to function as explorers, learning to use local transportation if it exists, see where people hang out, do business, shop, eat, dance? What informal sessions have faculty scheduled where students can share what they think of what the local press publishes during their stay? What exercises have faculty provided to push students to compare prices, quality, and goods and services and to begin to make their own maps of new territory that reveal who lives where, who has access to what? What expectation do students have that they should also be finding out who earns what salary, for what kind of work, and who lives in which parts of the towns and cities they are visiting? What questions are they generating to inquire into the lives and labors of field hands, clerks, and professional people waiting in line at the bank?

If faculty want students to dig deep and develop their own perspective on themselves as explorers, they need to design assignments that will help students to compare their own understandings with those of locals. S. B. Heath's groundbreaking work in *Ways with Words* makes the case that students of all ages learn better and come to see the way frameworks shape how and what they see by examining their own projects from the viewpoint of others. Coaching students to interview workers about their jobs, about their methods, and about their sense of possibilities in their cultural setting is one good way to move collegians into a textured perception of unfamiliar societies, and this process typically helps them to develop considerable empathy along the way. A modest proposal for preparing students might be that faculty engage in their own preparatory workshops at home. Faculty can move in small teams into areas off-campus where they can explore unfamiliar urban neighborhoods or visit nearby metropolitan areas to spend a day of exploring and discussing their observations. Learning how to look and see is what students are expected to master. Trying out analogous exercises before assigning students to their initial walkabouts abroad can help faculty greatly in refining their own language and pinpointing concerns that might shape preliminary assignments.

A rich text to use as background reading if cities are included in the travel study is Jane Jacobs' *The Death and Life of Great American Cities*. Her emphasis on street life (with some European examples), on how people move through urban spaces, on how to imagine that a city functions like an extension of a domestic living room or kitchen or backyard, and on how to see familiar streets in unfamiliar ways using this lens can be immeasurably rewarding, both during the preparation and during the travel study. Certainly reading her description of how people move through crowded urban areas sensitizes travelers to crowd behavior, which varies in different cities,

159

and encourages outsiders to pay attention to these phenomena. Do people queue up for buses? Do they jaywalk? Do they apologize for bumping into each other? Do they walk especially fast? Especially slowly? Do they greet others along the way? How do they relate to one another inside small stores? Once they are in streetcars, buses, underground trains? Do the answers to these questions vary with the age group or gender of the people observed? An excursion to someplace where a transportation network is established but new to the faculty could be a good site for preparatory sessions, and certainly such a trip is excellent for students who need to strengthen their sea legs. Often American students have never used public transportation in their own country, so faculty who familiarize themselves with what confuses students can potentially benefit when they frame assignments and think out itineraries for cities in foreign lands.

Metropolitan areas themselves could well intimidate American students, many of whom find campuses daunting and shrink when confronted by a metropolis. It helps, perhaps, to think of cities as complicated puzzles. Warren Weaver cites the organized complexity, which "are all problems which involve dealing simultaneously with a sizable number of factors which are interrelated into an organic whole" (qtd. in Jacobs 432). Students will notice (or not) patterns of traffic, garbage collection, street vendor activity (what they are selling and when, who is doing the selling), hours of business; their task is to sort these out, somehow, to generate their own mental maps of what is where and how things work. After a quick sorting of these fundamental elements, students can develop a sketch of where the money and power in a city show themselves on the street grid and of how local information travels.

Faculty accompanying students will have held orientation sessions, as mentioned, based on their own prior knowledge, but if the site is new to everyone, one productive approach is to engage in a field laboratory exercise in which everyone is an investigator. Discussions can reveal the significance of an observer's point of view, and variations of interpretation are a probable and desired outcome. Discrepancies serve as a perfect starting point for analysis and identification of evidence to support interpretation. The point of this kind of prep work is to develop a sense of what an explorer really *does* in new territory. Normally students are informed by prior readings and warned about weather, dangers, and attitudes to non-native speakers, but the raw experience of being lost or feeling lost is probably not the dominant sense of self the faculty bring with them into travel study. Disorientation is an important starting point, as much for faculty as for students: disorientation focuses the attention.

Composing a short list of articles, stories, and poems that should be read en route is another opportunity to turn students' attention to how they look and see, how they interact and with whom, and how they make maps of their uncharted wanderings. The list should include works by writers who feel like outsiders and talk about that experience and by social scientists who have come to be surprised by their own preconceptions, as William Whyte was when he discovered Jacobs, and then rediscovered, through using her lens, the social life in New York City. The theoretical readings suggested for faculty preparing to travel with students are also powerful for traveling students and, once read, they will be brought into discussion by the students themselves throughout their visit. Although students want to feel grounded, they relish their discoveries when they do feel a bit lost and can turn to their readings for vocabulary and conceptual framing.

Context is everything. Seeing details in context requires a stretch of the imagination, a good eye, and flexibility in interpretive engagement. If faculty want students to see what is out there, to see how individual elements fit into some local framework, and to figure out what all that means to people living in those worlds and to themselves, they must help their students develop an acute sensibility of place and of self in place. If instructors see the world they travel to in a fixed way that matches their own pre-existing image of it, they are less capable of setting the stage for students to discover for themselves what they think is out there. "In the last analysis, then, as in the first," writes Geertz, "the interpretive study of culture represents an attempt to come to terms with the diversity of the ways human beings construct their lives in the act of leading them" (16).

Students study the history, social structure, art collections, and foodways of a place while they are in it. They need to learn that each of these subjects is a window into local culture and that local culture is experienced not in terms of any one of them, but in terms of all of them—and more—as parts of a whole, which is where Geertz's sense of "Blurred Genres" becomes relevant (19). What students take home, if they have been immersed, is that sense of the whole, of the multi-disciplinarity of life as it is lived. So the final preparation instructors undertake should be how to think about that whole. Papers students submit following study abroad should not replicate the ones they write at home. Information, viewpoint, and perspective should all be infused with an understanding of that place as people live in it from day to day. To help students look for this depth, to see it captured in student writing, and to frame the trip as an exploration of text in context, faculty need to prepare their own lens in advance of traveling and to gird themselves for the shock of non-recognition when students see it all another way.

The final insight of travel study is for the travelers to see themselves as "human beings" who "construct their lives in the act of leading them," as Geertz suggests (16). If students come to see themselves as actively making sense of the world around them, and of themselves in that world, they have gained perspective, agency, and a deep knowledge of context. They have begun to construct an understanding of themselves among others. They have acquired skills of observation and interpretation that work everywhere, not just abroad.

Which leads back to "largeness of mind." This is both an objective faculty set out for their students and a starting point for themselves as they plan international study. An overlooked and fundamental point about planning experiential-learning opportunities is that any exercise outside the traditional classroom can be a laboratory through which students begin to acquire the skills of observation, interpretation, analysis, and reflection that are essential to the deep insights faculty hope their students will derive from international study. Context and detail in context are prerequisites to perceiving pattern. Interpreted and analyzed, pattern in turn yields the meaning students take away from their immersion.

There are many dimensions of learning from unmediated experience that faculty build into assignments and preparatory exercises. Included in the Works Cited are publications that deal with being elsewhere, the essential characteristic of active learning. Monographs and journal articles on Place as Text provide guides to organization and assignments. Other publications enlarge this topic and present theoretical constructs to clarify what the elements of immersion learning include. All site-specific learning is active learning, and as such can be analyzed in terms of the cognitive process outlined by David A. Kolb, who constructs his own understanding of the process as akin to that of scientific inquiry. Importantly, what is described here as preparation to lead a group of students to engage in experiential learning must be construed as a reiterative process: students explore new cities and countrysides in many, many forays. In between these trips students should write, describing what they have seen, comparing it to what they have read, and constructing hypotheses about what they think they have witnessed: they must interpret and analyze. And they must think about themselves in the process so that they can propose new hypotheses to test when next they move out into the environment. What emerges over time is a series of experiential immersions that are processed each time and distilled over time until what becomes a sense of place and self in place merges with a nose for evidence.

Perhaps the greatest challenge to faculty members is to consider themselves explorers, too, not the experts whose knowledge allows students to see whatever it is they end up seeing. Faculty need to think about ways to anticipate the unexpected, even if they are traveling with a group for the fiftieth time to the same city. One approach that might help is actually doing all the assignments given to the students: they can observe in minute detail at a street market, take notes, eavesdrop, describe what they heard and saw, and interpret all they discover and perhaps surprise themselves by their own observation. If that happens, they will have discovered themselves in a new way. The final challenge to faculty preparing to lead a group might well be to understand Geertz's maxim: "In the country of the blind, who are not as unobservant as they look, the one-eyed is not king, he is spectator" (58). Faculty need to figure out how to convey this understanding to students as an invitation and mean it.

WORKS CITED

Braid, Bernice. "Closing the Circle: Connected Knowing." *National Honors Report* 8.4 (Winter 1987). Print.

—. "Discursive Teaching and Higher Learning." *National Honors Report* 8.1 (Spring 1987): Print.

—. "Doing as Learning: Honors in an Experiential Setting." *Forum for Honors* 15.3 (Spring 1985): 3–13. Print.

—. "The Team and Higher Learning." *National Honors Report* 8.2 (Summer 1987). Print.

—. "Text, Context, and Cross-Cultural Conversation." *National Honors Report* 8.3 (Fall 1987). Print.

Geertz, Clifford. *Local Knowledge*. New York: Basic Books, 1983. Print.

Heath, S. B. *Ways with Words*. Cambridge: Cambridge UP, 1983. Print.

Jacobs, Jane. *The Death and Life of Great American Cities*. New York: Vintage Books, 1992. Print.

Kolb, David A. *Experiential Learning: Experience as the Source of Learning and Development*. Englewood Cliffs, NJ: Prentice Hall, 1984. Print.

Nooteboom, Cees. *Roads to Santiago*. San Diego, CA: Harcourt, 1992. Print.

Place as Text: Approaches to Active Learning. Ed. Bernice Braid and Ada Long. 2nd ed. Lincoln: National Collegiate Honors Council, 2010. NCHC Monograph Series. Print.

Whyte, William H. *City: Rediscovering the Center.* New York: Doubleday, 1988. Print.

—. Dir. *The Social Life of Small Urban Spaces.* Project for Public Spaces, 2001. Film.

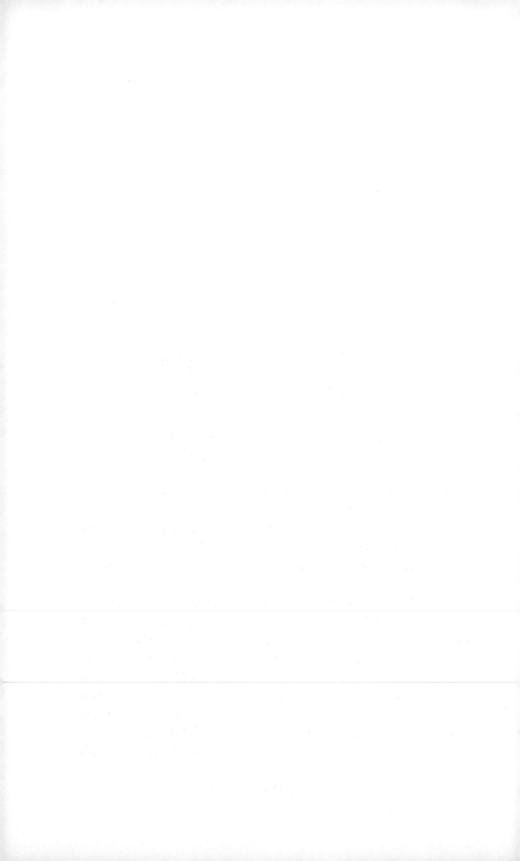

CHAPTER 9

Overcoming Obstacles to Studying Abroad for Honors Students

Philip Krummrich and Kayla Burton
Morehead State University

Judging by the number of sessions devoted to the subject at every national honors conference, honors administrators and faculty value overseas experiences as a part of honors education. Survey results suggest that college-bound students assign considerable importance to studying abroad. In 2001, John Marcum and David Roochnik reported that "more than 70% of high school seniors think it's important that their college offer study-abroad programs and almost half plan to participate in such programs" (1). And yet, unfortunately, according to Marcum and Roochnik, "less than 3 percent of U. S. undergraduates study abroad" (2). It would be natural to suppose, or to hope, that honors students would do better. When we redesigned the honors program at Morehead State University in 2009, we included a required overseas experience. When we reviewed other programs, however, we realized that such a requirement was highly unusual. The present study emerges from our wish to understand an apparent contradiction: despite broad agreement that study abroad for honors students is beneficial, common practice does not reflect this conviction.

Why, given the overwhelming support for the idea of study abroad, do so few students actually go? Why, considering our commitment to the principle of study abroad for honors students, do almost no programs require it? To research these questions, we developed separate surveys for honors students and administrators and distributed the survey links to honors programs and colleges via the NCHC listserv. To reach honors students, we asked honors administrators to forward the link to the student survey to their students. Forty-one administrators and 573 students completed the surveys. The surveys are included as appendices to this chapter. Our original intention was to focus on language barriers: the role they play and ways to minimize their negative impact. The answers to our survey questions provided a great deal of information about other obstacles, however, and we will give full consideration to those factors as well as we analyze the survey results.

Much of what we have learned may apply to undergraduates in general, but we believe that honors students may react more strongly than others to the common obstacles, especially language barriers and curricular concerns, to studying abroad. Understanding the obstacles and their effects is an indispensable prerequisite for useful action. In preparing our surveys, we consulted the literature, our experience, and common sense; the instruments are imperfect, and the results may therefore be incomplete or inconclusive, but we believe that they lead to a better understanding of the issues.

Table 1 summarizes the most common concerns, according to the responses received from honors administrators and honors students, regarding study abroad. Respondents could select more than one obstacle as they completed the survey. Administrators were not asked to speculate on the effects of "relationship status" (understood as romantic attachment) or other personal issues, but otherwise both groups were offered the same choices and given the opportunity to add others in their comments and open-ended responses.

TABLE 1: PERCEPTIONS OF MAJOR OBSTACLES TO
          STUDYING ABROAD

Obstacles to Studying Abroad	Honors Administrators	Honors Students
Financial concerns	97.5%	89.2%
Safety concerns	17.5%	33.6%
Language barriers	42.5%	31.1%
Curricular demands	32.5%	23.8%
Relationship status	N/A	14.9%

The following discussion examines these obstacles in order of importance according to the student responses. Of course, some honors administrators may have a clearer sense of the obstacles than their students because of their greater experience, but ultimately student perceptions are what matter, and they must be addressed if honors administrators hope to increase participation in study abroad among honors students.

The most common obstacle identified by honors administrators and students was financial concerns. Nearly all administrators and nearly 90% of students selected this option. Any suggestion that study abroad should be required immediately provokes fears that many students will face economic hardships that could possibly prevent participation. A proposal at our institution to require an overseas experience of all language majors, certainly a group that should make study abroad a high priority, was recently rejected because of concerns over the fiscal impact on students. No one disputes the need to be sensitive to students' financial situations. Still, academics must recognize, as April Stroud points out, that money may not be as powerful a factor as people think:

> the biggest obstacles to study abroad are not solely financial ones. After all, if finances were a major barrier to study abroad, the reauthorization of the Higher Education Act of

1992, which included provisions to allow the use of financial aid for study abroad if the student is enrolled in a program approved by the home institution, would have shown more dramatic effects on participation rates among traditionally underrepresented groups in American study abroad. (493)

That policy often makes affiliated semester and year-long programs very affordable through direct tuition exchange. Various overseas experiences, such as exchange programs, volunteering opportunities, and internships, in the final analysis, often cost no more than spending the same amount of time at the home campus. Because prioritizing may be problematic, administrators should encourage students to reduce or eliminate some personal expenditures in order to save for a study abroad experience. In short, some students who say that they cannot afford to study abroad may be using finances, consciously or unconsciously, to mask other concerns.

Eighty-four students mentioned financial concerns in their responses to the open-ended questions. Although a few students cited a reluctance to go into debt, they did not, in most cases, elaborate, perhaps because they believed that money requires no explanation or because their financial fears remained vague. The students' responses do not suggest that they had sought out accurate and detailed information about the true cost of overseas study. Further research on the financial realities of study abroad for honors students and their perceptions of the costs could be valuable.

The second most common obstacle cited by students was safety concerns. One-third of the students noted safety as a barrier while only one-sixth of the administrators did so. Since fewer administrators cited safety concerns, they may be underestimating the effect of these concerns on their students. Very likely those students who overcome their misgivings and go overseas will realize that the world is a safer place than they assumed; however, we cannot know how many are sufficiently discouraged by these concerns that they never study overseas.

Honors administrators and students rated "language barriers" high on the list of discouraging factors. Language anxiety refers to a strong sense of discomfort, much like that felt by those who suffer from math anxiety, that some people feel when confronted with the challenge of studying a second language. In our survey questions, we extended the meaning by implication to include the discomfort that many people feel when they find themselves in an environment in which most people are speaking a language that they understand imperfectly or not at all. Our findings regarding the importance of language barriers as a deterrent to studying abroad are consistent with our original hypothesis; indeed, it is reasonable to wonder if these percentages are misleadingly low. A student might intend all along to study in Ireland, for instance, and thus never worry about difficulties in communication.

Although the survey does not specify that the time abroad will necessarily be spent in a non-English-speaking country, many student responses seem to take that for granted. We may wonder if the concept of studying abroad is somehow linked in the minds of students to language barriers, even when no overt indication exists that another language will be involved. Students may avoid study abroad programs in non-Anglophone countries because they may be uncomfortable with the prospect of being surrounded by a language they do not understand. "Safety concerns" may overlap to some extent with "language barriers" because students might feel more trepidation about having to deal with dangerous situations if they do not speak and understand the local language fluently. Honors students might be more likely than the general population of college students to find these experiences unsettling: after all, honors students are driven to understand and function at a high level. They sometimes avoid classes in which they would not expect to do well or fear that they might feel incompetent. Perceived language barriers might discourage some honors students from selecting study abroad options outside the English-speaking world. That administrators marked this choice more frequently than students may imply that they are more conscious of the effects of language anxiety than their students, but the difference may also mean that they underestimate the willingness of their students to confront the unknown.

Despite some apprehensions expressed in the survey, 84.6% of the student respondents indicated that they would be willing to travel to a country where their native language is not spoken. In one sense, that figure is heartening because it strongly implies that students can overcome anxieties they may feel about language barriers and venture into the large portions of the world that are not English-speaking. On the other hand, the vast majority of college-bound students claim an interest in studying abroad and often end up doing nothing about it. That honors students say they would be willing to go is encouraging; however, evidence from deans and directors shows that the willingness does not always translate into a plane ticket.

A significant number of student respondents (114 of 461) cited "homesickness" as a fear; a number of related comments referred to a sense of family responsibility or to a fear of isolation. Some honors students may feel isolated through much of their academic life because of their unusual commitment to learning; having found, perhaps, a sense of community in their honors program, they may be reluctant to step away and risk returning to isolation. "Homesickness" can also be linked tentatively to language anxiety in this sense: language anxiety is one manifestation of students' natural preference for the safe and familiar.

In the open-ended responses explicitly related to language, forty-four of the 461 respondents mentioned "language barriers" as a fear without elaborating. Thirty-eight others referred to the same concern but offered explanatory remarks. One student worried about "being taken advantage of if [he] did not understand something [a local resident] said." This familiar fear of travelers in general is no doubt exacerbated by the special impatience of high-performing students with anything they do not fully understand. Other responses emphasize academic fears. "I wouldn't do well in the classes because of cultural and language differences." "I would have fears of not being able to communicate well and understand my assignments/lectures." "I would be afraid of being with an entire[ly] new group of people in a new place and having classes that were not taught in English." These comments show, first of all, that the students are not well-informed about study abroad options: they do not realize that they could choose from among many programs, even in non-Anglophone countries, in which the classes were conducted entirely in English, often by American faculty. We see also the fear of isolation and the anxiety of performing at anything below the highest level.

A more subtle discomfort is revealed by the student who worried "that [she] won't be able to pick up the language and won't be able to experience the country to its fullest." This response shows an intriguing combination of language anxiety and what we might call the anxiety of excellence. This student, apparently, would feel self-reproachful with anything less than experiencing the country "to its fullest." Those with experience of overseas study know that goal to be lofty, and they understand that even a limited experience can have great value, but one can certainly sympathize with the attitude of this student.

Honors deans and directors attributed more importance to the demands of the curriculum than did students (32.5%, as opposed to 23.8%). This difference may be in part because honors administrators have so often contended with the common perception among their institutional colleagues that honors classes and programs interfere and compete with the major. Students in some curricula may not be able to manage a semester or a year overseas without delaying graduation; just as often, advisors who are not supportive of honors programs or study abroad, or both, may exaggerate the difficulties. With pre-planning and summer options, students should seldom have a curricular reason for not studying abroad.

The open-ended responses related to curricular concerns were revealing and may be grouped into three categories. The most commonly expressed misgiving had to do with whether classes taken overseas would count towards requirements at the home institution in general education, the honors program, or the major or minor. That this doubt surfaced so often suggests that overseas programs do not coordinate well with the standard curriculum, that honors students need to be better informed about how classes taken abroad could fit, or that both factors are operating. Many students believe that studying abroad is not feasible because of their majors. One stated: "Courses offered in study abroad programs that sound interesting don't match up to Biochemistry." Students in professional programs with heavy clinical demands, such as nursing or education, had special concerns about studying abroad. Thus, one student observed: "Nursing does not leave much time for taking a semester off." And another student raised a troubling issue, recalling "education [requires] classes from [an] accredited program." For students sharing similar concerns, no easy answers exist because the challenges vary considerably from major to major and from school to school. With specialized and thorough advising, however, most students can identify feasible study abroad options. Finally, other students expressed concerns that participating in an overseas study program would delay their graduation. These students shared the assumption that they had to spend a full semester abroad; advisors need to identify possible short-term options. With the wisdom of hindsight, administrators and faculty members could assure students that the benefits of studying abroad outweigh any slight extension of the undergraduate degree program. Our educational system, however, has established four years as the norm, and honors students may view taking longer as a failure. The percentages of honors students electing overseas study are not likely to improve much until administrators clear up their misconceptions about the great range of study abroad programs available.

Students were asked whether their relationship status might constitute an obstacle, and 14.9% conceded that it might. Moreover, other circumstances, such as family illnesses and deaths, divorce, and relocation, may disrupt a student's plans. These factors constitute a general category of significant obstacles called "personal matters." In response to the open-ended question about fears, such unexpected individual reasons as "pet care" and "spiritual concerns" were also mentioned.

Upon analyzing the survey and interview results, reviewing the appropriate literature, and reflecting on our personal experiences, we offer the following suggestions for countering these obstacles and encouraging more honors students to study abroad. Although little can be done about the unpredictable personal issues that hold some students back, the other major obstacles can be made to seem less formidable by a combination of thoughtful publicity and positive action. We gained particularly valuable insights, to be shared later in this chapter, from program directors of the Kentucky Institute for International Studies (KIIS), a consortium that has provided successful programs in non-Anglophone countries for over thirty years.

The survey responses emphasize that honors students often lack accurate information about their study abroad options. They do not realize how affordable it can be or how much financial aid is available. They need to know more about how study abroad can mesh with their curriculum; they need to understand that safety concerns, although real and reasonable to some extent, can be diminished significantly by good preparation and common sense. Regarding language, they need to understand that being less than fluent is not a serious obstacle and that a range of overseas classes and programs are available in English. Honors students could easily discover this information for themselves, but the survey results demonstrate that many have not done so; honors administrators must actively promote this perspective. Academics experienced in attracting students to study abroad programs address common misconceptions in their recruiting materials. They explain the costs and financial aid options and emphasize the value of international education. They share syllabi for the proposed classes, clearly distinguishing between those taught in English and those conducted in other languages. Successful organizations such as KIIS, incidentally, strive to make coursework available in a wide range of fields, thereby addressing another common student concern. As part of the recruiting effort, program directors give prospective participants access to others who have already taken part through social media, testimonials on websites, and personal interviews; for example, Christine Shea of Ball State University invites former students in her program to a luncheon with recruits. These veterans of international experiences can allay the fears of prospective recruits about money, curriculum, safety, and language. Honors administrators could adapt these strategies to tailor programs specific to the needs of their student population.

Students could work at a remote research station in Costa Rica to study epiphytes or participate in an archaeological dig on a Greek island, devoting most of their time and attention to advanced fieldwork. David Keeling of Western Kentucky University, a veteran leader of student groups overseas, runs "geography field camps . . . where language skills are secondary to spatial science skills." Gayle Grout of Northern Kentucky University has been taking students to Salzburg for over twenty years, and she reassures students by making clear that they will be dealing mostly with a language they know very well: music. These programs overcome common concerns about studying abroad. They are usually reasonably priced and customized to fulfill curricular requirements, and the familiar company eases misgivings about safety and homesickness.

Such opportunities can be created specifically for honors students. The directors of most study abroad programs are actively seeking new recruits, and honors students are especially welcome. Honors administrators might also encourage their students to take the initiative: they could form groups, select destinations and programs, and lobby for classes designed to meet their needs. KIIS, for example, offers honors classes in several of its programs, which are open to students from all twenty-two member institutions of the consortium. Simply offering honors classes with no language requirement can be a boon for students worried about the demands of their curriculum or difficulties in communication. Such classes also allow honors students from different institutions to interact in a more sustained way than national and regional honors conferences permit.

If honors administrators believe that an overseas experience has value, they should be able to persuade honors students to consider pursuing non-credit experiences as volunteers. This statement implies no assumptions about the lofty-mindedness of honors students although experience suggests that many honors students are strongly motivated by a belief in service and might be favorably inclined towards a service experience instead of classes overseas.

Global Volunteers <http://globalvolunteers.org>, for example, offers students a multitude of opportunities to do meaningful work abroad. Especially for honors programs with a service-learning emphasis, volunteering may suit a student better than taking a class for credit. The linguistic challenges would be limited by the time frame and the nature of the volunteer work, and in any case English speakers would almost always be available to assist. Many honors students regularly volunteer their time, energy, and skills. Steering them towards overseas service opportunities may address most of the major concerns about study abroad: volunteering costs less because tuition is not a factor, interferes less if at all with progress towards graduation, and usually does not require proficiency in another language. Volunteer agencies offer a good support network, which reduces anxieties about safety and language. Almost half of the students in the recently redesigned honors program at Morehead State University, in which an approved overseas experience is required of all honors students, listed a volunteer program as one of their top two choices.

If they were aware of the remarkable exchanges available to them, the students might already be flocking out of the country in much greater numbers. The Magellan Exchange <http://www.magellanexchange.org>, for example, has member institutions in twelve countries; most are in the United States and Europe, but the consortium also includes Mexico, Costa Rica, and South Korea. Students spend a semester or a full year at the exchange campus, pay tuition to their home institution, and may take all of their classes in English, wherever they may be studying. In some respects, this solution is ideal: it is affordable, permits progress towards graduation, and combines sustained participation, without language barriers, in the host culture as part of an academic environment in which students can flourish. One member campus, Anyang University in South Korea, even offers scholarship support to attract students from the United States and Europe, so that the cost of spending the semester in South Korea is little more than that of staying home. By emphasizing coursework in business and technology, this organization provides one example of a practical response needed to overcome both the legitimate concerns and the ill-informed fears of honors students regarding study abroad.

In the interest of overcoming reluctance and attracting honors students into beneficial overseas experiences, we have suggested how honors administrators and advisors might address worries about money, curricular issues, safety, and language barriers. On an encouraging note, survey responses show that many honors students embrace the challenge of studying abroad and even the prospect of functioning in another language. Meg Brown of Murray State University exemplifies this positive attitude, indicating that "studying abroad in a country where the native language is NOT English looks great on a resumé and says so much about them as a person to a future employer: that they can work with different people and ideas, that they can think outside the box, that they can take reasonable risk." Even more students might take that attitude if they could overcome their fears and focus on what they can gain from studying abroad.

While soothing fears is necessary, persuading honors students to accept and relish the challenge of dealing with the world in a language other than English is the preferable approach. Obviously, the better prepared students are for the experience, the more they can learn from it. Program directors frequently offer crash courses in survival Spanish or German for travelers, and students will hear from others who have traveled that even a fifty-word vocabulary can make a difference. Sylvia Henneberg recommends that all programs include the option of a beginning language course; Christine Shea, who regularly takes groups to Greece, states: "We always suggest that they run through the really superior BBC language system for modern Greek." Whether the quick class in the language takes place before the trip or while students are abroad, it enhances the experience in practical and psychological ways.

Many honors students will be unable or unwilling to devote the standard minimum of four semesters to language study in preparation for an in-depth international program, but some clearly are willing to do so. To reinforce the value of this long-term commitment and to reward those honors students who make it, honors administrators should inform students about the U.S. government-sponsored Boren Scholarships and the Critical Languages Program, among others. Those students who are prepared to make a serious commitment—and the survey suggests that students recognize that a full semester is preferable to a short summer program or winter break program if the financial obstacles can be overcome—can use a study abroad program to develop an invaluable skill. Administrators can encourage honors students to accept the challenge and expand their capabilities. For example, music students from Morehead State University and Marshall University take part in a full-semester exchange with two universities in Brazil. The American students complete a not-for-credit introductory class in Portuguese, spend a month in intensive instruction in Brazil before the term begins, and then carry a normal course load taught entirely in Portuguese. They emerge from the experience with a solid working knowledge of another language, an impressive addition to their resumés, and greatly enhanced self-confidence and self-esteem. Although this program has the decided advantage of generous funding from FIPSE and the corresponding agency in Brazil, CAPES, the basic model could be adapted to other fields and exchange destinations.

CONCLUSION

Our nationwide survey of honors students and administrators establishes that the following factors reduce the number of honors students who study abroad: financial worries, safety concerns, language anxiety, curricular doubts, and personal issues. In most cases, these deterrents have more to do with perceptions and misconceptions than with reality. Many students seem not to know much about the experiences they are likely to have with other languages while out of this country, just as they labor under misapprehensions about money, curriculum, and safety. Some of the survey responses reveal notions about finances and language as misleading as the lurid fictionalization in *Taken*, the 2008 film about the dangers of foreign travel.

To the extent that misconceptions discourage the participation of honors students in study abroad, the remedy is clear: more and better information that is delivered in a timely fashion and from multiple sources. In response to the real obstacles, honors administrators should design distinctive opportunities for honors students, even involving them in the design process. With the right combination of straight facts and gentle suasion, administrators should be able to encourage many more honors students to confront and overcome their worries about money, curriculum, safety, and language and to get on that plane.

WORKS CITED

Brown, Meg. "Re: Research on Study Abroad and Honors." Message to the authors. 4 May 2011. Email.

Grout, Gayle. "Re: Research on Study Abroad and Honors." Message to the authors. 26 Apr. 2011. Email.

Henneberg, Sylvia. "Re: Research on Study Abroad and Honors." Message to the authors. 14 Apr. 2011. Email.

Keeling, David. "Re: Research on Study Abroad and Honors." Message to the authors. 13 Apr. 2011. Email.

Lenk, Sonia. "Re: Research on Study Abroad and Honors." Message to the authors. 21 Apr. 2011. Email.

Marcum, John, and David Roochnik. "What Direction for Study Abroad?: 2 Views." *Chronicle of Higher Education* 18 May 2001: B7. Web. 16 Feb. 2011.

Shea, Christine. "Re: Research on Study Abroad and Honors." Message to the authors. 13 Apr. 2011. Email.

Stroud, April. "Who Plans (Not) to Study Abroad?: An Examination of U.S. Student Intent." *Journal of Studies in International Education* 14.5 (2010): 491–507. Print.

APPENDIX 1

Survey for Honors Students

1. What is your gender?
- ☐ Female
- ☐ Male

2. What is your year of undergraduate study?
- ☐ Freshman
- ☐ Sophomore
- ☐ Junior
- ☐ Senior
- ☐ Other (please specify) _____

3. What is your major?

_____

4. What is your age?

_____

5. How important is study abroad in your honors program?
- ☐ Study abroad is required in my program.
- ☐ Information is easily available for students, and we are encouraged to study abroad.
- ☐ It is left up to students to find information on study abroad programs; it is rarely mentioned by faculty and staff.
- ☐ Study abroad is not encouraged at all by faculty and staff.

6. Are you interested in participating in a study abroad program?
- ☐ Yes
- ☐ No

7. **What are some of the reasons for which you would be interested in participating in a study abroad program? (Please check all that apply.)**
   - ☐ To make new friends and meet new people outside of my current peer group
   - ☐ To experience a new culture firsthand
   - ☐ To become familiar with a language other than my native one
   - ☐ To step out of my comfort zone in order to gain new experiences in life
   - ☐ To strengthen my resume
   - ☐ Other (please specify) _____

8. **What factors would stop you from studying abroad? (Please check all that apply.)**
   - ☐ Financial concerns
   - ☐ Language barriers
   - ☐ Safety concerns
   - ☐ The demands of the curriculum
   - ☐ Current relationship status
   - ☐ Other (please specify) _____

9. **Would the chances of your studying abroad increase if you could do it within a group with which you were already familiar, such as friends or peers?**
   - ☐ Yes
   - ☐ No

10. **How long would you want to study abroad?**
    - ☐ An academic year or more
    - ☐ A semester
    - ☐ A summer
    - ☐ A short term (three weeks or less)

11. **What positive experiences do you think you would gain by participating in a study abroad program?**

    _____

12. **What fears would you have about traveling to a new country for an extended amount of time?**

    _____

13. **Would you be willing to travel to a country where your native language is not spoken?**
    - ☐ Yes
    - ☐ No

14. **What is the level of anxiety you would feel about traveling to a country in which your native language is spoken very little, or not at all? (On a scale of 1–5, one being "no anxiety at all," and five being "very anxious.")**
    - ☐ 1
    - ☐ 2
    - ☐ 3
    - ☐ 4
    - ☐ 5

APPENDIX 2

Survey for Honors Administrators

1. **Which of the following statements most accurately represents the practices of your program in regard to study abroad?**

   ☐ We require it.

   ☐ We encourage it and offer funding to assist students.

   ☐ We encourage it although we can offer only limited financial support.

   ☐ We allow honors students to make their own decisions and arrangements regarding study abroad.

   Please add comments or clarifications if you can.

   _____

2. **Approximately how many of your honors students study abroad?**

   ☐ 100%

   ☐ 75–99%

   ☐ 50–74%

   ☐ 25–49%

   ☐ Under 25%

   Please add comments or clarifications if you can

   _____

3. **If your honors students participate in overseas programs, roughly how long do they elect to stay?**

   ☐ An academic year or more

   ☐ A semester

☐ A summer term

☐ A short term (three weeks or less)

Please add comments that will help to explain these preferences, if you can.

_____

4. **Please indicate the preferred destinations of your honors students who study abroad by writing the number in the blank (1 for "most popular" and so on).**

☐ England

☐ Europe

☐ Canada

☐ Other English-speaking countries

☐ Central and South America

☐ Africa

☐ Asia

☐ Other

Please mention any special factors that may influence the choice of destination.

_____

5. **Do you believe that language anxiety discourages your honors students from traveling and studying in non-Anglophone countries?**

☐ Yes

☐ No

Please add comments if you like.

_____

185

6. **Of your honors students who elect an overseas experience in a non-Anglophone country, how many have some prior knowledge of the language?**
   ☐ Over 50%

   ☐ 25–49%

   ☐ 5–24%

   ☐ None, or almost none

   ☐ Not known

7. **In your experience, what factors tend to discourage honors students from studying abroad? Please mark all that apply; if you can, please rank them in order of significance.**
   ☐ Financial concerns

   ☐ The demands of the curriculum

   ☐ Language barriers

   ☐ Safety concerns

   ☐ Other (please specify) _____

8. **Which of the following statements most accurately represents the role of study abroad in your honors program as compared with its role at your institution in general?**
   ☐ Study abroad is more important for honors students than for students in general at my institution.

   ☐ Study abroad is equally important for all students at my institution.

   ☐ Study abroad is less important for honors students than for others at my institution.

   ☐ Other (please specify) _____

APPENDIX 3

Questions for Directors of Study Abroad Programs

1. Please indicate where you take or have taken students.

2. Do you believe that language anxiety discourages a significant number of students from applying for your program?

3. Please describe briefly any specific strategies you use during the recruiting process to reassure students who are concerned about language barriers in the study abroad experience.

4. Please describe briefly any specific strategies you use to help students to deal with language barriers while they are participating in your program.

5. Judging by your experience, do language barriers cause many problems for students once they make up their minds to participate in your program?

6. What advice do you have for faculty and administrators who are trying to encourage more students to consider programs in non-Anglophone countries?

7. May we quote you in the monograph?
   ☐ Yes

   ☐ No

CHAPTER 10

Finding a Way:
Addressing the Financial Challenges of
Studying Abroad

Kim Klein
Shippensburg University

Mary Kay Mulvaney
Elmhurst College

As global perspectives and experiences become more highly valued attributes of university graduates, more students are weighing the benefits and costs of incorporating study abroad experiences into their undergraduate degree programs. Even though honors students generally place a high value on international experiences, they are often overwhelmed by the potentially steep expenses of studying abroad, especially in the context of steadily rising costs of higher education. Sometimes, a shift in perspective is required for students to understand how studying abroad represents an important investment in their future rather than a drain on their current finances. This chapter will present strategies for making study abroad experiences a financially viable option for honors students.

The costs of study abroad programs vary widely, and many factors influence these costs for students. The location of their study abroad experience is one of the first decisions that students make, and this decision often has the greatest impact on students' finances. Because they do not present language barriers, the United Kingdom and Australia are perennial favorites as study abroad destinations for U.S. students despite being among the most expensive locations. By recommending programs that are tailored to students' academic and professional goals in less popular but more affordable destinations, advisors can turn study abroad dreams into realities for cost-conscious students. Students who opt for a semester or year-long program in a destination where the costs of living are lower than those at their home campus in the United States may find that their living expenses, even when factoring in transportation costs to and from the overseas institution, are equal to, and sometimes even less than, housing and food costs at their home university. Latin American destinations are gaining in popularity because of their relative affordability and lower costs of living. For example, a home stay in Costa Rica or Mexico, where accommodations, meals, and laundry are included, can offer a substantial cost-of-living advantage compared to a student apartment in a major U.S. metropolitan area. Students and faculty often overlook Canada as a study abroad destination, but it is home to many outstanding and highly affordable universities that offer a range of world-class academic programs. And for students interested in cultural immersion experiences, studying in Quebec offers a similar opportunity for immersion in a Francophone culture than a potentially much more expensive study abroad experience in France.

Aside from location, the length of the study abroad experience is another important factor influencing price. Semester or year-long programs are often affordable options because a carefully chosen international program may cost no more, and occasionally less, than the equivalent time spent at the home university. Many universities have negotiated exchange agreements that allow their students to pay the same amount for tuition and possibly for other basic expenses, such as fees, housing, and meals, which they would pay at their home institution. Some especially advantageous exchange agreements make a semester or year abroad even more affordable than a semester or year at the home university. For example, Shippensburg University has an exchange agreement with Soonchunhyang University in South Korea that allows Shippensburg students to study abroad for less than they would pay for a semester at the home campus. During their semester abroad, students are charged the same tuition that they would normally pay at Shippensburg, but Soonchunhyang University provides housing and meals at no cost to exchange students. In addition to free accommodations and meals, students who take advantage of this exchange opportunity receive a stipend for leading English-language tutorials for Korean students. The stipend gives students the financial flexibility to travel throughout East and Southeast Asia during their semester abroad. These arrangements are growing increasingly common, and many universities post similar opportunities on their study abroad websites.

Universities that have made an institutional commitment to globalizing their campuses often provide significant resources to support students' international experiences. The most fortunate scenario is when an institution recognizes the inestimable value of study abroad for its students, makes a deliberate choice to identify study abroad as an institutional priority, and assists with funding through the general budget to underwrite its students' experiences. Dozens of colleges and universities promote study abroad as "part of their culture"; a recent *US News and World Report* includes more than fifty institutions where at least fifty percent of students participate in international experiences during the undergraduate years ("Most Students"). Arcadia University is one institution that has intentionally crafted its identity as a study abroad institution; students now seek admission with that goal in mind. The universities and programs requiring or strongly encouraging their students to study abroad recognize that they must provide financial support so that students can meet this institutional goal. Goucher College in Baltimore, for example, proudly proclaims on its website <www.goucher.edu> to be the first liberal arts college in the nation to require a study abroad experience of every undergraduate. To ensure that students can fulfill this requirement, Goucher provides vouchers, valued at a minimum of $1,200, to all students to defray their travel expenses. Augustana College in Illinois recently launched a similar program to finance experiential-learning opportunities, including international study, for its students. The program, "Augie Choice," provides students in their junior year or beyond with a one-time grant of $2,000 to offset the expenses of participating in international study, internships, and research experiences.

Another way that universities have institutionalized their commitment to promoting study abroad is through the implementation of fee plans. International education fees are similar to more common laboratory or technology fees that all students pay as part of their regular tuition each term, regardless of whether they ever take a chemistry class or set foot in a campus computer lab. For example, over twenty years ago, the Texas state legislature passed a law allowing state-supported institutions to assess a $1 per student fee, with the discretion to raise the fee (currently, it is $4), to support study abroad opportunities. Institutional fees range widely: a $15 international education fee is assessed at Southwest Tennessee Community College; a $100 globalization fee is charged at Howard University. Another fee-based possibility is a banking system. Institutions might, for example, charge students a $200 per semester international fee that becomes a bank account accumulating, with interest, nearly $2,000 for each student over four years to defray the costs of an international study experience.

An institutional commitment to study abroad can also provide the impetus for external fundraising efforts, such as capital campaigns that include funding initiatives for international education. Similarly, development offices may encourage donors to create an endowment designated to fund study abroad scholarships. Alumni and parents of students who have benefitted from studying abroad can be enthusiastic supporters of these fundraising initiatives. Parents of international students, some of whom have considerable financial means, may also be willing to underwrite a student seeking an international study experience because they recognize the value for their own offspring. Larry R. Andrews advises honors programs that are interested in pursuing internal and external funding opportunities to include international education support on their development wish list and in their annual reports (56–65). Frequently, administrators, faculty colleagues, trustees, and potential donors need some enlightened encouragement regarding the invaluable nature of an international component within a twenty-first-century students' higher education.

Less ambitious, internal possibilities for pursuing funding exist as well. Students can fundraise for specific international programs, especially service-learning experiences, because other people often recognize their value. By conducting the usual bake and book sales, walkathons, and bracelet distributions, students can accumulate funds to support group travel. Local chapters of Phi Beta Delta, the International Honors Society, may provide fundraising assistance. At Elmhurst College, student members of Phi Beta Delta drafted a proposal to the Student Government Association to support a campus-wide initiative to fund study abroad scholarships.

Honors students, of course, are strong candidates for competitive national scholarships to finance their international experiences. A valuable online resource for researching study abroad scholarships is a website hosted by the Institute for International Education <http://www.studyabroadfunding.org>. Students can search by field of study and destination to find descriptions of relevant scholarships, fellowships, grants, and paid internships. Several scholarship programs specifically target students with financial need. For example, the Benjamin A. Gilman International Scholarship <http://www.iie.org/en/Programs/Gilman-Scholarship-Program> provides awards of up to $5,000 to Pell Grant recipients to support their participation in international programs that are at least four weeks in length. Similarly, Freeman-Asia scholarships of up to

$5,000 are available to students with demonstrated financial need who plan to study in East or Southeast Asia for at least eight weeks. (See <http://www.iie.org/programs/Freeman-Asia> for details.)

Numerous foundations and national honors societies also offer funding for study abroad programs on a competitive basis. Rotary Foundation Ambassadorial Scholarships provide financial support for undergraduate and graduate students in all disciplines to study in destinations around the world <http://www.rotary.org>. Phi Kappa Phi, the interdisciplinary national honors society, awards fifty $1,000 grants each year to students attending institutions with active chapters, and these scholarships support students in any major who are traveling to destinations worldwide. More information is available at <http://www.phikappaphi.org>.

Other nationally competitive scholarships are ideal for students who are interested in studying in less traditional study abroad destinations. The National Security Education Program (NSEP) sponsors Boren Scholarships for undergraduate students. Boren Scholarships <http://www.borenawards.org> provide up to $20,000 to students who plan to study languages and cultures that the NSEP has defined as critical to U.S. national and security interests and in countries that are underrepresented as study abroad sites. Boren Scholarship recipients must commit to one year of service with the federal government. Similarly, the Critical Language Scholarship Program <http://www.clscholarship.org> provides a fully funded seven-to-twelve-week summer immersion experience for undergraduate and graduate students in strategically important nations, such as Turkey, China, and India, whose languages are understudied in the United States.

As students prepare their financial plans for studying abroad, they also need to be advised of the implications for their financial aid. Most forms of federal and state financial aid can be used to fund for-credit study abroad programs. Even students who do not normally qualify for financial aid may be eligible if their study abroad program is more expensive than their regular university. To facilitate the transfer of financial aid, some institutions have created direct tuition payment programs with nationally recognized study abroad providers, such as the Institute for the International Education of Students (IES) or School for International Training (SIT). Direct tuition payments allow for the transfer of all financial aid, including federal and state funds, as well as all local and need-based or merit scholarships.

Administrators, faculty, and students increasingly regard studying abroad as an invaluable component of a comprehensive degree program rather than a luxury add-on. Once students are advised of the factors that affect the costs of studying abroad and the extensive internal and external funding opportunities that are available to them, affording a study abroad experience often becomes less a matter of finances and more a matter of priorities. By furthering students' understanding of the many ways that study abroad experiences can advance their academic and professional goals, honors advisors can help students make study abroad a priority.

WORKS CITED

Andrews, Larry R. *Fundrai$ing for Honors: A Handbook*. Lincoln: National Collegiate Honors Council, 2009. NCHC Monograph Series. Print.

"Most Students Studying Abroad." *U.S. News and World Report*. 2011-2012 Annual Report. Web. 6 Feb. 2013.

"Open Doors 2011: Study Abroad by U.S. Students Rose in 2009/10 with More Students Going to Less Traditional Destinations." Institute of International Education. Web. 6 Feb. 2013.

CHAPTER 11

Mitigating the Challenges and Risks of International Travel: Preserving Opportunities for a Global Honors Experience

MARY ANN STUDER

DEFIANCE COLLEGE

The world is a difficult classroom, and faculty who want to use the global environment to educate their students are constantly learning how to effectively manage the risks. Indeed, in recent years, crisis management and, in some cases, evacuation of students has been necessary because of political unrest and natural disasters. Increasingly, knowing how to address risk management for study abroad is crucial. Faculty and administrators must recognize the difference between traveling by themselves and traveling with students. Those nagging suspicions about what could happen and those incidents that one hopes do not occur often do come to fruition. Students, as well as faculty on occasion, often travel with an identified sense of abandonment, a carefree attitude that is diametrically opposed to the heightened sense of awareness that would significantly contribute to their security and their ability to make safe choices. For a successful international study program, risk management is mandatory.

Those people who are experienced with risk management always consider what is most likely to happen and what can be most effectively managed. Developing training for students, faculty, and administrators that focuses on potential risks associated with college students traveling and with the specific locations involved, coupled with the development of protocols and plans that would effectively respond to those risks, is at the core of viable risk management. Four basic areas are critical to effective institutional management of risk with both short-term or long-term travel: (1) appropriate and continual training in crisis response for administrators and staff in support positions; (2) appropriate training of all faculty traveling abroad with students; (3) appropriate training of students traveling; and (4) appropriate use and monitoring of resources available from the U.S. government and support partners onsite at the location of study. Of course, many faculty members have traveled with students for years without experiencing a serious crisis, and many have traveled without any formal training. If they have had no serious incidents, they have been lucky. Today's world is different: the crises are more widespread; the threats are more numerous; and the targets, especially for U.S. citizens, are more explicit. Despite this challenging environment, international experiences, more than ever before, remain a critical mechanism for effectively preparing students to excel as professionals in the global environment of the twenty-first century; thus, addressing potential threats is more necessary than ever.

At Defiance College, a small liberal arts college in rural Ohio, faculty and administrators in the McMaster School for Advancing Humanity and the Carolyn M. Small Honors Program have been traveling with students for years to remote areas in developing countries, such as Belize, Cambodia, and Guatemala, as well as to culturally diverse urban areas throughout Europe. A large percentage of the students on these ventures are first-generation college students, many of whom have never flown before, let alone traveled internationally. They often enter college with no thoughts of even leaving the tri-state area. Yet, they have traveled and will travel in even greater numbers in the future. Defiance College has encouraged travel abroad for the last ten years through its honors program and its McMaster School for Advancing Humanity, which supports international community-based research. Most recently Defiance President Mark Gordon has instituted a commitment to all incoming students that they will have an opportunity to travel abroad sometime during their four years on campus. Defiance College is committed to preserving opportunities for its students to engage in what are truly life-changing experiences abroad.

The desire to fulfill this commitment, however, must be balanced against the myriad of risks involved. Institutions, like Defiance, that are promoting study abroad experiences must be committed to keeping students and faculty as safe as possible by having mechanisms in place for effective support and for appropriate response to threats.

RESPONSIBILITIES OF INTERNATIONAL EDUCATION ADMINISTRATORS AND STAFF

The administration of study abroad initiatives at Defiance College involves two major components: the initiative proposal and the Emergency Response Guidelines that specifically address international initiatives. The initiative proposal is probably similar to that used at many other institutions; the elements relative to safety and security are quite specific. The proposal requires a complete itinerary prior to travel; it should include all contact information associated with the initiative: hotel phone numbers, flight information, rental car agencies, contact information for community partners, and day-by-day itineraries. The proposal also lays out those elements that must be included in a pre-departure orientation conducted by the Program Director: logistics, academic information, legal considerations and procedures, health and medical information, personal safety, country/regional issues, and cross-cultural information.

The criteria for an onsite orientation are also included in the proposal. Students are more apt to take seriously the information relative to safety and security provided onsite than at a pre-trip orientation because the unfamiliar context of the host site helps them to comprehend their vulnerability. Therefore, onsite orientation is critical and should include:

- A review of emergency preparedness procedures and the locations of exits and emergency equipment;
- A list of the day and after-hour contact information for key personnel and the U.S. consulate or embassy;
- A review of relevant laws of the country;
- A review of personal safety issues;
- A discussion of safety and security measures and onsite rules;
- The location of medical facilities in the area;
- A meeting point in the event of an emergency or separation from the group;
- Acclimation and orientation to the location;
- A discussion of local transportation safety;
- Language negotiation—phrases needed for emergencies.

Initiative proposals require the Program Directors to agree in writing that they understand the institution's prescribed information and practices concerning safety and security monitoring while preparing for and executing any study abroad experience. The final element requires that the Program Directors list the potential risks associated with the initiative, excluding ones associated with normal modes of transportation. By constructing the international proposal, the Program Directors and faculty members clearly understand the training required once the program has been approved.

The second administrative component involves the Emergency Response Guidelines. (See Appendix 1.) These Emergency Response Guidelines clearly delineate between the protocols followed on campus in response to an emergency and the protocols followed by the onsite Program Director in response to an emergency abroad. Of course, these Emergency Response Guidelines align with the crisis response protocols Defiance College has developed to address on-campus crises.

Integral to the protocol for responding to an emergency abroad is having a committee, the smaller the better, for direct and immediate consultation in the event of an incident or a more widespread crisis. At Defiance College the first tier of this committee is composed of the Dean of the McMaster School (at other institutions this person would likely be the Director of the Office of International Education), the Provost/Chief Academic Officer, the President of the College, and the designated Single Point of Contact for any international initiative. Although this first tier may look completely different at a larger institution, the committee should be kept to a minimum of three or four people. Criteria in the emergency response protocols define the rationale for expanding the response team to a tier-two group that would include the Vice President of Student Engagement (or perhaps the Dean of Students at other institutions), the Chief Financial Officer, and the Director of Public Relations in addition to the tier-one members.[1] For each international initiative, Defiance designates an on-campus person to be the Single Point of Contact (SPC); whenever possible, the SPC is the Dean of the McMaster School or the Director of the Study Abroad Office. The SPC is always a faculty member or administrator who has had extensive experience traveling abroad with students. The SPC responds to any concerns or questions the group traveling may have and serves as the liaison with the families of the students and faculty who are traveling should they need to contact a participant. The SPC meets with the faculty traveling pre-trip, reviews the itinerary, and maintains the emergency contact and medical disclosure paperwork, passport copies, and other required information for all participants on his or her person during the initiative. The SPC is on call 24-hours-a-day for the duration of the trip. In addition, the SPC monitors the U.S. Department of State and other sources of information and news relative to the area where the group is traveling. Defiance encourages parents of the students traveling to meet the SPC prior to the trip as well. This meeting helps parents to become familiar with and to develop confidence in the program staff.

The highly structured nature of the emergency response protocol means that the SPC can function effectively and methodically during volatile situations. The Emergency Response Guidelines include an appendix that helps the SPC to determine whether or not the situation is an emergency and then provides a series of standard question sets to address each of the following incidents: accident/injury, medical emergency (physical or mental), physical/sexual assault, missing person, death, incarceration, political/civil unrest, terrorist attack or threat, and natural or human disaster. Thus, the SPC can systematically gather the information necessary to initiate action even in an emotionally charged context. Although the Emergency Response Guidelines clearly establish that the onsite faculty Program Director is first and foremost responsible for maintaining the safety and welfare of the group, the SPC is responsible for notifying the appropriate persons to aid in the response and provide advice on an appropriate course of action. Included in the Emergency Response Guidelines is a two-page protocol for the onsite Program Directors; it provides information that guides the immediate response to a local emergency, an individual emergency, a worldwide crisis, program cancellation, or withdrawal from the program. All faculty directors must acknowledge in writing that they have read carefully and understood the Emergency Response Guidelines.

Developing and disseminating the Emergency Response Guidelines are not sufficient: these guidelines must be reviewed annually and modified as necessary. The study abroad faculty need to conduct annual drills or simulations with both the tier-one and tier-two committee members as well as with staff who may answer an incoming call to the Study Abroad Office. Practice contributes significantly to the ability to mount an effective response. Communication is also a key component of an effective response as well as an integral factor in how the response will be perceived by others. Having an explicit understanding of (1) what to say; (2) who is going to say it; and (3) who is hearing it will be important at the time of the incident. The institution's response to a crisis will be judged by students, parents, the community, and perhaps the press. Therefore, it is critical that the institution consistently provides information relative to the crisis, that the information released is congruent, and that the exchange between the institution and families remains honest and caring.

TRAINING OF FACULTY TRAVELING ABROAD WITH STUDENTS

Drills and role-playing exercises in which the Emergency Response Guidelines are reviewed and various protocols implemented cannot be limited to administrators and staff. All faculty traveling with the McMaster Fellows and Scholars Program participate in a day-long workshop in which about 60% of the training relates to safety and security. Safety and security issues addressed in the workshop include: (1) a discussion of topics of concern as reported by the Overseas Security Advisory Council;[2] (2) a review of the Emergency Response Guidelines accompanied by a drill; (3) an updated list of contact information for sources for monitoring situational conditions pre-trip and while onsite; (4) the guidelines for conducting onsite safety and security orientations; (5) an update of health concerns specific to the locations slated for travel; (6) the development of a potential threat list specific to each location and a plan of action to address each threat; and (7) a review of concerns or questions that emerged during the last year of travel.

Developing a potential threat list specific to the location of travel is imperative. Because hypothetical situations can be overwhelming, faculty and staff may just succumb to hoping that nothing bad happens. This attitude is extremely dangerous and irresponsible. The institution has effectively prepared for risks if faculty members can identify threats that a reasonable person could foresee and develop a plan to address them. On the other hand, if the itinerary involves potential threats that cannot even be effectively handled in a workshop when there are options to avoid the risk, then the institution should consider revising the travel plans. The faculty workshop also reviews the agenda for student training, which is conducted during monthly collaborative sessions held throughout the academic year for McMaster Fellows and Associate Fellows and again just prior to travel to voice concerns or garner new information. (See Appendix 2.) If institutions follow these steps, their faculty and administrators can feel confident that they have done everything in their power to keep students safe.

TRAINING OF STUDENTS TRAVELING

Currently, all students traveling abroad through Defiance College participate in a learning community. For McMaster Scholars, the learning community operates for a year and begins at least one full semester prior to travel. For other honors program students, the learning community lasts for one semester, and the travel takes place toward the end of the semester. While these learning communities focus on many other areas such as the political, economic, cultural, and social aspects relative to the location of travel, they also reinforce and constantly update safety and security information. All McMaster Scholars must attend a day-long workshop that is 90% focused on issues surrounding safety and security. (See Appendix 3.) A series of exercises intentionally moves students to a greater understanding of possible difficult circumstances while studying abroad. The Scholar Workshop agenda includes: (1) an opportunity to develop a personal profile; (2) information on trusting instincts and the power of the subconscious to warn of imminent danger; (3) a definition of professionalism and its dictates for appropriate behavior; (4) an exercise that helps students to define their motivation for travel; and (5) coverage of health concerns related to international travel and concerns specific to the locations slated for travel in the upcoming academic year. In addition, students also participate in a scenario in which the Program Director is incapacitated or they are separated from the group.

The mechanism for facilitating students' ability to profile themselves as possible victims is based largely on the "Travel Wise Personal Inventory" proposed in Ray Leki's *Travel Wise* (27–39). Modified to suit short-term travel abroad, this exercise, followed by extensive discussion, helps students to envision themselves as possible victims and to overcome the notion that they are somehow immune to personal violence. It may encourage them to modify their behavior, dress, or demeanor in ways that will make them less of a target, whether that is changing the way that they carry themselves or by appearing less American. Even if they do not modify their profile, at least they will gain the ability to view themselves from the perspective of a predator.

Developing a heightened situational awareness is a valuable everyday skill. Gavin de Becker's *The Gift of Fear* is an excellent resource and required reading for all students studying abroad and for all faculty leading any international program. This text teaches readers to develop a heightened sense of situational awareness based on the recognition that people subconsciously process information that contributes to those gut feelings of imminent danger they cannot afford to disregard. After reading and discussing *The Gift of Fear*, students realize the increased risk of wearing earphones when traveling because they have completely eliminated their sense of hearing as well as the risk associated with disclosing one's hotel location to a friendly stranger. In fact, students often recommend this book to family and friends because its relevance reaches well beyond their international experience.

During the workshop students also focus on professional behavior as it pertains to their academic discipline, their role as Defiance College students, and their specific value set. Since implementation of this particular part of the training, Defiance has witnessed a reduction in instances of inappropriate attire and alcohol consumption. This session also contributes to the overall success of having students think of themselves as professionals with expertise and responsibility onsite, an attitude that influences, albeit indirectly, their ability to care for themselves and make sound decisions.

Part of making good decisions is recognizing that there is no way to assess risk without a defined purpose. The cost or risk must be weighed against the benefit or purpose. As an institution Defiance cancelled an academic tour to Egypt several years ago because of a series of bombings in local tourist spots seemingly targeted at student groups. In contrast, several years ago Defiance approved, with location restrictions, travel to Israel for a group to conduct significant training in an art school. This was perceived safer, despite some unrest in the region, because of the close affiliation with a local educational institution and the area restrictions. Students may be more at risk because they are not clearly motivated to undertake the challenge of applying their expertise in the often remote or even harsh conditions in which they find themselves. During their training workshop, students explore their true motivation for travel. When students are clearly motivated, they become resilient and embrace the host culture, including local food and cultural traditions. Promoting an understanding of why they are participating in the experience does not lessen their surprise if they need to evacuate their living space in the middle of the rainforest in Belize as army ants scour the area, but it does help them to understand why the experience is all worthwhile. Their ability to embrace the host culture allows them, in some cases, to move more consciously, observe more critically, and be more cognizant of their surroundings.

Students should realize the strength of their own instincts. They must take care of themselves, eat properly, take medications appropriately, and avoid over-indulging. If they follow these tenets, the team, of which they are a critical part, will be successful. Obviously, students must take responsibility for themselves and for keeping themselves safe, but this obligation does not mean that faculty have any less responsibility: it simply means that the primary responsibility and most effective mechanism to ensure their safety reside within students themselves.

EXTERNAL RESOURCES OF SUPPORT ON LOCATION

Institutions sponsoring groups of students who are traveling internationally should definitely register their excursions with the U.S. Department of State's "Smart Traveler Program." The U.S. Department of State website <http://www.state.gov> and the Smart Traveler Program provide access to up-to-date official country information, travel alerts, travel warnings, and embassy locations. Defiance College's policy insists that if a travel warning has been issued for a given location, travel in the location must be curtailed or limited; in some cases, the trip is cancelled. If the travel initiative is in progress and imperiled, the group is brought home as soon as it is safe to do so. Defiance seriously considers emergency messages (formerly known as warden messages) issued by the U.S. Department of State along with other travel advisories issued by countries such as Australia, Canada, and the United Kingdom. All those traveling under the auspices of the college must be provided with the day and after-hours contact information for the closest U.S. Embassy. If the location is one where the institution has been working for a long period of time or repeatedly, the Program Director should make an appointment to visit the Embassy and make face-to-face contact with the Regional Security Officer. This practice will lay the groundwork for effective action should the need arise or, at the very least, for open communication for less serious incidents.

The Overseas Security Advisory Council (OSAC) allows subscribers to access daily bulletins about political, civil, and social unrest around the world. OSAC holds training sessions annually for administrators and faculty, as well as for other entities in the private sector, traveling internationally with students. These seminars are well worth the travel to Washington, D.C. OSAC understands that more and more students are studying abroad and that an increasing number of these initiatives are short-term. Unfortunately, short-term study abroad is much more dangerous because these programs often lack the infrastructure that would otherwise support a long-term visit in country. OSAC has developed seminars offering preventative information to rectify that situation. These seminars explore topics such as initial preparation, culture shock, security abroad, crisis management, alcohol awareness, fire safety, sexual assault, terrorism, evacuation, and natural disasters. Notification of training seminars appears in the daily OSAC briefings or is available at the OSAC website <http://www.osac.gov>.

Another excellent source of information is the Centers for Disease Control (CDC) accessed at <http://www.cdc.gov>. The CDC lists information on both required and recommended immunizations for those traveling to a specific location. Faculty and students should check the website and its recommendations prior to seeing their personal physician. Many times their personal physician does not have the experience necessary to make a sound recommendation to a student journeying to the remote areas of Cambodia or does not know that a particular anti-malaria drug will not be effective in Belize. Obviously, faculty and students should access various websites that provide them with information about potential threats specific to their location of travel.

Travel insurance is imperative for everyone traveling abroad, and the travel insurance company's website is often another excellent source of good information. Fortunately, travel insurance companies are becoming more responsive to the spate of recent crises. Where just a few years ago, many did not cover trip cancellation or evacuation costs incurred because of political unrest, some of them now do. Many insurance companies do not cover accidents/injury if the student was intoxicated, which is precisely when the majority of accidents happen—an observation worth stressing to students and faculty prior to traveling. Obviously, reading the policies carefully is prudent; one of the best ways to identify a good insurance company is asking for recommendations from similar institutions with similar programs and trying to determine if the company has knowledgeable staff and medical personnel in case an incident occurs.

Interestingly, at a recent seminar sponsored by the U.S. Department of State, an administrator from another university said that if he laid out all the risks to his faculty and students they would probably be too frightened to travel at all. The director of the seminar responded that if this information scared them off, then they probably should not be traveling. He went one step further saying that failing to recognize potential threats is, in fact, a threat to being able to take appropriate action. Adequate preparation is crucial.

PARENTAL PREPARATION

Because of the demographics of Defiance's student population, parents rarely have experience traveling internationally, and, understandably, many are leery. In order to develop parents' confidence in the Program Director and the programs themselves, as well as to provide support for their daughter or son who is traveling, Defiance schedules a meeting with parents before the trip. This meeting is not mandatory, and indeed some parents do not participate, but the option is there. The sessions address the logistics of travel, but they also candidly discuss the potential threats associated with the specific location to which their daughter or son is headed. Most parents are actually relieved to know that a risk assessment is an integral part of trip preparation and continues onsite and that plans have been developed to respond to or remediate threats. The Program Director reviews the travel insurance policy with parents and specifically addresses the issue of drinking. The response to these sessions has been excellent. The parents gain an understanding of the mechanisms in place to ensure the safety and security of students, and they gain an understanding of the purpose of the initiative as well. This information allows them to conduct their own risk assessment.

CONCLUSION

Fortunately, at Defiance College the level of training, planning, and preparation has evolved as international travel supported by the McMaster School and the honors program has evolved. As study abroad grows significantly at Defiance College, the expectation that faculty and students comply with these safety and security measures is entrenched. In today's world where so many safety and security concerns exist and even inhibit travel, creating and maintaining an effective infrastructure for handling safety and security issues are no longer optional.

NOTES

[1]The rationale for the activation of the second tier of the emergency response team would be that the crisis has escalated to the point that the first-tier cohort anticipates (1) a crisis response that may involve the larger student body; (2) the need for financial resources; (3) the ability to spread out responsibilities over various administrators, thus providing consistent personal dialog as the crisis progresses; and/or (4) media attention surrounding the crisis. A larger emergency response team may also facilitate outreach to the individual families when a large group is involved.

[2]The Overseas Security Advisory Council began in 1985 with the mission to facilitate security cooperation between the U.S. Department of State and the American private sector. The OSAC website <http://www.osac.gov> contains unclassified global security reports, coverage of worldwide events, searchable regional security information, and a resource library with information on contingency planning. Most of the information shared through this website and OSAC training sessions offered to the private sector mirror that which is provided to U.S. Department of State personnel.

WORKS CITED

de Becker, Gavin. *The Gift of Fear: Survival Signals That Protect Us from Violence.* New York: Little, Brown, 1997. Print.

Leki, Ray S. *Travel Wise: How to Be Safe, Savvy, and Secure Abroad.* Boston: Intercultural P, 2008. Print.

APPENDIX 1

Emergency Response Guidelines and Procedures

These guidelines outline the steps that the Defiance College, the McMaster School, and study abroad program participants will follow in the event of a study abroad emergency. The use of the term "participants" in this document refers to all students, staff, and faculty directly associated with a Defiance College and/or McMaster School-sponsored study abroad program.

The Defiance College *Crisis Response Team* consists of persons from the following list—the *President of the College*, the *Vice President of Academic Affairs/Academic Dean*, the *Dean of the McMaster School*, and the *Vice President of Student Engagement*. The *Crisis Response Team+* includes the College's *Crisis Response Team* and the following personnel—*Director of Public Relations* and (when appropriate) legal counsel for the institution. The added personnel comprising the *Crisis Response Team* provide the expertise unique to handling a crisis that may occur as faculty and students travel abroad.

The Defiance College *Crisis Response Team* in conjunction with the *McMaster School* is charged with the responsibility of coordinating the management of emergencies affecting participants in credit-bearing and non-credit-bearing study abroad programs that Defiance College and/or the McMaster School sponsors. The safety and well-being of students, faculty, and staff who are participating in these programs abroad are of the highest importance, and all reasonable actions are, and will be, taken to accomplish this goal.

While acknowledging that no single plan can address all emergency contingencies, the Defiance College *Crisis Response Team* recognizes the importance of establishing, in advance, policies and procedures that are designed to safeguard the safety and well-being of study abroad participants. These procedures coordinate with the Defiance College *Crisis Response Protocol* as identified in the College's Emergency Plan where appropriate, while recognizing that incidents taking place outside the United States are unique in nature and require management by professional staff trained in the field of education abroad.

Emergencies are those situations or incidents that pose a genuine and sometimes immediate risk to study abroad program participants or that have already disturbed the safety and well-being of study abroad program participants. (See Appendix 1 for full description.*) There are other situations that may be disturbing and threatening to participants or family and friends back home but which pose no risk to the safety and well-being of participants. By following the procedures outlined below, the designated *Single Point of Contact* for the initiative will be able to gather information that will allow that individual to respond efficiently and effectively to emergencies and to place other situations in appropriate context and respond to them accordingly.

These procedures incorporate the existing Study Abroad Program Cancellation Policy. (See Appendix 2.*) The Study Abroad Program Cancellation Policy governs both programs in which participants have not departed for the abroad location and programs on location at the study site when there is an emergency affecting all participants.

The designated *Single Point of Contact* is on-call 24 hours a day, seven days a week, and will provide the director of the study abroad initiative multiple phone contacts to ensure availability. The *Single Point of Contact* will be agreed upon by the director of the initiative, the *Dean of the McMaster School*, and the person being selected as the *Single Point of Contact*. All staff/faculty who handle emergency calls will have: 1) an overseas contact list; 2) a domestic contact list; 3) a complete itinerary of the trip; 4) a complete trip file including travel abroad applications, student medical disclosure information, and copies of participants' passports; and 5) a copy of the Emergency Response Guidelines and Procedures. In addition, the *Single Point of Contact* on emergency phone duty shall remain in the Northwest Ohio area and thus will have access to all information on file at the McMaster School. For calls into the *McMaster School Office* reporting an emergency during regular office hours, office staff will follow guidelines for handling the call as stated in Appendix 3.* Outline forms are readily available at the front desk to guide staff through the process and included in this document as Appendix 4.* For calls after hours the *Single Point of Contact* will follow guideline for handling the call as stated in Appendix 3.*

Onsite Program Directors and other onsite staff at the study abroad location need to be ready to act in an emergency and to be in regular communication with the *Single Point of Contact or the McMaster School* should an emergency occur in order to develop the most effective course of action in emergency situations. Specific guidelines for Program Directors are attached to these guidelines in Appendix 5.* At program sites where there is not Defiance College faculty/staff specifically hired to manage the program, the local institutional contact can act as a resource.

Operating principles:

1. All responses to an emergency will be governed by the highest concern for the safety and well-being of students, faculty, and staff participating in a Defiance College-sponsored study abroad program.

2. All reasonable and prudent measures will be taken to gather information necessary about the emergency.

3. The *Single Point of Contact/ Crisis Response Team+* will exercise caution and restraint in deciding how information about an emergency should be shared.

4. The *Single Point of Contact/Crisis Response Team+* will respond to emergencies by following the procedures outlined below, except when otherwise dictated by circumstances or agencies outside the College's control.

5. The College through the *Director of Public Relations* and the *Office of the President* will make a conscious effort to inform parents of the participants in a timely manner of any issues affecting the study abroad program or its participants in the event of an emergency or a perceived emergency.

We acknowledge consulting the "Emergency Response Guidelines and Procedures" from the Study Abroad Center of the International Education Service of Iowa State University. Their guidelines credit "Managing Real and Perceived Emergencies Abroad," which is issued by the Office of International Studies and Programs of the University of Wisconsin–Madison. That work, in turn, was based upon emergency management procedures established at Michigan State University. Finally, we acknowledge the "Emergency Response Plan for Education Abroad Participants" of the Education Abroad Office of Bowling Green State University.

* **Editors' Note:** For the full text of Defiance College's Emergency Response Guidelines and Procedures, including all appendices referred to above, contact Mary Ann Studer.

APPENDIX 2

McMaster Fellow Faculty Workshop Agenda

This portion of the workshop focuses on safety and security and changes annually to respond to the needs of the group and current activity worldwide. Faculty who are new to traveling internationally with students receive more extensive training than experienced faculty and usually partner with an experienced faculty member for their first trip.

Health, Safety, And Security
- Travel Abroad Study Guide
  - Using the travel guide
- Emergency protocols
  - Single Point of Contact
  - Handling a crisis and the response
  - Case studies exercise
- Updates on issues, scams, and threats
  - Social networking threats
  - Lightning kidnappings
- Travel must haves
  - Flashlights
  - Smoke detectors
  - Additional passport photos
- Focus on onsite orientation
- Lessons learned

APPENDIX 3

McMaster Scholar Student Workshop Agenda

This portion of the workshop focuses on safety and security and is about four hours in length. Included here is a broad outline that does not include every aspect that is covered during this workshop.

- Self-assessment
  - Personal Profile—(R. Leki, *Travel Wise*)
- Travel Health
  - Articles on travel health
  - Country-specific resources
- Travel Application
  - Full disclosure
- Safety and Security for International Travelers U.S. Department of State Advice
  - Situational awareness, trusting your instincts, self-defense (avoidance), fire-safety, emergency protocols, what to watch for, your self-preservation information, Smart Traveler enrollment, embassies and consulates
- Social Media and Your Safety.
  - Current dangers and trends, stay off Facebook
- "What if" scenarios
  - Real scenarios—checking your response

CHAPTER 12

Exploring the Synergies between Undergraduate Honors Theses and Study Abroad Experiences

Lisa Markus, Jill McKinney, and Anne M. Wilson
Butler University

Research on the impact of study abroad experiences has demonstrated numerous positive influences on the general development of undergraduate students.[1] International study can significantly enhance foreign language acquisition, have a positive impact on the study of a diverse number of academic majors, and increase student awareness of global issues.[2] Mary M. Dwyer and Courtney K. Peters note that scholars generally agree that studying abroad has a positive impact on undergraduate students, especially in the areas of personal development, academic commitment, intercultural development, and career development (1–4).

In Robert M. Gonyea's study of senior-year engagement, participants who studied abroad reported higher levels of integrative and reflective learning. The study did not, however, specifically explore how this learning applied to the generation of an undergraduate thesis. Honors programs expect their students to derive more than their non-honors cohorts from their academic experiences, including study abroad, and directors hope that participation in study abroad experiences influences the undergraduate thesis in both subtle and overt ways. A study by Karen W. Bauer and Joan S. Bennet assessing undergraduate research surveyed students on engagement and collected data on student activities including research, study abroad, and the production of an undergraduate thesis (219). The study focused solely on the perceptions of benefits gained from performing undergraduate research and not on the potential synergistic effects of study abroad and undergraduate thesis production on those benefits. Highly motivated honors students build upon experiences, fostering a synergistic impact on their undergraduate career. In particular, an undergraduate thesis can be inspired by or directly influenced by an honors student's study abroad experience. George D. Kuh et al. have identified studying abroad (126) and undergraduate thesis production (188) as high-impact educational practices. The absence of published examples that explore the connections between studying abroad and the production of an undergraduate thesis is surprising. Desiring to fill that gap, this essay argues that the undergraduate thesis can provide direct evidence of gains made through study abroad.

Butler University has a vigorous study abroad program. Approximately one-third of all graduating seniors have studied abroad during their undergraduate years. In the past ten years, approximately 400 of 1500 honors students (about 28%) studied abroad. Although the number of undergraduates studying abroad has increased significantly over the past two decades, the majority of American students, according to the Institute for International Education (IIE), still graduate from college without ever having studied abroad ("Open Doors" 22). In real numbers, about fourteen percent of undergraduates study abroad during the pursuit of their bachelor's degree ("Open Doors 2011"). When compared to the general undergraduate population, the Butler student population offers a statistically relevant number of students on which to perform deep analyses of the impact of studying abroad. Furthermore, the honors program has a required thesis component as the capstone for completion of the program. Between thirty and fifty undergraduate theses are produced annually; fewer students complete this final hurdle than are eligible, which is a phenomenon common to honors programs with this requirement. Many undergraduate theses have an international flavor, but the number of projects incorporating study abroad experiences directly into the production of the undergraduate thesis is not clear from the completed thesis. A follow-up study was performed to determine the impact of study abroad on the production of the undergraduate thesis.

STUDY

A retrospective analysis of the undergraduate thesis collection from 2001 to 2010 was undertaken to determine the impact of studying abroad on the production of the honors undergraduate thesis by searching for international themes in the titles and abstracts. The transcripts of students with international themes were evaluated to determine if they had a transcripted (academic semester or summer study) experience abroad. Students who traveled abroad independently were excluded from the study since the academic content of their experience could not be known. This analysis identified twenty-eight Butler University alumni who had studied abroad and completed an undergraduate thesis between 2001 and 2010. These alumni were asked a series of questions to determine the impact of their study abroad experience on their undergraduate thesis. Ten alumni responded to the requests for information. The questions included the following:

- Had you thought about your thesis topic before you studied abroad or after?

- Did your thesis topic change/evolve while you were abroad?

- Did you perform specific research, visit particular sites, talk to certain individuals while abroad with your thesis topic in mind? Please describe.

- Did your thesis change/evolve upon your return to Butler?

- Were there challenges to your thesis that you did not anticipate?

- Would you recommend combining study abroad with undergraduate thesis preparation to a current student? Why or why not? What advice would you have for that student?

- Is there anything else you would like to share?

All of the undergraduate theses were examined for direct evidence of the impact of studying abroad on the undergraduate thesis. Examples of direct evidence include reference to studying abroad in the text; reference to studying abroad in the acknowledgments; and reference to resources available only abroad, such as sites, libraries, faculty members, or interviews. Theses that contained a direct link or a connection reported in the alumni survey were coded as "linked." The study abroad experience clearly influenced several of the undergraduate theses: for example, the thesis reflected some aspect of the country where the student studied abroad. If no direct evidence linked the two, they were designated as "possibly linked." In addition, if alumni reported that their study abroad experience impacted their thoughts about their thesis, even in broad terms, their work was also designated "possibly linked." Last, if the alumni indicated no link in the survey, their work was designated "not linked."

FINDINGS

Of the twenty-eight theses examined, seven had no link; eight were categorized as possibly linked; and thirteen were directly linked to the study abroad experience. The majority of the undergraduate theses were moderately to significantly influenced by the student's study abroad experience. See Table 1.

Table 1: Results of the Links of Study Abroad to
Undergraduate Thesis

Relationship of Study Abroad to Thesis Topic	Total	Writers' Study Abroad Sites
Linked	13	Costa Rica, France, Germany, Hong Kong, India, Indonesia, Kenya, Scotland, Spain
Possibly linked	8	England, Finland, France, Peru, Spain
Not linked	7	China, England, France, Ghana, Latvia, Switzerland

DISCUSSION OF FINDINGS

The majority of students identified clear links between their study abroad experience and their undergraduate thesis. The alumni questionnaires, as well as comments in the individual undergraduate theses, provide great insight into how the students connected study abroad with the creation of their undergraduate thesis. In addition, comments from some students who did not combine the study abroad experience with their thesis provide plausible explanations for the absence of a link.

No Link

An analysis of the thesis collection revealed seven undergraduate theses that appear to have no relationship to the study abroad site. All did have a direct relationship to the academic major of the thesis writer, which is not a requirement of our program, but the majority of our students do combine their thesis with at least one of their academic majors of study. This group includes one student who studied abroad as noted on the transcript, but the university did not record the student's study abroad site and the student did not respond to our survey.

Three students who had no link responded to the alumni survey. Helen Momoko Wilson was an international student from Malawi who studied in Switzerland. Her thesis centered on educational disparities in this southern African country. She commented: "I am an international student and my thesis was driven by my background and the country that I come from. My study abroad in Geneva, Switzerland, did not contribute to my thesis" (Wilson, "Re: Honors and Study Abroad"). The undergraduate thesis can serve many purposes, including reflecting the personal background and academic program of the student. In this case, Wilson combined her international studies major and biology minor to produce a study of girls' education and sustainable development ("Education and Girls' Development in Malawi: Promotion of Girls' Education in Relation to Sustainable Development").

Another student drew from a different experiential-education program, Butler's semester in Washington, D.C., program, to inform his undergraduate thesis. While outside the purview of this study, drawing from out-of-classroom experiences can be a real asset for the undergraduate thesis. Matthew J. Rogier wrote:

> I had thought quite a bit about my thesis topic before I studied abroad, [but] it was actually my internship experience in Washington that gave me the idea for my thesis. In fact, it was my work in D.C. that got me really interested in China and Climate Policy. . . . I did, however, have the opportunity [while abroad] to do a bit of work that prepared me for my thesis. For a course on the economics of the European Union my term paper was about the European Union Emissions Trading Scheme, which gave me my first chance to write a long, serious paper about environmental policy.

Another alumnus, Jarod M. Wilson, studied abroad in France the summer after his sophomore year. The summer after his junior year, he traveled to Uganda for fourteen days. Students view international travel differently after they have had a study abroad experience; not surprisingly, Wilson found his African experience helpful for his thesis preparation:

While this wasn't a study abroad experience, I think that it actually helped me to determine my thesis topic—"The effects of war on children in post-colonial, sub-Saharan Africa." I wouldn't say that my thesis topic evolved while I was in Uganda, but I was able to put a face on some of the stories I had been hearing back in the U.S. about child soldiers and wars that were happening in Africa. . . . I was unable to actually interview people [who] had been affected by war. I could only use accounts that were from reporters, which made it hard to get the answers that I needed to ask that would better fit my research. . . . I think that doing research in the location that you are doing your thesis on can make it that much better.

Finally, an alumna who did not draw upon her study abroad in Latvia for her thesis work at all did utilize her anthropology major to explore the Day of the Dead, and her study abroad experience for several months after graduation was greatly enhanced by her undergraduate thesis work. Sarah M. Morales states:

I actually completed my thesis prior to doing my second study abroad experience in Oaxaca. Since I did my thesis about Day of the Dead, it would have been wonderful to have that abroad experience prior to completing my work. Unfortunately it didn't work that way for me. However, I have continued to pursue this topic further simply out of personal interest and found my experience abroad really enriched my understanding of the research I did prior. Plus, I got to experience the Day of the Dead celebration firsthand with my host family.

Clearly, even alumni who report no relationship between studying abroad and the undergraduate thesis have a broader understanding of the world around them through these experiences. The holistic incorporation of study abroad, the undergraduate thesis, and the entire academic experience often combine in unexpected ways. Students may not realize the connections until after completion of their undergraduate program, even students who participated in abroad programs and wrote a thesis on an unrelated topic. Future research could explore these two high-impact experiences and the potential unanticipated effects beyond graduation.

Possibly Linked

Eight students completed theses that were possibly linked to their international study experiences. As with those whose theses were not linked, all theses reflected the students' majors. These students' majors included journalism, political science, theatre, psychology, chemistry, and communication studies. All but one student had two majors. For five of the eight students, the majors included French or Spanish. The category of possibly linked study abroad and undergraduate theses comprises two classes: (1) those that suggest linkage given the topic, site of study abroad, and/or student major; and (2) those defined by the thesis writers themselves as possibly linked.

Students with non-obvious connections between their study abroad experiences and undergraduate theses were more difficult to detect. Some alumni were willing to make statements that clearly indicated a relationship even if it was not evident from the undergraduate thesis. Other alumni had more contradictory and complex interactions between their study abroad experiences and the production of their undergraduate theses.

One alumnus, Carlos Miguelez Monroy, returned to Spain to pursue graduate study in international law and international relations. In addition, he is an accomplished journalist with Solidarity Center Collaborations, a journalistic awareness project that is part of an NGO partnership for development (*Centro de Colaboraciones Solidarias*). His undergraduate thesis examined the journalistic writing style of Gabriel Garcia Marquez, which may have had an impact on his career.

Erin Alexander Heaney reported a subtle link between her thesis work and her study abroad experience. While studying in France in fall 2001, she played on the men's university soccer team because there were no women's teams. She reported that the French were surprised that she was athletically inclined as a woman. This revelation eventually led her to study gender bias in the career of Marie Curie.

Samantha E. E. Hyler proclaimed a lack of any relationship between her thesis and study abroad experience in her alumni survey:

> I unfortunately did not do any fieldwork for my thesis, nor could I really draw on my experiences abroad as I wrote on the Sami culture, of which I had no real contact during my studies in Jyvaskyla. . . . I think it is really unfortunate, because my study really would have been much more well-grounded if I had supported it with fieldwork, transitioning my thesis from a very theoretical project to one grounded with ethnographic perspectives. ("Re: Honors and Study Abroad")

Yet in her thesis, she clearly acknowledges exchanges with her study abroad host family. Hyler consulted them about her project, and they answered general questions about Finland and served as non-experts about the Saami people ("Saami" 3). Hyler limited herself to a rigorous anthropology definition of fieldwork and concluded that the impact of her study abroad experience on her undergraduate thesis did not meet her academic standards, yet her undergraduate thesis provides evidence for gains in two of Dwyer and Peters' areas, academic commitment and intercultural development. Hyler is currently working on her Master's of Applied Cultural Analysis in Sweden; her graduate work deals with city planning and "urbanness" ("Re: Honors and Study Abroad"). Perhaps her graduate research is providing the opportunity to perform the field study that she felt was lacking in her undergraduate thesis.

Jared Linck performed research on grammar corrections by adults on language acquisition. He comments:

> My undergraduate thesis was only indirectly related to my study abroad experience. . . . For this work, I coded transcriptions of native Spanish care-givers interacting with

children aged 2–5 years; my semester abroad in Salamanca, Spain, helped me to acquire sufficient proficiency in Spanish to understand and adequately code these transcriptions. (Linck)

Linck goes on, however, to acknowledge a long-term impact of his study abroad on his life after college, declaring that his "study abroad experience had a much more dramatic and direct impact on [his] Master's thesis research" and indicating that his "study abroad experience was the single most influential experience that guided the entire direction of [his] career—not just [his] Master's research topic." This kind of relationship to study abroad is exactly what college faculty members hope their students will have: a high-impact experience that students can build upon following graduation.

These examples clearly illustrate the long-term impact of both studying abroad and the production of an undergraduate thesis. Even though the two are not directly related in these examples, the intersections between studying abroad and the undergraduate thesis can have ongoing and unforeseen influences on the evolution of the student, the graduate, and the lifelong learner.

Linked

Those theses directly influenced by study abroad are clearly acknowledged by the authors in the undergraduate thesis or the alumni survey. In some cases, the alumni survey reinforced statements in the undergraduate thesis. For example, even students who traveled to their study abroad sites with clear ideas about what they wanted to study often made adjustments. One student, David P. Thielmier, went to Africa, planning to focus his thesis research on the impact of the Amboseli National Park on the Maasai (4–5). Upon immersion in the culture of the Maasai, however, a more interesting problem surfaced. Thielmier became interested in the differences between the Real Maasai and the Saved Maasai, ultimately focusing his research on examining what it meant to be Maasai (6–9). His thesis verifies his growth in intercultural development.

Several students studied abroad in two different sites during their undergraduate careers, so it is not surprising that two graduates in this study did so as well. Samantha (Keith) Ski's first study abroad experience informed both the choice of her second experience and her undergraduate thesis topic. She took advantage of her second study abroad experience to specifically explore a topic in her major, biology, and international policy through an examination of bio-prospecting in Costa Rica (Ski). Ski found that Costa Rica was a model for doing it "right" (Ski). Ski's thesis provides evidence of her gains in academic commitment and intercultural development.

Some students elaborated on their original idea to create an unanticipated final project. Daniela N. Diamente described her experience as an evolution from an ethnographic study, which does make up one chapter of her thesis, to a study of the impact of Catholicism on a small community in Costa Rica (1–3, 16–24). Interestingly, she describes herself as a pseudo-member of the community that she studied. This progression to community member is a common theme for students who study abroad; by including this idea in the content of her thesis, Diamente is acknowledging her own transformation. Her thesis work indicates that she has made gains in personal development and intercultural development.

In another instance, the study abroad site did not seem to have a direct connection to the thesis topic; however, the student was able to make full use of the international experience even though it was not the site of study. Samantha Atkins explains, "I think living abroad helps you think outside the box" (Atkins). Her thesis was on meditative practice, and working through some homesickness, Atkins developed the discipline to focus on her practice, which then provided the basis for her undergraduate thesis. Clearly, this discipline indicates improvement in her self-reliance and personal development.

Many students traveled to their study abroad site with the general idea that they would develop a thesis topic during this time and perform some type of fieldwork. Deborah I. Tamulonis combined her two majors, communication studies and political science, and her international destination, London, in her undergraduate thesis. The thesis evaluated rhetorical criticism of Liberal Democrat general election manifestos. These experiences eventually led her to earn a Master's degree in Public Administration from the London

School of Economics and attain permanent employment in London (Tamulonis). While not all students who study abroad spend significant time overseas after graduation, this graduate leveraged her study abroad experience to pursue an international career. Tamulonis's undergraduate thesis work suggests progress in her academic commitment, intercultural development, and career discernment.

A student can also develop the idea for a thesis topic while being immersed in a culture as an outsider. Susanna Foxworthy was intrigued by the complex relationship that the French have with food and refined her thesis topic to explore France's rejection of genetically modified food. Foxworthy described her experience in the alumni survey, claiming that her "study abroad experience affected [her] thesis topic and directed [her] thoughts" (Foxworthy). She "began to understand the culture more, thus narrowing the topic of the thesis" (Foxworthy). Cultural awareness of both the students' home culture and the culture of the study abroad site is a key aspect of intercultural competence.

Esther E. Farris studied in Indonesia with the general idea of utilizing her religion and English majors in her thesis. While visiting schools there, she was inspired: "[T]he Indonesian government requires religion to be taught in the public schools. I wondered about the goals and effects of such an education, especially in Bali, where religion is so broad and all-encompassing as to [be] hardly definable" (2). This undergraduate thesis highlights one of the perennial challenges of education: how to teach diversity in religion. This student's work successfully achieves the important goal that students who study abroad identify universal themes that unite humans.

The students who explore and refine their topic while abroad can enjoy an extraordinary academic experience. The path taken to discovery becomes the subject of the undergraduate thesis. Catherine R. Tapp describes this process:

> I reached the point in my research I knew that the observations and responses that I had recorded were not wrong, but fair representations of Sufi life. . . . Additionally, my

project took me to a myriad of places, some of which I had not planned to visit. . . . This flexibility really allowed me to explore areas that I had not previously considered, [and] thus broadened the base of my research. (5–6)

In this case, thesis research allowed a student to adapt and change her itinerary to visit a variety of sites. A flexible travel schedule allowed her to maximize her travels and benefit intellectually from her study abroad experience. Tapp's gains in academic commitment through her travels were documented in her thesis, and she also improved her intercultural awareness through her study of the Sufi.

Occasionally, the study abroad experience itself becomes the subject of the undergraduate thesis. This choice was especially appropriate for one student who was a Spanish and international studies double major. Sarah Hundt explains:

Prior to study abroad, I had tossed around a few ideas for my thesis . . . but had not come up with anything concrete. I assumed that I would have an epiphany of some sorts while . . . in Spain. . . . Then it dawned on me that I should just write a thesis about studying abroad. . . . I decided that I would base my thesis on whether or not study abroad programs affect the way that students perceive culture and those who are different from themselves. (Hundt)

Hundt's thesis centered on intercultural development; she was able to focus academically on the study abroad experience. Many researchers have noted how studying abroad in a non-English-speaking country frequently has a significant impact on language acquisition. Dwyer and Peters have observed that immersion in the culture allows for intensive language study through continued language usage (4). Dwyer has also noted immersion leads to greater confidence in language facility (156); similarly, Valerie A. Pellegrino found immersion contributes to competent language development (112). This immersion often directly affects the academic major, but other consequences can be realized as well, including on the undergraduate thesis.

Elizabeth Newton spent her third semester abroad; she explains: "At the time, I was not yet thinking about my honors thesis topic. . . . While the specific topic [of the thesis] did not evolve, my love for the Spanish language did. It was this core interest that ultimately led me to my thesis topic of Spanish/English code switching" (Newton). In this case, the immersion in a non-native language ultimately led to the genesis of the undergraduate thesis topic.

Students at Butler often use the undergraduate thesis to blend multiple passions. This combination can allow the student to maintain the energy required to complete such a daunting task, but it can also provide a motivational outlet for academic areas of interest, as Amy L. Gackenheimer did, "combin[ing] two passions--one for Scotland and the other for school—to develop an intensive thesis comparing and contrasting the approaches to teaching between Scottish and American schools" (1). Because education majors typically find it challenging to combine undergraduate thesis preparation with the rigors of student teaching, students who combine study abroad with these two activities remain exceptionally rare. Nevertheless, Amy Hunter (Gackenheimer) describes her experience in her alumni survey:

> I volunteered at an elementary school in Glasgow, Scotland, while . . . studying abroad. The arrangement was special because volunteers in classrooms were not as common as they were here in America. Once I developed the topic, the teacher with whom I volunteered played a critical role in providing firsthand information on education in Scotland. (Hunter)

Hunter's undergraduate thesis demonstrates gains in all four of Dwyer and Peters' areas of development.

For Butler students in the creative disciplines of theatre, dance, and music, the undergraduate thesis has not been a point of academic emphasis. It often takes special inspiration for these students to contemplate undertaking an undergraduate thesis; like education majors, these students rarely combine their study abroad experience and undergraduate thesis. Yet Ronald Gilliam describes how spending one semester at the Hong Kong Academy for the Performing Arts inspired his undergraduate thesis, and he characterizes his experience as "amazing" (Gilliam). He adds, "the influence of [his] study abroad experience has traveled with [him] to the present day." Gilliam further explains that he decided to tackle an undergraduate honors thesis after returning "because [he] was so inspired by [his] exposure to Chinese culture, especially the diverse mixture of cultures in the global city of Hong Kong" (Gilliam). Clearly, this student's thesis work provides another example of gains in all four of Dwyer and Peters' desired outcomes for a study abroad experience. He was so moved that he completed an undergraduate thesis to document his newfound passion in his academic major.

CONCLUSIONS

Both studying abroad and the production of the undergraduate thesis can have a strong impact on the development of an undergraduate student. All of the experiences that shape an undergraduate student's academic career are complex, but clearly, the thesis work and study abroad experience enhance students academically, personally, and interculturally.

The survey of undergraduate theses reveals that the majority (twenty-one out of twenty-eight) were influenced by study abroad experiences; thirteen of the twenty-eight were significantly influenced. The theses demonstrated that students became more aware of their own and the host country's culture, became more self-reliant, utilized travel to learn more about the host country, and wrestled with big questions and themes common to the human condition. Very few students began their study abroad experience with a clear idea of their thesis topic or a plan to combine their thesis with their study abroad experience. Several alumni lamented this lack of intentionality during their semesters abroad. Indeed, alumni suggested that academic advisors should at least raise the opportunity with advisees prior to their semester or year abroad so that undergraduate thesis writers have the opportunity to consider all of their options.

Students who utilized the study abroad experience to deepen their thesis research were academically engaged while abroad. This engagement included in-depth academic writing, cultural and language immersion, ethnographic studies, and experiential-education activities such as visiting museums and historical sites. Study abroad orientations should address the possibility of combining this experience with thesis preparation. Based on these findings, the Butler University Honors Program is considering emailing reminders to students overseas to encourage them to take advantage of the experiences in preparing their theses.

A larger question posed by this study is why only twenty-eight out of the approximately four hundred thesis writers who studied abroad in the past ten years wrote a thesis with an international theme. This number seems remarkably small given the large number of students who have second majors in languages or international studies. Judy T. Bates also observes challenges in the use of the experiences of study abroad returnees (135–36). Like the work of Bates, this study reveals the challenges of having students integrate their study abroad experiences with the rest of their thesis and academic curriculum. Further study could identify and investigate other reasons study abroad participants do not incorporate their study abroad experiences into their undergraduate theses.

For those students whose study abroad experience influenced their undergraduate thesis, this study indicates that the interaction was positive. Alumni reported that researching and writing an honors thesis in conjunction with studying abroad deepened and enriched their interests. Just as studying abroad inspired some students to pursue a thesis, having plans to write a thesis enticed a wider exploration of the world while abroad for others. In some cases, students contributed to their study abroad sites by sharing their perspectives through cultural exchanges, donating time or expertise, or sharing data while exploring their thesis topic. Writing the thesis, usually upon return, fostered critical thinking and reflection on some aspects of students' foreign experience and allowed them to share the acquired knowledge with their academic community in the form of an undergraduate thesis in their own corner of the world. Some alumni who linked honors thesis work with studying abroad were inspired to continue pursuing scholarly work abroad for their graduate studies. For many graduates, the study abroad experience, without a doubt, had a long-lasting impact.

NOTES

[1]Judy T. Bates notes positive foreign language development, personal development, and intercultural development for students who participated in Lander University's Honors International Program (129–34). Growth in intercultural development and personal development are also noted by Mary M. Dwyer and Courtney K. Peters. Nadine Dolby determined that students from the United States who study abroad critically reflect on the national identity of the United States (152). Kimberly S. Gray, Gwendolyn K. Murdock, and Chad D. Stebbins suggest that the long-term benefits of study abroad include confidence, maturity, and empathy (41). Benjamin L. Hadis demonstrates that alumni who had studied abroad showed signs of personal development (16). A study by Anastasia Kitsantas reports that cross-cultural awareness and global understanding are enhanced (Kitsantas). Ann Lutterman-Aguilar and Orval Gingerich utilizes the pedagogy of experiential education to assist students in making personal connections to the study abroad experience (75). Dennison Nash finds that students who studied abroad showed an increase in autonomy (200). Marilyn E. Ryan and Renee S. Twibell observes that students reported increased academic knowledge and "serendipitous learning outside the classroom" (427).

[2]Three studies of nursing students who participated in study abroad listed the benefits: learn cultural differences, compare healthcare systems and nursing practice, and personal development (Button, Green, Tengnah, Johansson, and Baker 323); cognitive development (Frisch 12); and substantive knowledge, perceptual understanding, and cultural competence (Kollar and Ailinger 30–31). Business students showed enhanced cross-cultural tolerance (Black and Duhon 142). Language students show an improved linguistic profile, according to Martin Howard, "between the pattern

of contextual use of specific forms by the learner in both a study abroad setting and the foreign language classroom" (137).

WORKS CITED

Atkins, Samantha. "Re: Honors and Study Abroad." Message to the author. 16 Dec. 2010. Email.

Bates, Judy T. "The Effects of Study Abroad on Undergraduates in an Honors International Program." Diss. U of South Carolina, 1997. Print.

Bauer, Karen W., and Joan S. Bennett. "Alumni Perceptions Used to Assess Undergraduate Research Experience." *Journal of Higher Education* 74 (2003): 210–30. Print.

Black, H. Tyrone, and David L. Duhon. "Assessing the Impact of Business Study Abroad Programs on Cultural Awareness and Personal Development." *Journal of Education for Business* 81 (2006): 140–44. Print.

Button, Lori, Barbara Green, Cassam Tengnah, Ines Johansson, and Christine Baker. "The Impact of International Placement on Nurses' Personal and Professional Lives: Literature Review." *Journal of Advanced Nursing* 50.3 (2004): 315–24. Print.

Centro de Colaboraciones Solidarias. Web. 16 Jan. 2013.

Diamente, Daniela N. "*La Casa de Todos*: Localizing Catholicism in Quepos, Costa Rica." Undergraduate thesis. Butler U, 2001. Print.

Dolby, Nadine. "Reflections on Nation: American Undergraduates and Education Abroad." *Journal of Studies in International Education* 11.2 (2007): 141–56. Web. 24 Aug. 2011.

Dwyer, Mary M. "More Is Better: The Impact of Study Abroad Program Duration." *Frontiers: The Interdisciplinary Journal of Study Abroad* 10 (2004): 151–64. Web. 22 Sep. 2011.

Dwyer, Mary M., and Courtney K. Peters. "The Benefits of Study Abroad: New Study Confirms Significant Gains." *Transitions Abroad* 37.5 (2004): 56. Web. 22 Sep. 2011.

Farris, Esther E. "Interreligious Relations in Bali, Seen in the National Context and in a Balinese School." Undergraduate thesis. Butler U, 2001. Print.

Foxworthy, Susanna. "Re: Honors and Study Abroad." Message to the author. 18 Oct. 2010. Email.

Frisch, Noreen C. "An International Nursing Student Exchange Program: An Educational Experience That Enhanced Student Cognitive Development." *Journal of Nursing Education* 29 (1990): 10–12. Print.

Gackenheimer, Amy L. "An Investigation About Teaching in Scotland and America." Undergraduate thesis. Butler U, 2001. Print.

Gilliam, Ronald. "Re: Honors and Study Abroad." Message to the author. 5 Oct. 2010. Email.

Gonyea, Robert M. "The Impact of Study Abroad on Senior Year Engagement." Annual Meeting of the Association for the Study of Higher Education. Jacksonville, FL. 6–8 Nov. 2008. Conference Presentation.

Gray, Kimberly S., Gwendolyn K. Murdock, and Chad D. Stebbins. "Assessing Study Abroad's Effect on an International Mission." *Change* (2010): 37–41. Print.

Hadis, Benjamin L. "Gauging the Impact of Study Abroad: How to Overcome the Limitations of Single-Cell Design." *Assessment & Evaluation in Higher Education* 30.1 (2005): 3–19. Print.

Heaney, Erin Alexander. "Re: Honors and Study Abroad." Message to the author. 9 Dec. 2010. Email.

Howard, Martin. "The Effects of Study Abroad on the L2 Learner's Structural Skills: Evidence from Advanced Learners of French." *EUROSLA Yearbook* 1.1 (2001): 123–41. Print.

Hundt, Sarah. "Study Abroad/Undergraduate Thesis." Message to the author. 5 Oct. 2010. Email.

Hunter, Amy L. (Gackenheimer). "Re: Honors and Study Abroad." Message to the author. 15 Oct. 2010. Email.

Hyler, Samantha E. E. "Re: Honors and Study Abroad." Message to the author. 11 Nov. 2010. Email.

—. "Saami Reindeer Herding: 'Traditional' Practice in Modern Scandinavia." Undergraduate thesis. Butler U, 2008. Print.

Keith, Samantha M. "Sovereign Rights and Conservation in the Bioprospecting Industry." Undergraduate thesis. Butler U, 2003. Print.

Kitsantas, Anastasia. "Studying Abroad: The Role of College Students' Goals on the Development of Cross-Cultural Skills and Global Understanding." *College Student Journal* 38 (2004): 441–52. Web. 31 Jan. 2013.

Kollar, Shelly J., and Rita I. Ailinger. "International Clinical Experiences: Long-Term Impact on Students." *Nurse Educator* 27.1 (2002): 28–31. Print.

Kuh, George D., et al. *Student Success in College: Creating Conditions That Matter.* San Francisco: Jossey-Bass, 2005. Print.

Linck, Jared. "Re: Honors and Study Abroad." Message to the author. 25 Oct., 2010. Email.

Lutterman-Aguilar, Ann, and Orval Gingerich. "Experiential Pedagogy for Study Abroad: Educating for Global Citizenship." *Frontiers: The Interdisciplinary Journal of Study Abroad* 8 (2002): 41–82. Web. 15 May 2011.

Morales, Sarah M. "Re: Honors and Study Abroad." Message to the author. 30 Sep. 2010. Email.

Nash, Dennison. "The Personal Consequences of a Year of Study Abroad." *Journal of Higher Education* 47 (1976): 191–203. Web. 16 Aug. 2011.

Newton, Elizabeth. "Re: Honors and Study Abroad." Message to the author. 12 May 2011. Email.

"Open Doors: Report on International Educational Exchange." Institute of International Education. 2010. Web. 15 May 2011.

"Open Doors 2011: Study Abroad by U.S. Students Rose in 2009/10 with More Students Going to Less Traditional Destinations." Institute of International Education. 2011. Web. 23 Jan. 2013.

Pellegrino, Valerie A. "Student Perspectives on Language Learning in a Study Abroad Context." *Frontiers: The Interdisciplinary Journal of Study Abroad* 4 (1998): 91–120. Web. 22 Sept. 2011.

Rogier, Matthew J. "Re: Honors and Study Abroad." Message to the author. 19 Oct. 2010. Email.

Rowles, Connie. J., Daphene C. Koch, Stephen P. Hundley, and Sharon J. Hamilton. "Toward a Model for Capstone Experiences: Mountaintops, Magnets, and Mandates." *Assessment Update* 16 (2004): 1–15. Print.

Ryan, Marilyn E., and Renee S. Twibell. "Concerns, Values, Stress, Coping, Health and Educational Outcomes of College Students Who Studied Abroad." *International Journal of Intercultural Relations* 24 (2000): 409–35. Print.

Ski, Samantha (Keith). "Re: Honors and Study Abroad." Message to the author. 18 Oct. 2010. Email.

Tamulonis, Deborah I. "Re: Honors and Study Abroad." Message to the author. 18 Oct. 2010. Email.

Tapp, Catherine R. "In Search of the Sufi: An Ethnographic Account of Sufism in North India." Undergraduate thesis. Butler U, 2005. Print.

Thielemier, David P. "Cattle People: An Examination of Maasai Identity." Undergraduate thesis. Butler U, 2000. Print.

Wilson, Helen Momoko. "Education and Girls' Development in Malawi: Promotion of Girls' Education in Relation to Sustainable Development." Undergraduate thesis. Butler U, 2010. Print.

—. "Re: Honors and Study Abroad." Message to the author. 5 Dec. 2010. Email.

Wilson, Jarod M. "Re: Honors and Study Abroad." Message to the author. 15 May 2011. Email.

CHAPTER 13

"New Ways of Seeing": Internationalizing An Honors Program

CHRISTOPHER J. FROST
ST. JOSEPH'S COLLEGE

TIMOTHY L. HULSEY
VIRGINIA COMMONWEALTH UNIVERSITY

KAREY SABOL
SAN DIEGO STATE UNIVERSITY

In discussing the depth of a particular piece of music, Marcel Proust writes that "the only true voyage of discovery, the only fountain of Eternal Youth, would be not to visit strange lands but to possess other eyes, to behold the universe through the eyes of another, of a hundred others, to behold the hundred universes that each of them beholds, that each of them is . . . " (657). For Proust, art leads to new ways of experiencing the world. His focus is not on the senses, but rather "beholding" in a metaphorical sense (657). True enough, and yet after decades as teacher-scholars, including years of international experience, academics often still fail to heed Proust's advice. They can move through strange lands as they would a more familiar place, interpreting everything they see through their own prefabricated lenses. On the other hand, an excursion into a strange land can jolt people from habitual ways of seeing as they encounter differences in meaning, language, and culture; it can become a "true voyage of discovery" (Proust 657).

It seems that the issue is not simply one of moving around, but of a particular type of engagement that is essential to "behold[ing] the universe through the eyes of another . . . [or] a hundred others" (Proust 657). This notion of a particular form of engagement, as one travels and encounters multiple layers of difference, suggests the potential for study abroad as an intentional way of engaging with difference, a different way of learning. When designed well, study abroad experiences differ qualitatively from courses delivered at home. A meaningful study abroad experience requires students to modify the way they perceive and engage the world. Study abroad experiences should change their students not merely in the content or amount of their learning, but in the way they think about the world and themselves in that world. As Jody Jessup-Anger notes, "Not only does study abroad serve to enhance students' understanding of other cultures, it may be influential to the formation of self " (360). Her assertion that an intentionally designed study abroad experience extends beyond acquisition of cognitive content is another way of suggesting that it may so reliably alter a student's sense of self, that a student now views both self and world differently.

Like study abroad, honors education also should be defined in qualitative terms. Properly constructed honors courses represent a distinctly different form of student engagement; they challenge academically talented students to enter course material directly and, in doing so, to be changed by what they learn. Ideally, and at its best, an honors education provides students with both increased knowledge and an understanding, beyond that of a non-honors experience, of the context from which that knowledge sprang. In other words, it encourages complex connections and in-depth critical thinking.

A FRAMING QUESTION

What happens when courses combine the attributes of honors classes with the experiences that only studying abroad can provide? As Rosalie C. Otero observes, study abroad programs that are designed and led by honors faculty "tend to be customized both to the students and to the honors program, assuring that field pedagogy will replicate the standards and quality that students can expect in their home classes, seminars, and colloquia" (41). Combining the challenging nature of the honors classroom experience with the exploratory and experiential elements of studying abroad paves the way for life-changing educational experiences; a careful integration of the two modalities yields a promise of transformation.

Accordingly, the purpose of this essay is three-fold: (1) to address the role that honors programs and honors colleges can play in promoting international education; (2) to explore the link between honors education and study abroad, using specific honors study abroad programs as illustrations; and (3) to examine the student-learning outcomes of such programs.

Proust's "possessing other eyes" suggests at least part of the challenge (657). Indeed, the crux of the issue stems from a dialectic: the goal of offering students new eyes through which to view the world versus the practices essential to designing and implementing programs that facilitate that goal. Proust is sure that visiting strange lands is not enough. Melding the best of honors education with the highest purposes of study abroad provides an opportunity to change students' perspectives, but it does not, of itself, guarantee that outcome.

Among the greatest challenges to creating and sustaining honors study abroad programs are flawed beliefs: the notion that international experiences are essentially elitist undertakings, the idea that study abroad automatically increases students' understanding of other cultures and counters their ethnocentric views or their conception of globalization exclusively in terms of business and economics, the perception that students' motivation for study abroad is résumé building, and even the perception that study abroad is an opportunity to party. Disparate perceptions of study abroad may be inevitable, given the sheer number of educators who deal with internationalization and the diversity of agendas that underpin international activities. That said, the reality of an honors study abroad program, such as the one at San Diego State University (SDSU), counters the generalizations outlined above.

At SDSU, study abroad participation has increased nearly 1,000% in the span of 15 years. In 1996, fewer than 150 students went abroad, and in 1997, 167 students did so; in 2009, 1,835 students studied abroad, and the upward trend continues. These numbers represent an increase from under 5% to almost 30% of students who study abroad on their way to graduation; thus they represent quantitative indicators that document a qualitative change in the institutional culture. Administrators, for example, no longer see study abroad as an optional add-on experience for select students: it is an essential component of the undergraduate experience. SDSU now boasts 37 majors and academic programs that require or will soon require study abroad; one of the earliest and most prominent of which was SDSU's University Honors Program. Figure 1 shows the spread of student participation by academic college.

Staggering growth aside, the number of students going abroad is only part of the story. During that same interval (1996–2011), San Diego State University has significantly improved its six-year graduation rates. In a recent article in the *Chronicle of Higher Education*, Rachel Louise Ensign cited SDSU as among the top four public research universities with the highest increase in graduation rates in the country (17% during a five-year span). The diversity of SDSU has increased during this interval, and there now exists no majority population. White students currently comprise less than 50% of the overall population. Importantly, the diversity of students studying abroad closely tracks the diversity of the campus, as depicted in Figure 2.

This information demonstrates that some of the common beliefs about study abroad outlined above are demonstrably false. Study abroad need not be an elitist undertaking, the domain of a select few, or the privilege of white students only. And far from being an optional add-on experience, study abroad has been

Figure 1: SDSU Study Abroad Numbers by Academic College/Division, 2010

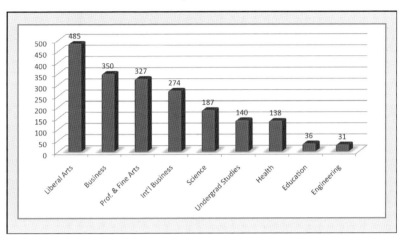

Figure 2: Percentage of SDSU Study Abroad Students Compared to Enrollment, by Ethnicity

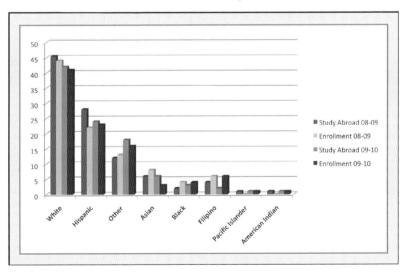

carefully integrated into the very fabric of intellectual inquiry and contributes to the ever-increasing success rates of SDSU students. Indeed, the empirical work of the American Association of Colleges and Universities' educational researcher George Kuh supports the transformative potential of international experience.

SAN DIEGO STATE UNIVERSITY:
AN INSTITUTIONAL CASE STUDY

The methods and strategies that allowed SDSU to achieve such phenomenal success in sending students abroad are subtle and nuanced, and they parallel the explanation for how graduation rates increased so significantly: these results are more an artifact of cultural change than evidence of the effects of programmatic silver bullets. Changing institutional culture begins with vision and values. Indeed, a key role for honors programs resides precisely there. At SDSU, open-mindedness and a willingness to ask questions reside at the core of inquiry and discovery. Accordingly, the honors program positioned itself to begin not with answers, but with questions: What kind of world do you want? What kind of difference will you make? What kind of future will you map? The choice of the word "world," as opposed to "society" or "culture," was intentional, as was the commitment to melding honors education and international experience.

The SDSU Honors Program hit upon the notion of "Honors Without Borders" to develop a distinctive vision. This definition includes at least four senses of border crossing: crossing academic disciplines; moving beyond boundaries defined by race, ethnicity, and class; bridging the gap between knowledge and life; and crossing geographic borders. One concrete example of infusing the vision and values of an honors without borders approach into the larger university culture is this: the honors program formed a new honor society, "Scholars Without Borders," that is open to faculty, staff, and students from across the campus. This organization serves as a catalyst for advancing the ideals of academic engagement, experiential learning, service learning, and international experience. More specifically, it provides study abroad scholarships funded by members' dues and external donations; sponsors lectures on international themes on campus; provides opportunities for students to connect with faculty involved in research and other projects abroad; gives awards for undergraduate research that is international in scope and to honors faculty members engaged in international research and creative activity; sponsors an international photo contest, which includes a narrative connected to the year's common experience theme; and features student international experiences in media, both local and national.

The SDSU transformation would not have been possible without the leadership of top administrators. One of the key members of Scholars Without Borders is the Provost, Nancy Marlin. Provost Marlin leads by example; she engages in international experiences herself by articulating an international-themed narrative for the university and by allocating resources to support international activity across multiple levels, including undergraduate education, graduate education, and faculty travel and research. In governance parlance, the vision and values of the honors program represent a bottom-up move in changing institutional culture while the leadership of senior administrators provides top-down support of intentional cultural change.

Provost Marlin established an Office of International Programs (OIP), headed by an Academic Affairs administrator, the assistant vice president. OIP directly stimulates international activity by (1) administering a yearly funding cycle (fall and spring) for faculty travel grants; (2) coordinating international faculty and student exchange programs; (3) providing assistance to visiting faculty from universities abroad; (4) serving as an advocate for international research and exchange programs; (5) serving as an information clearinghouse for international projects, funding opportunities, and academic programs; and (6) supporting the university-wide goal of a global campus by promoting internationalization in everything from curricular content to cultural campus activities and speakers. In its latter role, OIP works closely and collaboratively with Scholars Without Borders.

Additionally, an International Programs Council at SDSU provides overall guidance and policy direction for the continuing development of international activities. The Council features representatives from all academic colleges and includes students, faculty, administrators, the College of Extended Studies, the SDSU Foundation, and the Campanile Foundation. OIP, the International Programs Council, the University Honors Program, and Scholars Without Borders allocate financial resources for international travel; thus, a great deal of funding hinges upon whether an academic program requires study abroad. Although academic departments determine whether or not to require study abroad and how to define that requirement if implemented, the OIP offers financial incentives to support the decision to require study abroad.

In like manner, faculty interest generally drives agreements with partnering institutions and exchange programs. This model has allowed SDSU to establish 335 cooperative and exchange agreements featuring universities in 52 countries worldwide. Student programs are open to all full-time SDSU students for resident credit for a semester or full-year exchange. These agreements are generally of three types, or some combination thereof: cooperative agreement, student agreement, and faculty agreement. The agreements can encompass joint research, exchanges of cultural value, study abroad, internships, and service, and faculty in particular departments or OIP manage the various incarnations.

Faculty research has been a high priority at SDSU for decades, and many faculty members were already engaged in research that crosses geographic borders. While a research without borders strand was implicit in the intellectual culture, these intentional moves toward international experience, both bottom up and top down, precipitated an explicit commitment to connecting research to the creation of study abroad opportunities for undergraduate and graduate students. One starting point for encouraging faculty members to take students abroad or to promote student participation in an exchange is to involve faculty who already work beyond geographic boundaries. Another option is to identify faculty members involved in service learning or honors education.

Outreach to connect students to these vast opportunities begins at freshman orientation with optional workshops designed to excite students about the possibility of spending a summer, semester, or year abroad. While SDSU's international advising is decentralized, a centralized Education Abroad Office provides general information sessions coupled with specialized advising via international coordinators in the academic colleges. Advisors help students to identify study abroad opportunities that align with curricular requirements. An additional partner is the Travel Study Office, located within SDSU's College of Extended Studies, which helps to market and administer many of SDSU's faculty-led study abroad programs. Organizations like Scholars Without Borders are also instrumental in connecting students to potential experiences abroad as well as integrating international resources situated across the campus.

FROM AFRICA TO OXFORD:
CASE STUDIES IN FACULTY-LED PROGRAMS[1]

A bias seems to emerge from a belief that the junior-year abroad model represents the gold standard. Karin Fischer challenges that belief when she discusses one large-scale study (6,400 graduates of 22 colleges) reported in the *Chronicle of Higher Education*: "The findings of the Study Abroad for Global Engagement project . . . suggest that students who go overseas for a short period of time, four weeks or less, are just as likely as those who study abroad for several months or even a year to be globally engaged" (Fischer). Moreover, faculty-led international programs tend to be intentional, providing specific experiences designed to maximize student engagement with the culture. Those students in longer-term programs are often left to their own devices in planning how they will engage with the host culture, frequently resulting in *ad hoc* tourist itineraries that produce little or no meaningful interaction with the culture. Fischer references Marlene Torp of the Danish Institute for Study Abroad, who emphasizes, academics must "carefully integrate both academic and cultural content" into programs. She continues: "You see what you know. If you don't know anything, you don't see anything"; or as Proust would have it, people cannot behold the universe through the eyes of another (qtd. in Fischer).

By taking the key features of a quality honors experience—small seminars, interactive pedagogy, use of primary texts, multidisciplinary perspectives, and team teaching—and melding those components into a quality study abroad experience, instructors increase the likelihood that students who study abroad return transformed. Melding the honors approach of City as Text™ and Place as Text pedagogy to a particular location facilitates what may be one of the most critical roles for honors programs on a college or university campus: providing a tangible model for integrating academic knowledge and life experiences across disciplinary and cultural boundaries. City as Text™ and Place as Text courses and programs align with efforts to integrate knowledge and emphasize cultural content. (See Chapters 3, 8, and 17 of this monograph.) While the SDSU/VCU "Oxford Experience" and the SDSU "Tanzania Project" are not City as Text™ programs per se, they incorporate exemplary interdisciplinary syllabi that are intentionally tailored to connect carefully to context. And because both programs feature months of rigorous academic work on campus prior to departure, they represent a model different from many study abroad experiences, including a hybrid component.[2]

The Oxford program offers original course collaborations. "Religion, Science and the Quest for Meaning" featured eight to ten primary texts; an intentional crossing of disciplinary boundaries; and team-taught, seminar-style pedagogy. An additional course, "Literature, Art, and the Quest for Meaning," requires five to six primary texts, as well as poetry, films, art, and cultural experiences. By integrating the works of Sigmund Freud and C. S. Lewis into each course, the two courses richly cohere.

Given the immense reading load, the courses actually begin six months before the summer experience. Students enroll by October of the prior year and begin monthly class sessions and discussions, including the reading of a book per month, plus they participate in online forums. This hybrid approach ensures that students connect the academic content to the upcoming trip to St. Hilda's College,

Oxford. Upon the students' arrival in Oxford, the program is immediately intense: 24/7, for just over three weeks, with seminars, excursions, guest lecturers, and films. Past programs have featured seminar discussions of Richard Dawkins's *The Devil's Chaplain*, led by Richard Dawkins; theological responses to Dawkins from Richard Swinburne and Alister McGrath; lectures on C. S. Lewis from Walter Hooper; an analysis of the meanings of nonverbal communication by Peter Collett; discussion of a new frame from which to view C. S. Lewis's *Narnia Chronicles* by Michael Ward; and talks by additional Oxford dons who vary year to year.

The richness of these seminars stems from an array of experiences: taking private, sunrise/sunset tours of Stonehenge; standing in the yard of Shakespeare's Globe Theatre, like the Groundlings in the early seventeenth century, for a play connected to the course; visiting museums; and experiencing the cities and architecture of Oxford and London. Last year's C. S. Lewis Symposium in Oxford featured a staged version of Mark St. Germain's *Freud's Last Session*, to which the SDSU/VCU students were invited. The event proved to be one of the most appropriate and powerful culminating experiences that the Oxford program has offered.

The power of this model, which melded carefully crafted interdisciplinary courses with a particular international experience to achieve carefully delineated learning outcomes, led the co-authors to develop a study abroad program that would integrate an interdisciplinary seminar with both study abroad and service learning, carefully built upon a foundation of collaborative scholarship on moral reasoning. (See Hulsey and Frost for the book that ensued from discussions with honors students and honors faculty colleagues over a six-year span.) For the Oxford program, the course begins with a question, grounded in the moral reasoning work, that challenges honors education, international programs, and education *in toto*: How many people wake up each morning and say to themselves: "What am I going to do about destroying the environment today?" The answer is not many, and yet human habits that destroy habitat are engrained, ubiquitous, and ongoing. The gap here points to a phenomenon that our scholarly work has been exploring: the harm that is committed by individuals who do not perceive the harm or who even see toxic outcomes as morally justified.

This point is crucial: If human beings cannot solve problems by using the same kind of thinking employed in creating them (to paraphrase Einstein's proverbial statement), then a radical re-thinking of what people mean by "education" is in order. As David W. Orr notes early on in *Earth in Mind*:

> It is worth noting that [the ecological state of the earth] is not the work of ignorant people [but] the results of people with BAs, BSs, LLBs, MBAs, and PHDs. Elie Wiesel once made the same point [about the Holocaust, where] educa-tion did not serve as an adequate barrier to barbarity. (7–8)

Advocating for a new kind of thinking is problematic and suspect unless academics can at least sketch the contours for a new kind of education, one that provokes meaningful moral reasoning. If morality begins at the first moment of perception, then this new kind of thinking hinges on new ways of perceiving. This under-standing compels people to investigate the conditions under which they are most able to switch perceptual frames and attend to a dif-ferent subset of information and, in so doing, perceive the moral dimensions of a situation more accurately. In particular, educators need to understand more clearly how and when this frame switch-ing can occur even in situations where people suddenly perceive what they are motivated *not* to see.

Put another way, these questions return to Proust's challenge: only instead of developing new ways of seeing as defined by an abil-ity to behold through the eyes of others, the challenge is defined by provoking new ways of seeing nature and one's relationship to the natural world. The challenge is one of understanding what it means to "behold the lilies of the field" (*New Jerusalem Bible,* Matt. 6:28), which implies comprehending how "beholding" differs from "seeing."

"Nature and the Quest for Meaning," an interdisciplinary course, addresses these issues; it integrated a credit-bearing service-learn-ing course (defined by service-learning outcomes) and connected to a study abroad project in Tanzania. The context of the course is the broader dialog on nature and humanity as situated within the natural order, particularly as that discourse overlaps the human quest for meaning. The course explores a variety of perspectives on ways of seeing nature and human beings as positioned within or aside the natural world through texts, poetry, films, discussions, and experiential options. The course challenges students to consider alternative readings of the nature of human beings vis-à-vis the natural world and to shift perspectives as they examine nature from multiple vantages: as if looking out a window with nature as object of study, as if looking into a mirror with nature reflecting back something of themselves, and as if peering through a lens with nature serving as a filter through which they derive meaning for their lives. Students read a number of works on nature, on the state of the planet, and on various approaches to service learning, including a year-long effort to collect backpacks, books, and other educational staples for a village school in Kongwa, Tanzania.

Upon venturing into Africa, students put a full year's preparatory work, both intellectual and service oriented, into action by working on the school grounds, transporting thousands of books to the school library, and interacting with the schoolchildren and villagers. Additionally, they toured large game preserves and beheld wildlife in their natural habitats. They even swam in the pool of a waterfall, where a toad's very existence, according to Cornelia Dean, is threatened (Dean). Prior to departing Tanzania, the students had learned that these tiny spray toads were saved from extinction by transporting them to the Bronx and Toledo zoos. Upon swimming in a pool that was once the toad's natural habitat, the students could perceive clearly their absence. This perception led to deep discussions regarding a new type of thinking demanded by ecological crisis. Put another way, the tiny toad became a stimulus object that provoked frame switching.

ASSESSING INTERNATIONAL OUTCOMES

Anecdotal evidence of student learning through the study abroad experience is rich. According to Teresa Donahue, Kathleen

Krentler, Bruce Reinig, and Karey Sabol, "students returning from study abroad frequently describe their experiences as 'life-changing' and 'transformative,'" and "report improved academic and cognitive growth, along with intercultural competencies and psychosocial development" (170). Having been involved in honors education for over twenty-five years, led study abroad programs for the past decade (Canterbury, Oxford, Mexico, Tanzania, Greece), and engaged in international teaching in settings as diverse as Romania and Morocco, we have seen firsthand both the quantity of transformations (percentage of participating students transformed) and the quality of transformation (the deep impact of these programs) that these efforts have produced. But these are anecdotal accounts.

Given the reality that study abroad does not automatically increase students' understanding of other cultures and challenge ethnocentric views, educators are beginning to see a need to assess more accurately the impact of study abroad as an academic endeavor, according to Donahue and her colleagues (170). Michael Steinberg argues that international educators should be able to "demonstrate that the students on our programs return home having grown intellectually and personally, having developed a greater measure of global and intercultural competence . . . [and that] they are much better prepared for careers in a global environment" (19). Here is where honors programs can pave the way. In order to better understand what students learn through study abroad experiences, SDSU's Honors Program has attempted to document the value of study abroad in more than just anecdotal fashion.

SDSU designed a set of learning outcomes for study abroad that would cross disciplinary, cultural, and programmatic boundaries. Of course, the design of these learning opportunities was to adopt Proust's goal of helping students to see with new eyes. Many institutions begin by setting forth a slate of admirable international activities and then observing the results. A more effective approach is beginning with the end in mind and then designing specific programs and activities to meet those learning outcomes. SDSU attempted to discern, at root, what all students should learn in six main goal areas through these international encounters. Students should experience growth in the following arenas, as evidenced by changes in the skills and abilities listed:

1. Disciplinary Knowledge:
   - Synthesize academic/disciplinary concepts with real-world phenomena.
   - Improve critical-thinking skills.
   - Gain an international perspective of career/discipline.

2. Social/Emotional Growth:
   - Build independence.
   - Gain self-confidence.
   - Build self-awareness.
   - Develop empathy.
   - Increase tolerance for ambiguity.

3. State-of-the-Planet Awareness:
   - Develop awareness of the political and economic state of the planet.
   - Increase awareness of alternative transportation and housing arrangements.
   - Increase tolerance for living in regions of the world with alternative or more challenging physical environments.

4. Intercultural Competence:
   - Explore the nature of culture in general.
   - Gain specific knowledge of host culture.
   - Become conscious of one's own cultural perspective.
   - Engage diverse expressions of culture.
   - Develop international goodwill and global citizenship.
   - Adapt effectively in cross-cultural settings.

5. Language Learning:

- Improve language competency in speaking, listening, reading, and writing.

- Engage with others in the host language.

6. Lifelong Learning:

- Pursue continuous global learning.

- Explore international opportunities after graduation.

While these learning outcomes are geared toward study abroad and other international experiences, they are goals towards which most honors programs aspire.

Fueled by a mini-grant from the University System of Georgia, SDSU participated in a small-scale piece of that institution's multi-faceted GLOSSARI (Georgia Learning Outcomes of Students Studying Abroad Research Initiative) Project.[3] Although the GLOSSARI Project focused only on academic growth and did not cover all areas of possible student transformation, it gauged student development in a few key dimensions of learning: functional knowledge, knowledge of world geography, knowledge of global interdependence, interpersonal accommodation, and cultural sensitivity. The SDSU replication study by Donahue, Krentler, Reinig, and Sabol, which employed the GLOSSARI ILO survey instrument made available by the University System of Georgia, measured change via self-reported assessments of knowledge, skills, and abilities both before going abroad and in a post-test of those same knowledge, skills, and abilities once participants returned (172). The researchers ran demographic statistics on the pool of study abroad students, and from the data, they designed a representative control group that would remain on campus during the corresponding semester (controlling for ethnicity, sex, student level, and academic college). The researchers administered the same pre-test and post-tests at either end of the on-campus semester. Students in the Oxford Experience program, including students participating in semester and yearlong programs, as well as exchange and immersion programs and the representative control group of students who did not study abroad, took the pre- and post-tests. (See the Appendices for the tests.)

Although the two groups reported statistically similar abilities prior to departure, students who studied abroad perceived that they had experienced learning and growth across all five dimensions; the control group believed they had achieved growth in just one area (knowledge of world geography). Among the study abroad group, no statistical differences were attributable to ethnicity, sex, or academic college. The use of a representative control group that did not travel abroad addressed the argument that students who study abroad are simply different and more academically elite. In the future, the analysis will explore data across study abroad program types in order to assess any differences in learning between short- and long-term programs, study abroad locations, or program types.

Assessment of student learning in study abroad can and should be multifaceted. Survey instruments that measure student self-perceptions of learning, like the one mentioned above, can be valuable in obtaining information about a large number of students and in comparing student learning across courses, program types and lengths, locations, and other variables. At the same time, course-level assessment is better at directly measuring student learning. In addition to the GLOSSARI ILO survey, Oxford and Tanzania students are assessed at the course-level through rubric-based evaluation of extensive journal entries, evaluation of participation in onsite experiences, and evaluation of culminating or integrative projects. Moreover, graduating honors program students who elect to do a culminating senior portfolio rather than a thesis or project are required to complete a reflective essay addressing their personal development as defined by student-learning outcomes as a result of their international experiences.

These attempts at assessment are important for a number of reasons. They measure the success of internationalization efforts by perception of learning, rather than by an increase in the number of study abroad participants. Darla K. Deardorff argues that although participation rates are useful, they are not themselves a meaningful outcome of internationalization and international education, just as a bigger honors program is not an accurate indicator of program quality (26). Study abroad is a relatively new field of research, and most institutions offer a wide range of programs; hence, knowing which of the many types of study abroad programs advance student-learning outcomes is important. At SDSU, such evidence has provided information to those in charge of designing and implementing study abroad programs about the features and characteristics that promote student learning. This evidence, in turn, has allowed faculty and study abroad leaders to improve learning in current study abroad programs by adding new pre-departure and re-entry components to supplement learning opportunities. One example of a new feature is a recently piloted SDSU Global Scholars Blog, wherein honors students abroad respond to a variety of challenging prompts about their learning and engagement with the host culture, thus creating a virtual classroom of students in various locations around the globe.

Donahue, Krentler, Reinig, and Sabol found that empirical evidence is also useful in responding to critics of international education who feel that resources are better directed toward on-campus programs (170). These critics may be skeptical about the value of study abroad in the same way that many are skeptical of the value of an honors program. "Empirical evidence of increased student learning," observe Donahue, Krentler, Reinig, and Sabol, "reduces the likelihood that study abroad will be seen as 'party abroad,' and substantiates the intrinsic value and depth of these programs" (170).

CONCLUDING DISCUSSION

Current conversations are exploring complex ways beyond the specific connections between honors and international education to comprehensively internationalize campuses. SDSU and VCU have settled upon different positions along an internationalization continuum, but they have carefully collaborated on the design of programs that feature the most successful practices of the short-term, faculty-led model. In terms of the design of particular programs, such as the Oxford Experience and the Tanzania Project, the core of this model is the careful integration of the highest purposes of honors education with a specific set of student-learning outcomes tied to international experience. These experiences had significant impact, enhancing student skills across multiple dimensions. Beyond providing gains in intercultural competencies, these programs clearly advance the goals of honors education. In essence, they enable the vision, endorsed by Proust, that requires new eyes through which to see and prepares students for true voyages of discovery.

NOTES

[1]We are assuming that readers are familiar with the basic tenets of honors education. We focus on a particular study abroad program model, rather than on the program goals of an honors program *in toto*, using two different faculty-led programs as illustrations. This model was developed by the co-authors and bridges experiences from three honors programs: San Diego State University, Texas State University, and the Honors College of Virginia Commonwealth University.

[2]Because programs at Oxford are featured elsewhere in this monograph, we address the Oxford Program only briefly here.

[3]For a more complete discussion of this study on study abroad learning outcomes, see the report of Richard Sutton and Donald Rubin. We would like to thank Donald Rubin for allowing us to reprint the survey instruments in the appendices to this chapter.

WORKS CITED

Ashwill, Mark A. "Developing Intercultural Competence for the Masses." *Nafsa.org*. NAFSA, 1 Apr. 2004. Web. 22 Apr. 2011.

Collett, Peter. *Book of Tells*. London: Bantam, 2004. Print.

Dawkins, Richard. *A Devil's Chaplain*. New York: Houghton Mifflin, 2003. Print.

Dean, Cornelia. "Saving Tiny Toads Without a Home." *New York Times* 2 Feb. 2010. Web. 25 March 2013.

Deardorff, Darla K. "A Matter of Logic?" *International Educator* 14.3 (2005): 26–31. Print.

Donahue, Teresa, Kathleen Krentler, Bruce Reinig, and Karey Sabol. "Assessing the Academic Benefit of Study Abroad." *Journal of Education and Learning* 1.2 (2012): 169–78. Print.

Ensign, Rachel Louise. "Fast Gainers: Four Ways That Colleges Have Raised Graduation Rates." *Chronicle of Higher Education* 5 Dec. 2010. Web. 18 Jan. 2013.

Fischer, Karin. "Short Study Abroad Trips Can Have Lasting Effect, Research Suggests." *Chronicle of Higher Education* 20 Feb. 2009. Web. 20 Apr. 2011.

Hooper, Walter. *C. S. Lewis: A Companion and Guide.* New York: Harper Collins, 1996. Print.

Hudzik, John K. "Comprehensive Internationalization: From Concept to Action." *Nafsa.org.* NAFSA, 9 Jan. 2011. Web. 20 Apr. 2011.

Hulsey, Timothy, and Christopher Frost. *Moral Cruelty: Ameaning and the Justification of Harm.* Lanham, MD: UP of America, 2004. Print.

Jessup-Anger, Jody. "Gender Observations and Study Abroad: How Students Reconcile Cross-Cultural Differences Related to Gender." *Journal of College Student Development* 49.4 (2008): 360–73. Print.

Kuh, George D. *High-Impact Educational Practices: What They Are, Who Has Access to Them, and Why They Matter.* Washington, D.C.: American Association of Colleges and Universities, 2008. Print.

McGrath, Alister. *Dawkins' God: Genes, Memes, and the Meaning of Life.* Oxford: Blackwell, 2005. Print.

New Jerusalem Bible. Ed. Henry Wansbrough. New York: Double-day Religion, 1999. Print.

Orr, David W. *Earth in Mind: On Education, Environment, and the Human Prospect.* Washington, D.C.: First Island P, 2004. Print.

Otero, Rosalie C. "Faculty-Led International Honors Programs." *Journal of the National Collegiate Honors Council* 12.1 (2011): 41–45. Print.

Proust, Marcel. "The Verdurins Quarrel with M. De Charlus." *Remembrance of Things Past.* Trans. C. K. Scott Moncrieff and Stephen Hudson. Vol. 5. Hertfordshire: Wordsworth Editions, 2006. Web.

"Securing America's Future: Global Education for a Global Age." *Nafsa.org.* NAFSA, 13 Mar. 2003. Web. 20 Apr. 2011.

"Standards of Good Practice for Education Abroad." *Forumea.org.* Forum on Education Abroad, 2011. Web. 21 Apr. 2011.

Steinberg, Michael. "The Place of Outcomes Assessment in Higher Education Today and the Implications for Education Abroad." *A Guide to Outcomes Assessment in Education Abroad.* Ed. Mell C. Bolen. Carlisle, PA: Forum on Education Abroad, 2007. 7–22. Print.

Sutton, Richard, and Donald Rubin. "The GLOSSARI Project: Initial Findings from a System-Wide Research Initiative on Study Abroad Learning Outcomes." *Frontiers: The Interdisciplinary Journal of Study Abroad* 10 (2004): 65–82. Print.

Swinburne, Richard. *Is There a God?* Rev. ed. Oxford: Oxford UP, 2010. Print.

Ward, Michael. *The Narnia Code: C. S. Lewis and the Secret of the Seven Heavens.* Carol Stream, IL: Tyndale House, 2010. Print.

APPENDIX 1

GLOSSARI ILO Pre-Study Abroad Survey

1. Today's Date (MM/DD/YYYY): _____

2. What institution do you currently attend? _____

3. Your Full Name (first and last):_____

4. Gender (please circle):   Male   Female

5. Which of the following ethnic/cultural labels best fits you? (please circle)

   - White

   - Asian American

   - International Student

   - Africa American

   - Native American

   - Hispanic American

   - Multiracial/multiethnic

6. What is the highest level of education achieved by your father and/or mother?

   - Less than high school diploma

   - High school graduation

   - Post high school technical certificate

   - Some college

   - Bachelors degree

   - Professional or graduate degree

   - Don't know

7. What is your native (home) language? _____

8. Foreign Language(s) studied in college: *(please list Language, highest-level course taken and final grade)*

   • First Studied Language: _____

   • Second Studied Language: _____

   • Third Studied Language:_____

9. Your estimated overall GPA: _____

10. Your present or intended major:_____

11. Your present or intended minor (if any): _____

12. Your intended career: _____

13. In what geographic locality would you like to live and work for most of your career?

   • In or near my home town

   • Away from my home town but in state

   • Away from my home state but in the USA

   • Outside the USA

   • No particular preference

14. Approximately what percentage of your current *good friends* were *not* born in the US? _____%

15. Approximately what percentage of your current *daily acquaintances* were *not* born in the US? _____%

16. Approximately what percentage of your current *good friends* were born in the US but come from a background or *culture substantially different* from your own? _____%

17. Approximately what percentage of your current *daily acquaintances* were born in the US but come from a background or *culture substantially different* from your own? _____%

18. What institution will be sponsoring your study abroad program?

19. In what foreign country or countries will you be studying this semester?_____

20. What is the primary language of the host country? (If English, please proceed to question #22): _____

21. What is your proficiency in the language of the host country? Rate your proficiency PRIOR to studying abroad from 1–10 on the following scale: (please circle number)

   1   Highest Language Proficiency: native speaker proficiency.

   2

   3

   4

   5   Moderate Language Proficiency: able to grasp the basic topic of most conversations directed toward you, & could make your opinions or needs basically understood.

   6

   7

   8

   9

   10   Lowest Language Proficiency: essentially no knowledge of the language except for a few stock phrases.

22. What is the title of your study abroad program?_____

23. What is or will be the date you are leaving home for this trip? (MM/DD/YYYY) _____

24. For what course(s) will you be earning credit? _____

25. Have you studied abroad in a different program prior to this term?   YES   NO

26. For how long will you be studying abroad this semester? (please circle)

- Fewer than 4 weeks

- 4–8 weeks

- 8–12 weeks

- Semester (more than 12 weeks)

- 1 Academic/Calendar Year

- Other

For questions 27–55, please circle how strongly you agree or disagree with each of the following statements.

27. I understand how foreign manufacturing affects the prices of consumer goods (e.g., clothing) in the US.

Strongly Disagree   Disagree   Neutral   Agree   Strongly Agree

28. I know how to use a public telephone in a foreign country.

Strongly Disagree   Disagree   Neutral   Agree   Strongly Agree

29. I know how to take a train or bus between cities in a foreign country.

Strongly Disagree   Disagree   Neutral   Agree   Strongly Agree

30. When interacting in a foreign country, I know how to talk my way out of difficult situations.

Strongly Disagree   Disagree   Neutral   Agree   Strongly Agree

31. I am sensitive to differences among languages and cultures.

Strongly Disagree   Disagree   Neutral   Agree   Strongly Agree

32. I know how to buy toothpaste or a can opener in a foreign country.

Strongly Disagree   Disagree   Neutral   Agree   Strongly Agree

33. I know enough about a foreign language and culture to compare and contrast it with my own.

Strongly Disagree Disagree Neutral Agree Strongly Agree

34. I know the names of the seven continents.

Strongly Disagree Disagree Neutral Agree Strongly Agree

35. I know the names of at least four rivers in Europe.

Strongly Disagree Disagree Neutral Agree Strongly Agree

36. I know the names of at least three rivers in Asia.

Strongly Disagree Disagree Neutral Agree Strongly Agree

37. I know how to give coherent, logical directions in a foreign country.

Strongly Disagree Disagree Neutral Agree Strongly Agree

38. I know how to explain US foreign policy to my peers.

Strongly Disagree Disagree Neutral Agree Strongly Agree

39. When interacting in a foreign country, I know when it is to my advantage to take risks.

Strongly Disagree Disagree Neutral Agree Strongly Agree

40. I know what kinds of jokes would be funny to a person from a foreign country.

Strongly Disagree Disagree Neutral Agree Strongly Agree

41. I am sensitive to my own reactions to people from different language and cultural backgrounds.

Strongly Disagree Disagree Neutral Agree Strongly Agree

42. I know how the political and personal freedom experienced by US citizens compares and contrasts with the degree of freedom experienced by citizens in another country.

Strongly Disagree Disagree Neutral Agree Strongly Agree

43. When interacting in a foreign country, I know how to lead discussions and conversations.

Strongly Disagree   Disagree   Neutral   Agree   Strongly Agree

44. I understand how world markets overseas can affect my intended career.

Strongly Disagree   Disagree   Neutral   Agree   Strongly Agree

45. I am sensitive to how specific settings affect my style of interacting with others.

Strongly Disagree   Disagree   Neutral   Agree   Strongly Agree

46. I know how to locate a safe and comfortable nightclub or bar in a foreign country.

Strongly Disagree   Disagree   Neutral   Agree   Strongly Agree

47. I know how to pacify an angry person (e.g., shopkeeper) in a foreign culture.

Strongly Disagree   Disagree   Neutral   Agree   Strongly Agree

48. I know how to be patient when interacting with people.

Strongly Disagree   Disagree   Neutral   Agree   Strongly Agree

49. I know how to be flexible when interacting with people.

Strongly Disagree   Disagree   Neutral   Agree   Strongly Agree

50. I understand why US troops are concerned about the military situation in North Korea.

Strongly Disagree   Disagree   Neutral   Agree   Strongly Agree

51. I know how to locate basic information in a foreign newspaper.

Strongly Disagree   Disagree   Neutral   Agree   Strongly Agree

52. I know enough about the essential norms and taboos (greetings, dress, behavior) of a foreign culture to adjust my behavior appropriately.

Strongly Disagree   Disagree   Neutral   Agree   Strongly Agree

53. I know how to find different ways to express an idea that I am having trouble saying to a foreigner.

Strongly Disagree   Disagree   Neutral   Agree   Strongly Agree

54. I know the names of at least 6 countries in Africa.

Strongly Disagree   Disagree   Neutral   Agree   Strongly Agree

55. I know the capital cities of at least four countries in South America.

Strongly Disagree   Disagree   Neutral   Agree   Strongly Agree

APPENDIX 2

GLOSSARI ILO Post-Study Abroad Survey

1. How long did you study abroad (How long did your classes last?) (please circle)
   - Fewer than 4 weeks
   - 4–8 weeks
   - 8–12 weeks
   - Semester (more than 12 weeks)
   - 1 Academic/Calendar Year

2. Today's Date (MM/DD/YYYY): _____

3. Your Full Name (first and last): _____

4. Your Email Address: _____

5. What is the official language of the nation in which you were studying? If the official language is English, please skip to Question 9. _____

6. While you were studying abroad, which language were you required to use in class? (please circle)
   - English
   - Mostly English, some Host National Language
   - Mostly Host National Language, some English
   - Host National Language in almost all activities
   - Predominantly Host National Language

7. While you were studying abroad, which language did you use outside of class? (please circle)

- English
- Mostly English, some Host National Language
- Mostly Host National Language, some English
- Predominantly Host National Language
- Host National Language in almost all activities

8. AFTER studying abroad, what is your CURRENT proficiency in the host national language? Rate your proficiency from 1–10 on the following scale: (please circle number)

1   Highest Language Proficiency: native speaker proficiency.

2

3

4

5   Moderate Language Proficiency: able to grasp the basic topic of most conversations directed toward you, & could

6   make your opinions or needs basically understood.

7

8

9

10   Lowest Language Proficiency: essentially no knowledge of the language except for a few stock phrases.

9. What was the date you left home for this study abroad experience? (MM/DD/YYYY) _____

10. What was the date you returned home from this study abroad experience? (MM/DD/YYYY) _____

11. During the study abroad program, which courses were you enrolled in for academic credit? Enter course number(s) below. (e.g., BIOL 1101) _____

12. How was your study abroad program administered? (Please make a selection based on the descriptions below.)

   a A faculty member from my college took a group of students from my college abroad.

   b A group of students from my college were all taught as a group by host national instructors.

   c I participated in a study abroad program with a group of students from many different countries; the program was run by an independent study abroad agency or institute.

   d I participated in a study abroad program with a group of students from many different countries; the program was run by the host national university.

   e I directly enrolled as a temporary student at the host national university.

13. What was your housing situation during study abroad? (Please make a selection based on the descriptions below.)

   a I lived in a dorm or residence hall.

   b I lived in a dorm with a brief opportunity for homestay.

   c I lived in a dorm part of the time, and in a homestay part of the time.

   d I lived in a room that I rented from my homestay family.

   e I lived as a member of the family in a homestay.

14. How much opportunity did you have for interacting with people from the host culture and interacting with them in daily life, experiencing their way of life?

    a None: No opportunities

    b Isolated: Almost none or very limited opportunities

    c Optional: Optional participation in occasional integration activities

    d Required/Extensive: Required regular participation in cultural integration program, extensive direct cultural contact via service learning, internship

15. To what degree were you encouraged to think about or reflect upon your study abroad / cultural experience?

    a None: No provisions for cultural reflection at all

    b Initial Guidance: Orientation was provided prior to departure for this program

    c Some Guidance: Orientation was provided prior to departure and is ongoing

    d Extensive Guidance: Pre-departure orientation, mentoring, ongoing orientation or course in cross-cultural perspectives, reflective writing, and research

16. Which phrase best describes the majority of the faculty who taught you in your study abroad program?

    • Only faculty from my home university

    • Faculty from home university/other US university

    • Faculty from host country alone

    • Faculty from host culture & home university

    • Faculty from all over the world

17. On average, how many hours per week did you spend interacting primarily with members of the host country? _____ hours/week

18. Approximately what percentage of your current good friends were not born in the US? _____%

19. Approximately what percentage of your current daily acquaintances were not born in the US? _____%

20. Approximately what percentage of your current good friends were born in the US but come from a background or culture substantially different than your own? _____%

21. Approximately what percentage of your current daily acquaintances were born in the US but come from a background or culture substantially different than your own? _____%

For questions 22–50, please circle how strongly you agree or disagree with each of the following statements.

22. I understand how foreign manufacturing affects the prices of consumer goods (e.g., clothing) in the US.

    Strongly Disagree   Disagree   Neutral   Agree   Strongly Agree

23. I know how to use a public telephone in a foreign country.

    Strongly Disagree   Disagree   Neutral   Agree   Strongly Agree

24. I know how to take a train or bus between cities in a foreign country.

    Strongly Disagree   Disagree   Neutral   Agree   Strongly Agree

25. When interacting in a foreign country, I know how to talk my way out of difficult situations.

    Strongly Disagree   Disagree   Neutral   Agree   Strongly Agree

26. I am sensitive to differences among languages and cultures.

    Strongly Disagree   Disagree   Neutral   Agree   Strongly Agree

27. I know how to buy toothpaste or a can opener in a foreign country.

    Strongly Disagree   Disagree   Neutral   Agree   Strongly Agree

28. I know enough about a foreign language and culture to compare and contrast it with my own.

Strongly Disagree   Disagree   Neutral   Agree   Strongly Agree

29. I know the names of the seven continents.

Strongly Disagree   Disagree   Neutral   Agree   Strongly Agree

30. I know the names of at least four rivers in Europe.

Strongly Disagree   Disagree   Neutral   Agree   Strongly Agree

31. I know the names of at least three rivers in Asia.

Strongly Disagree   Disagree   Neutral   Agree   Strongly Agree

32. I know how to give coherent, logical directions in a foreign country.

Strongly Disagree   Disagree   Neutral   Agree   Strongly Agree

33. I know how to explain US foreign policy to my peers.

Strongly Disagree   Disagree   Neutral   Agree   Strongly Agree

34. When interacting in a foreign country, I know when it is to my advantage to take risks.

Strongly Disagree   Disagree   Neutral   Agree   Strongly Agree

35. I know what kinds of jokes would be funny to a person from a foreign country.

Strongly Disagree   Disagree   Neutral   Agree   Strongly Agree

36. I am sensitive to my own reactions to people from different language and cultural backgrounds.

Strongly Disagree   Disagree   Neutral   Agree   Strongly Agree

37. I know how the political and personal freedom experienced by US citizens compares and contrasts with the degree of freedom experienced by citizens in another country.

Strongly Disagree   Disagree   Neutral   Agree   Strongly Agree

38. When interacting in a foreign country, I know how to lead discussions and conversations.

Strongly Disagree   Disagree   Neutral   Agree   Strongly Agree

39. I understand how world markets overseas can affect my intended career.

Strongly Disagree   Disagree   Neutral   Agree   Strongly Agree

40. I am sensitive to how specific settings affect my style of interacting with others.

Strongly Disagree   Disagree   Neutral   Agree   Strongly Agree

41. I know how to locate a safe and comfortable nightclub or bar in a foreign country.

Strongly Disagree   Disagree   Neutral   Agree   Strongly Agree

42. I know how to pacify an angry person (e.g., shopkeeper) in a foreign culture.

Strongly Disagree   Disagree   Neutral   Agree   Strongly Agree

43. I know how to be patient when interacting with people.

Strongly Disagree   Disagree   Neutral   Agree   Strongly Agree

44. I know how to be flexible when interacting with people.

Strongly Disagree   Disagree   Neutral   Agree   Strongly Agree

45. I understand why US troops are concerned about the military situation in North Korea.

Strongly Disagree   Disagree   Neutral   Agree   Strongly Agree

46. I know how to locate basic information in a foreign newspaper.

Strongly Disagree   Disagree   Neutral   Agree   Strongly Agree

47. I know enough about the essential norms and taboos (greetings, dress, behavior) of a foreign culture to adjust my behavior appropriately.

Strongly Disagree   Disagree   Neutral   Agree   Strongly Agree

48. I know how to find different ways to express an idea that I am having trouble saying to a foreigner.

Strongly Disagree   Disagree   Neutral   Agree   Strongly Agree

49. I know the names of at least 6 countries in Africa.

Strongly Disagree   Disagree   Neutral   Agree   Strongly Agree

50. I know the capital cities of at least four countries in South America.

Strongly Disagree   Disagree   Neutral   Agree   Strongly Agree

Creating International Opportunities for Honors Students in the Health Professions: A Nursing Case Study

Ellen B. Buckner
University of South Alabama

Lygia Holcomb
University of Alabama at Birmingham

Although international experiences are an expanding component of honors education, the challenge of creating study abroad programs that fulfill the expectations characteristic of honors education remains. Various strategies exist, as this monograph attests, for accomplishing this objective. Carolyn Haynes advocates creating study abroad honors experiences that promote meaningful engagement and feature "research opportunities, internships, community service projects, coursework with host-country students or other intensive opportunities for engagement" (21). Bernice Braid and Gladys Palma de Schrynemakers concur, proposing that honors

275

study abroad experiences inexorably "link scholarly depth with perspective," and they describe the significance of cross-disciplinary inquiry in preparing students to be "observant, creative, analytical, conscious of nuance, aware of context, and alert to themselves in interaction with others different from them" (27). Lynne Clark Callister, Geraldine Matsumura, Sandra Lookinland, Sandra Mangum, and Carol Loucks have described a variety of educational strategies to promote synthesis of outcomes from international experiences, including student presentations of articles and reflective journals. Sheila Greatrex-White adds that assignments during the experience should include, at a minimum, opportunity for reflection in a journal or log. This essay describes how the University of Alabama at Birmingham (UAB) Nursing Honors Program integrated these pedagogical approaches into a study abroad course for nursing students that combined undergraduate research and service learning.

INTEGRATING STUDY ABROAD INTO THE NURSING HONORS PROGRAM

The UAB Nursing Honors Program began to explore the possibilities of engaging honors students in study abroad experiences in 2007, six years after it was established. Several forces converged to support these explorations. Fortunately, at the time, UAB's Office of Study Abroad was well-established and assumed responsibility during the planning and implementation phases for the budget, international travel, and safety arrangements for students and faculty. The nursing honors program had gained invaluable experience the previous year in developing an international undergraduate research project when a student from Kenya successfully completed her honors project in her home country. The UAB School of Nursing is a World Health Organization Collaborating Center for Nursing (WHOCC) with an active agenda to build international relationships, especially in Central America. In support of that initiative, nursing faculty members were seeking ways to strengthen their relationships in Honduras by developing a site for study abroad in a small village in the Western Region of Honduras that had a school of nursing, a regional hospital and community agencies, and non-governmental organizations (NGOs).

Nursing faculty members developed a summer study abroad course for honors nursing students, "Health, Education and Social Welfare in a Global Community," whose purpose was to expose students to a cross-cultural health care experience in a global community. The course objectives included immersion in an international experience and increasing undergraduate student awareness of ethical multiculturalism, cross-cultural health issues, and international health concerns. The course incorporated online modules and discussions to prepare students for their international health care experience. Individual and group course assignments included examining the role of the nurse in global health, ethical practice, global health goals of the World Health Organization (WHO), epidemiology and environmental impact on a population, global health issues (social, political, economic, and environmental), Honduran partnerships, international travel, and the long-term effects of international nursing experiences. Students and faculty traveled to Honduras at the end of the summer term and immersed themselves in activities in the regional hospital, urban and rural communities, and a school of nursing. They interacted with nursing students from the local auxiliary nursing program, Honduran nursing faculty, local nurses and health care workers practicing in the hospital, public health officers, and the staff and volunteers of several NGOs. They also worked daily with young translators from the local bilingual school. Partnering was clearly an important component of this study abroad course because it increased student exposure to experiences across cultures and directed learning toward providing culturally sensitive care. The opportunities for group and individual reflection while in Honduras were carefully structured to engage students fully in the experience: students participated in an end-of-the-day huddle, and each student kept a daily reflective journal.

The program and reflection were designed to contribute to students' professional growth in the affective (emotional) domain as described in Bloom's Taxonomy. Bloom and colleagues identify the highest stage of development in the affective domain as characterization by the values of the profession (Krathwald, Masia, and Bloom). By participating in the collaborations with international colleagues, students had direct opportunities to collaborate. They had opportunities to realize a human connection between peoples of differing cultures. They could see firsthand the shared values of nursing.

RESEARCH IN INTERNATIONAL SETTINGS

International education in honors is, of course, not new; however, because of the small number of honors nursing programs, honors study abroad options in nursing are rare. Michelle L. Edmonds reports that only a few published studies describe the experiences of American nursing students who study abroad and discuss the benefits or barriers to their educational experiences. Central to these study abroad initiatives and experiences is creating opportunities for research and service learning. Nursing research is an integral part of the professional nursing role. With the increasing emphasis on evidence-based practice (EBP) worldwide, nursing faculty must find new ways to incorporate nursing research into their classes. Providing students with opportunities to actively develop clinical questions, analyze recent findings, and integrate knowledge from those studies into new approaches to care is essential. Study abroad programs that incorporate service learning offer great opportunities to practice research skills and integrate the scholarship characteristic of honors while allowing nursing students to experience different cultures and develop as caregivers and medical practitioners.

To increase the success of the honors research projects, nursing students relied on the work of Nancy J. Crigger, Lygia Holcomb, and Joanne Weiss, who coined the term, "Ethical Multiculturalism" (460). Crigger, Holcomb, and Weiss have identified protocols for working with populations in developing nations that decrease the risk of unintentional, unethical practices in research or insensitive treatment of participants when conducting research (460). They identify three strategies to facilitate ethical multiculturalism:

(1) respect the community and its values: begin and end with the community; (2) minimize conflict of interest and role confusion by keeping roles and goals simple; and (3) inform optimally; going the extra mile to inform participants (465–66). In the following sections of this discussion, each strategy is addressed in relation to this honors research and service-learning program.

RESPECTING THE COMMUNITY AND ITS VALUES

Beginning with formulating a research question and concluding with disseminating results, the ethical multicultural researcher involves the community as a partner throughout the research project. The heart of successful international research is collaboration. Developing ongoing relationships with contacts in the host country facilitates quality experiences. The support for collaboration in the nursing honors program was provided by the WHOCC and Sparkman Center for Global Health at UAB, Central American Medical Outreach in Honduras, and the nursing faculty at the Escuela de Auxiliaries de Enfermeria Maya de Occidente in Honduras. Governmental and non-governmental agencies also supported the collaboration, and students and faculty worked together throughout the process, which had stages occurring in both the USA and Honduras.

To establish the foundation for a successful program, students and faculty developed and maintained relationships with their international partners via email discussions about the feasibility of pursuing certain topics and projects. The students identified interests and engaged their partners and faculty mentors to initiate and follow through with arrangements and approval processes. All of the students in the honors course proposed their research in the form of a written prospectus. They developed studies that used instruments with universally recognized applicability to minimize risk and inconvenience to the research participants. Students had to obtain approval for their research from the Ministry of Health Ethics Committee in Honduras and UAB's Institutional Review Board (IRB). During the 2006–2009 academic years, the projects that students completed in Honduras included nurses, nursing students, other health professionals, and community members. The 2007 Honduran projects focused on nurse burnout, nurses' and students' use of sexual history, and autonomy preferences in health decision-making in Hispanic women. The 2008 projects addressed nursing students' attitudes on care of persons with HIV, women's perceptions of natural birth, emotional indicators in children in orphanages, and perceptions of community violence. In 2009, a service-learning project demonstrated ways to support childbearing women in labor.

Following the completion of their research studies, the students disseminated their research findings in ways that provided further connections to strengthen the Honduran partnership. They developed posters and PowerPoint presentations and translated them into Spanish. The posters were sent to the nursing school in Honduras. UAB's Honduran partners stated these were very well received and even mounted on walls near classrooms so their students could see examples of evidence-based practice in action.

Students presented their findings at the National Conference on Undergraduate Research (NCUR) and the Biennial Convention of the Honor Society of Nursing, Sigma Theta Tau International. They also submitted selected papers to peer-reviewed journals. The most significant experience in dissemination was the opportunity to participate in *Project Honduras*, an international conference that highlighted collaborative community-based activities across Honduras. In fall 2008, several nursing faculty and students traveled back to the Western Region of Honduras to share findings at the conference with colleagues and professionals representing a variety of disciplines and occupations from across the country. Students and faculty gave presentations in Spanish on two topics: community violence and children's emotional risk in out-of-home settings. Other students who could not attend in person sent posters, which had been translated into Spanish, on the topics of health decision-making, gender roles, and perceptions of natural birth. Honduran nurses who worked with UAB honors students and who had been part of the collaboration also presented their work. They spoke about the need to increase community awareness of the problem of community violence and to develop partnerships to build community support structures. Following the presentations, the *Project Honduras* organizing committee designated community violence as the theme for its next conference.

MINIMIZING CONFLICTS OF INTEREST AND ROLE CONFUSION

In order to support and control such an extensive integrated program, faculty members and students needed protocols to govern numerous educational decisions; they used an ethical multicultural model. Under this model, participants kept the protocols simple: the topics were straightforward, and all had variables that were limited to one or two elements. The topics included attitudes of nurses, health decision-making processes, and perceptions of birth in pregnant women. The studies utilized measures that were readily understood and could work with different populations. For example, one narrative tool was open-ended: "Tell me a story about why you became a nurse." This strategy resulted in responses that could be easily compared with nurses from different countries. When students used questionnaires, they contained only a few questions, and they were precisely directed toward the primary clinical issue. When appropriate, students used an interpreter during interviews, and a bilingual-certified translator from the local area translated the written questionnaires. The methods that students used were chosen because they had been successfully used in international settings. These strategies also included using human figure drawings for children as a simple screening tool for emotional risk and forming focus groups to discuss sensitive topics such as concerns about community violence. Following implementation, students stated that the methods had been effective and that most participants had no difficulty responding to or completing the instruments.

INFORMING OPTIMALLY

One of the key strategies contributing to the success of the Honduras expedition was clear communication. Participants were informed about studies in Spanish, and all documents were translated and verified by a certified translator. UAB's IRB required local context review and approval, and that requirement was fulfilled by the Western Region Ministry of Health, which holds a federalwide assurance (FWA) listed on the Office of Human Research Protections (OHRP) website <http://www.OHRP.gov>. This is a critical point in international work. Institutional Review Boards in the USA recognize those international agencies that hold a FWA with OHRP. Collaboration with the Ministry of Health at this level demonstrates the significant level of international partnership that was required and established in this program. All consent forms and questionnaires were translated into Spanish, and the translation was checked by officials at the Ministry of Health, with reviews provided by the Minister of Health, who serves as the chairman of the Ethics Committee. Whenever the IRB expressed concerns that translations were not appropriate, this objection was overcome by using a certified healthcare translator in Alabama who verified all translations of consents and letters. At the end of the project, researchers communicated their results and analysis to all the community partners.

INSURMOUNTABLE BARRIERS

Unfortunately, even with support from multiple collaborators, the honors nursing program in Honduras had to be discontinued. The university IRB approval process became incredibly laborious: they did not always accept international letters of support, even though they were standard forms from the Honduran health agencies. Possible solutions, such as a videoconference or the travel of an IRB representative to meet with the partners, were not implemented. Because of a political coup in Honduras on June 28, 2009, that summer's study abroad trip was cancelled. The cancellation of the study abroad course and the continuing IRB issues led to the decision to discontinue offering an international option for students in the nursing honors program.

ASSESSING INTERNATIONAL OPPORTUNITIES FOR HONORS STUDENTS

In their evaluations, students reported that they had life-changing experiences. Students, faculty, and even the partners in the Honduran communities participating in these honors study abroad collaborations evidenced growth in the following ways:

1. Students engaged in significant inquiry, studying universal concepts such as nurses' burnout, nurses' knowledge and attitudes, community residents' health decision-making, needs and interventions for at-risk women and children, and community awareness and prevention of violence for communities. Their presentations at local, national, and international forums made significant contributions to the discipline. (For a list of student projects conducted during the Honduran collaborations, see the Appendix.)

2. Faculty identified the collaborations as being effective in addressing significant health issues. Honduran nursing colleagues came to the USA in reciprocal educational programs as part of the WHOCC. Nursing faculty from the Escuela de Auxiliaries de Enfermeria Maya de Occidente completed a survey through the hospital emergency room to document incidents of domestic violence in the community. The NGO developed a shelter for women at risk of abuse, and nursing students at UAB assisted by providing personal care items and other supplies for the shelter. Healthcare provider practice in the labor and delivery ward began to include comfort measures and some privacy for laboring women.

3. Student-investigators reported building skills for future leadership roles. They reported increased confidence and assertiveness.

4. Students described personal growth in obtaining a broad global perspective on persons, cultures, nations, health, and nursing. Their experiences reflected those described by Marsha Atkins and Kathleen S. Stone, who describe study

abroad as promoting understanding of self, of others in reciprocal relationships, and of nursing.

5. Students responded to the opportunity in ways that demonstrated ethical multiculturalism in their research. Because of the study abroad context, students recognized the need for nursing initiatives with international relevance, and they developed projects that required international collaborations. In their commitment to navigate the lengthy processes of internal and external approval, students demonstrated cultural awareness, and they accounted for the need to protect and optimally inform research participants as they followed through with projects in international settings. In their journal reflections, students discussed the benefits of the international experiences as they were developing the values of the nursing profession. They also recognized the similarity of values shared with partners around the world.

6. The collaboration resulted in strengthening a reciprocal relationship between nurses and faculty in two countries. The projects developed scientific and problem-focused approaches to improving health care in an international setting and initiated dialog between nursing students in two countries on the importance of evidence-based practice.

7. Students became increasingly committed to further international experiences. One went on to enroll in a joint MSN-MPH degree program.

8. Students expanded their skills and their appreciation of nursing as a discipline as they participated in the international collaboration in nursing. Students described significant personal growth in journals. As hoped, the international experience contributed to their professional growth in the affective domain (Krathwald, Masia, and Bloom). For nursing honors students, the transition from novice to newly emerging global leader in nursing began with experiences supporting their international work and scholarship in

nursing. This work had a cross-cultural impact on students' lives and relationships.

The honors study abroad courses in Honduras were an unqualified success for the students in the UAB Honors Nursing Program and incredibly valuable for the in-country partners. The combination of evidence-based research, careful analysis, service learning, and rich community engagement and collaboration with a large cross-section of the Honduran people profoundly changed people's lives and health options and care. Unfortunately, all too often in honors education, valuable programs and activities must be suspended or discontinued because of depleted resources, especially in tough economic times, or other factors beyond anyone's control, such as political instability or changes in personnel or mission. Nevertheless, the faculty in the UAB Honors Nursing Program hope for the opportunity to reinstate a service-learning study abroad option in the future for their students, and they hope that this project will inspire others to create similar programs for their own students. Clearly, this opportunity to engage in an honors project in an international collaboration fostered development of global perspectives, international scholarship, life-changing relationships, and improved health care. The Honduran initiative attained the shared vision and the desired goal of honors, service learning, and international study: they should be transformational experiences.

WORKS CITED

Atkins, Marsha, and Kathleen S. Stone. "Undergraduate and Graduate Students Partnering in a Short Term Transcultural Experience in Honduras." *ABNF Journal* 17.4 (2006): 147–51. Print.

Braid, Bernice, and Gladys Palma de Schrynemakers. "A Case Among Cases." *Journal of the National Collegiate Honors Council* 12.1 (2011): 25–32. Print

Callister, Lynne Clark, Geraldine Matsumura, Sandra Lookinland, Sandra Mangum, and Carol Loucks. "Inquiry in Baccalaureate Nursing Education: Fostering Evidence-Based Practice." *Journal of Nursing Education* 44.2 (2005): 59–64. Print.

Crigger, Nancy J., Lygia Holcomb, and Joanne Weiss. "Fundamentalism, Multiculturalism and Problems of Conducting Research with Populations in Developing Nations." *Nursing Ethics* 8 (2001): 459–68. Print.

Edmonds, Michelle L. "An Integrative Literature Review of Study Abroad Programs for Nursing Students." *Nursing Education Perspectives* 33.1 (2012): 30–34. Print.

Greatrex-White, Shelia. "Uncovering Study Abroad: Foreignness and Its Relevance to Nurse Education and Cultural Competence." *Nurse Educator Today* 28 (2008): 530–38. Print.

Haynes, Carolyn. "Overcoming the Study Abroad Hype." *Journal of the National Collegiate Honors Council* 12.1 (2011): 17–24. Print.

Krathwohl, David R., Bertram B. Masia, and Benjamin Samuel Bloom. *Taxonomy of Education Objectives, the Classification of Educational Goals: Handbook 2, Affective Domain*. New York: D. McKay, 1964. Print.

Saenz, Karen, and Lygia Holcomb. "Essential Tools for a Study Abroad Nursing Course." *Nurse Educator* 34.4 (2009): 172–75. Print.

APPENDIX

Student Research Projects

Blackburn, Michelle Feliciana. "Perceptions of Community and Family Violence: Examining the Views of Hispanic Women in Honduras and USA." 2008.

Boswell, Shannon. "Autonomy Preference and Central American Women: A Comparison of Two Populations." 2007.

Debiasi (née Chamlee), Laura B. "A Collaborative Approach to Assess and Improve the Emotional Well-Being of Children in Honduras." 2008.

Frazier, Sarah. "How to Ease the Pain of Labor with Different Techniques." 2009.

Herring, Kristin. "Perceptions of Positive Birth: Honduran Women's Definitions Pre- and Post-partum." 2008.

Little, Amy. F. "Enthusiasm or Exhaustion? Nurses' Motivations and Experiences of Burnout in Two Comparison Countries." 2007.

Mullin, Heather Simechak. "Sexual History and Follow Up: What Drives Practice? A Comparison of USA and Honduras." 2007.

Pelotto, Brittany. "Caring for Mental Health Patients: Perceptions of Generalist Nurses in Two Countries." 2008.

Slater, Larry Zuendel. "Knowledge and Attitudes Toward Caring for HIV/AIDS Patients and Families Among Nursing Students in Honduras and USA." 2008.

Yartins, Nicole. "Gender Role Related to Acculturation in Central American Women: A Comparison Between Honduras and USA." 2008.

CHAPTER 15

Honors Overseas with an International Population

CECILE HOURY

FLORIDA INTERNATIONAL UNIVERSITY

The emphasis on globalism in higher education today has increased the significance of international experiences for students' personal, academic, and career development. An understanding of global issues enhances students' education; broadens their personal and educational perspectives; familiarizes them with second or third languages; contributes to healthier exploration, appreciation, and understanding of different cultures; enhances preparation for careers in a global society; and strengthens the networking and relationships between universities and countries. Because university administrators and faculty recognize these benefits, they have increased the resources for study abroad programs and sent a strong message to their students about the essential nature of international education in their preparation for life. Because of the increasing emphasis on studying abroad, the number of students participating in such programs has grown rapidly over the years. Some students participate in short-term international experiences, in summer or alternative spring breaks, or in lengthier exchange programs through their home institution; others opt to complete their entire degree at a foreign university.

Research and publications on international education programs have also expanded to the point where various aspects, benefits, and challenges of these programs are now well-documented and analyzed.[1] Much of the literature, however, focuses on two specific groups of students: American students participating in study abroad programs outside of the U.S. and international students participating in study abroad programs in the U.S. Little has yet been published on international students enrolled for four-year degrees at American universities who travel with those universities' study abroad programs.

Honors study abroad programs often attract international students. Several factors explain this phenomenon. Because international students understand the value of being exposed to different cultures, languages, and ways of life, they tend to be naturally attracted to study abroad programs. International students come to the U.S. to obtain the best education possible. Because most honors colleges or programs are the institutions' focus for academic excellence, offering challenging coursework that fosters intellectual curiosity, critical thinking, problem solving, experiential learning, and community engagement, international students are often interested in participating in honors learning experiences, such as honors study abroad programs. Finally—and this pertains to many public institutions—international students pay out-of-state tuition, which may be five or six times more than what in-state students pay, for the classes they take. When multiplied by the number of credits, this financial obligation is a major burden for many international students. At many public universities, however, when international students register for a study abroad class, they pay in-state tuition, which often makes a three- or six-credit study abroad class more affordable than a regular three- or six-credit class. Participating in an honors study abroad program, then, might allow international students to earn the credits they need at a more affordable rate while giving them an enriching cultural and educational experience. Of course, they usually represent only a small percentage of the students enrolled in study abroad programs.

The term "international education" suggests any academic experience that takes students across national borders with the intention of preparing students to be active and engaged participants in a global world. Although most honors programs and colleges are involved in a range of such opportunities, this chapter focuses primarily on short-term study abroad programs, distilling some of the key logistical and cultural issues that honors administrators and faculty should be aware of as they design study abroad programs and embark on international experiences with international students.

Determining the immigration status of international students is essential. Traveling outside the United States with a non-U.S. passport places students in a special and, unfortunately, often complicated and unstable situation. Two crucial questions must be answered well in advance: Can the international student enter the country of destination? Certain countries might not require visas for American travelers based on existing partnerships with the U.S., but they might require visas for citizens of other countries. Will these students, at the end of the program, be able to reenter the United States without any problems? Administrators should take several measures to address these issues, but the key is to be proactive in working with international students traveling abroad with the program.

The first step is to develop and maintain a strong ongoing relationship with the university or college's Office of Education Abroad and International Students and Scholar Services (OEA and ISSS— the names may vary at each institution). The director of honors study abroad programs should not wait for problems to surface to contact these offices. University policies for study abroad programs and U.S. State Department immigration regulations are, by nature, extremely fluid. Today, international students may need to fill out two documents to reenter the country; the next day, they may need three. One day, various formalities take one month; the next, they take half a year. Moreover, what is required for citizens of one country might differ for citizens of other countries. For the honors director to provide general answers regarding the immigration status and requirements of students is virtually impossible. The best option is to refrain from answering any immigration-related questions and to refer students to the experts in the international studies office, while staying in the loop regarding the answers and their implications for the students.

The second step comes at the point when students officially apply to the program. Students must be prepared to provide key documents, including a copy of their passports and any other immigration papers, such as I-20 or Green Card. This step ensures that, months before the actual departure, the program director and appropriate institutional offices are aware of the students' specific immigration status, are tracking their situations and addressing them appropriately, and are maintaining a comprehensive list of the international students enrolled in honors study abroad programs.

Shortly after students turn in their program applications, the honors study abroad director should, as a third step, invite all international students to a meeting with the institutional travel offices. Their staff should review with the students the regulations they need to know before taking the trip. Numerous glitches can disrupt their plans. For instance, the U.S. State Department does not usually accept any photocopies of legal documents, so students need to make sure that they travel with the original paperwork. Also, students who are seniors graduating in May and traveling the summer after are usually not allowed back in the U.S. since they are officially no longer students. Another example involves international students who graduate in May and have previously applied for Occupational Practical Training (OPT).[2] It usually takes three to six months for these students to receive their OPT cards. Since students apply before graduating, they may not receive their card until August or even later. For international students to leave the U.S. without the OPT card is risky. Their participation in a program that would require them to leave the country without this critical immigration document is therefore inadvisable. Although the study abroad directors for both honors and the larger institution have the responsibility for ensuring that students understand the policies and regulations, ultimately the students must decide whether to risk not being allowed back into the United States.

After the directors have reviewed the main immigration policies, they should set aside time at the meeting for students to ask questions of the staff. The staff should record minutes of the meeting and distribute them to the students so they can refer to them to check what they need to do to remain in good standing with the U.S. State Department. Having minutes contributes to the clear paper trail that documents the situation for all the students and the recommendations they have been given. Finally, all immigration documents should be scanned and stored on a USB drive or mobile device so that the faculty director on the trip can easily access copies of the students' immigration documents if the need arises.

The final step is emailing the international students two weeks before departure to remind them of the particular documents they need to take on the program. The most efficient mechanism is having a checklist of the necessary documents. Requiring students to sign this list and turn it in the day before leaving underscores the significance of having the documents. Another important factor to consider when dealing with the immigration status of international students participating in study abroad programs is the point of departure and return for the trip. Some programs ask students to meet at the school or local airport so they can travel together to the country of destination. Similarly, at the end of the program, the whole group usually travels back together. Although this approach has positive aspects, it might not be ideal for international students. If the program does not start immediately after the end of a semester, international students may have already returned to their home countries. Obviously, for them to travel to the U.S. and then on to the destination country, which may be closer and cheaper to reach from home, would be an expensive inconvenience. The same concerns apply at the end of the program. Having students return directly to their home countries rather than to the U.S. and then home again may well be faster and cheaper. Allowing international students to travel separately also means that if they experience complications when entering the destination country or re-entering the U.S., the whole group is not detained at the airport indefinitely while the situation is addressed. Of course, this scenario also means that students are on their own in dealing with such complications.

From a logistical point of view, the students' ability to finance their program costs and personal expenses while on the trip should also be discussed. Many students rely on financial aid, scholarships, or travel grants to finance their study abroad experiences. Surfing the internet or contacting the international study office demonstrates that the opportunities for financial support are plentiful; however, the vast majority of financial options are reserved for U.S. citizens only. As a result, international students must often rely on personal funds, such as parental support or work income, to cover the expenses involved with studying abroad. Stating the financial aid options clearly on the program website and application is advisable so that international students do not apply, pay a deposit, and then discover that they are unable to pay the balance of the costs. Not only would they miss out on the program and likely lose their deposits, which are usually non-refundable, but they would also end up dropping the class, losing its credits, and jeopardizing their academic status. Being clear about all expenses involved in the program is always the best option.

One non-logistical but essential consideration is the individual and collective cultural implications of having international students on an American honors study abroad program. Directors of such programs need to ensure, prior to departure, that the international students and the group as a whole are ready for the challenge. This preparation can be achieved via readings, reflection, and discussions inserted in a spring semester seminar or series of workshops.

Richard D. Lewis's *When Cultures Collide* is a good starting point to address issues of culture and how people's own cultural makeup impacts how they perceive others.[3] The first section of the book is especially pertinent for any student or group preparing for an international experience. It introduces the concept that from infancy, people are conditioned to think, feel, and perceive reality in a certain way. Influential factors include families and friends; educational, religious, and political institutions; national language; and history. Through this conditioning process, individuals are provided with a specific code of behavior and core values—what is right and wrong, polite and impolite, acceptable and unacceptable, appropriate and inappropriate—as well as the cultural interpretation of essential concepts such as truth, time, space, and communication. These components shape not only who people are, what they believe, and how they behave, but also how they perceive others and deal with difference. To help people understand, respect, and appreciate others' cultural makeup and consequent view of reality, Lewis groups different cultural characteristics into three main categories:

1. Linear active cultures—those who plan, schedule, organize, pursue action chains, do one thing at a time. Germans and Swiss are in this group.

2. Multi-active cultures—those lively, loquacious people who do many things at once, planning their priorities not according to a time schedule, but according to the relative importance that each appointment brings with it. Italians, Latin Americans, and Arabs are members of this group.

3. Reactive cultures—those cultures that prioritize courtesy and respect, listening quietly and calmly to their interlocutors and reacting carefully to the other side's proposals. Chinese, Japanese, and Finns are in this group. (xviii–xix)

Lewis does not include citizens from the United States of America in his cultural categorization process, perhaps because most U.S. citizens have varied ethnic roots, thus making it difficult to highlight a uniform cultural pattern. Some U.S. citizens have retained many elements of their cultural heritage. Someone traveling in Miami, for example, may find that its large Hispanic population influences the way that people behave in ways similar to those of people in multi-active cultures, but that traveling through, say, Wisconsin would be a different experience. Americans of different origins, then, might fit into Lewis's first, second, or third categories.

Although Lewis's classifications are problematic, his approach can be useful when discussing the impact of cultural upbringing on the way people feel and behave on a daily basis. Students do not need to agree with Lewis's characterizations, but they can enrich a discussion about the different characteristics people use to categorize others and can push students to wonder about whether that process is ethical or beneficial. In the end, students should reach the conclusion that such categorization inevitably leads to unfounded generalizations and reinforces stereotyping.

That international and American students explore such issues is essential because they will influence the internal functioning of the group as well as what they live and learn while abroad. This process is all the more important for students visiting non-European countries, where the customs may differ greatly from those familiar to American students. Adequate preparation will ensure that students are ready to encounter different cultural elements and are willing to adapt positively to linguistic, behavioral, and cultural challenges.

This readiness is especially important for international students traveling with a group of Americans because differences in cultural and national background place these students in a unique position. During the preparation phase of the program, they will often be considered—except for immigration paperwork issues—"Americans" by default. These non-American students will then often hear or read instructions about the position of the U.S. in the post-September 11 (and now, post-Bin Laden) world. The general advice to U.S. students traveling abroad is to avoid gathering at American places abroad, wearing American university gear, and identifying themselves as part of an American group—in other words, to draw as little attention to their national status as possible. Once abroad, international students' status will affect their stay insofar as they are considered "Americans" by default.

When students from a U.S. university travel abroad, they are welcomed, perceived, interacted with, and treated quite specifically as Americans. For good or bad, people assume these students embody whatever their countrymen typically think of the United States. During free time in these countries, however, international students can decide to more clearly represent their countries of origins. Although affiliated with an American university, they may identify themselves as French, Italian, or Peruvian. This self-identification, in turn, will have an impact on how they are perceived and treated. That these students are not Americans and yet are at times in the position of Americans forces them to navigate between or combine different identities. Although this process certainly will increase these students' national and global awareness, it also means that they and their fellow students must explore, negotiate, and reconcile additional cultural, national, and identity conflicts.

At the collective level, the participation of international students influences different aspects of the program. At the logistical level, international students might find themselves, voluntarily or involuntarily, separated from the rest of the group. They may be grouped together in one hotel room/apartment or one study group. Although this separation may be natural and not problematic in itself, the director of the program should be aware of this proclivity and discreetly ensure that it does not become an issue or a barrier to all the students' learning and sense of community. Time, for example, has precise quantitative values and measures, but it is also a cultural concept, and dealing with different approaches to time can become a collective issue. When analyzing Americans' perception of time, Lewis concludes that for an American, time "is clock- and calendar-related, segmented in an abstract manner for convenience, measurement, and disposal" (53). For Arabs and Latin people, however, "time is event—or personality—related, a subjective commodity which can be manipulated, molded, stretched, or dispensed with, irrespective of what the clock says" (Lewis 57). These different approaches to time can create logistical issues while abroad. If the director asks students to report at a specific time every morning and different students show up at different times because, for them, 9:00 a.m. means 8:30 or maybe 9:30-ish, this behavior can become a source of frustration for other students who may feel disrespected. It can, of course, cause logistical nightmares as well. The same kind of dilemma can surface with space, language differences, eating, personal hygiene, and a plethora of other issues. The faculty director should capitalize on these possible conflicts by using them to stimulate discussions about cultural diversity and understanding, rather than letting them become grounds for conflict. In any case, they will need to be addressed.

International students participating in study abroad programs with American universities also bring different perspectives since they are not discovering a new culture with only an American sensibility. The experience is not the same, for example, for a Swiss student to go on a study abroad program to Italy with an American university as it is for an American student to do so. An important component of study abroad programs is learning about other countries' histories, cultures, and economic and political systems. When discussing these issues, American students usually have only their own experiences and national heritage to rely on; their views are therefore limited. When touring Italy, for instance, students often discuss different political and economic regimes, including fascism, communism, monarchy, and capitalism. But American students' perception of communism has largely been shaped by the post-World War II U.S. response to communism. The images from that perspective are highly negative: the 1950s Red Scare, the Cold War, Fidel Castro (still a major cause of concern in Miami), and the rise of the Chinese economy. A French student, however, may have a different perspective on communism, which enjoys legitimate political status there. For that student, communism did not result in the suppression of human rights in France. Indeed, it produced the right to five weeks of paid vacation per year, which is a policy no government since then has dared to change despite several economic crises. When French students express these ideas, they shape the critical thinking of the other students. In that sense, the participation of international students in study abroad programs clearly broadens other participants' intellectual horizons, deepening their knowledge and understanding of international political, economic, and socio-cultural issues as well as their awareness of the critical nature of personal and national perspectives on identity formation and global appreciation and cooperation.

The growing presence of international students in American universities' study abroad programs, then, influences all aspects of the programs, from their design to their organization and development to the outcomes of the experience. It creates some logistical challenges, stimulates discussion and debate about issues of nationalities and identities, and introduces enlightening perspectives for the participating students of all nationalities. Honors study abroad program directors need to be proactive to overcome the logistical concerns while capitalizing on the unique opportunities that traveling with international students can create.

NOTES

[1]See David J. Comp's "Research and Literature on U.S. Students Abroad" and "Research on U.S. Students Study Abroad" for useful summaries of recent literature. Major research journals in the field include *Frontiers: The Interdisciplinary Journal of Study Abroad* and *Journal of Studies in International Education*.

[2]OPT refers to a period during which students with F1 status who have completed or have been pursuing their degrees for more than nine months are permitted by the United States Citizenship and Immigration Services (USCIS) to work in their fields for at most one year on a student visa without needing to acquire a work H1B visa.

[3]Richard D. Lewis's work can be downloaded as a PDF file, free of charge, at <http://fast-file.blogspot.com>. Part 1, entitled "Getting to Grips with Cultural Diversity," goes from pages 3 to 100. Part 2, "Managing and Leading in Different Cultures," focuses on the impact of cultural diversity on business practices (pages 101 to 178). Part 3, "Getting to Know Each Other," analyzes the cultural characteristics of over seventy countries (pages 179 to 575). It might be interesting to assign the sections dealing with the country of origin of the international students in the program, the United States, and the country of destination.

WORKS CITED

Comp, David J., ed. "Research and Literature on U.S. Students Abroad: A Bibliography with Abstracts, 2000–2003." UCLA Center for International and Development Education and UCLA Center for Global Education. Web. 19 Mar. 2013.

—. "Research on U.S. Students Abroad: An Update, 2004–2011." UCLA Center for International and Development Education and UCLA Center for Global Education. Web. 19 Mar. 2013.

Lewis, Richard D. *When Cultures Collide: Leading Across Cultures.* Boston: Nicholas Brealey, 2006. Print.

PREPARING TOMORROW'S GLOBAL LEADERS

Honors International Education

PART III:

ADVICE FROM EXPERIENCED FACULTY LEADERS

CHAPTER 16

Lessons Learned:
An Idiosyncratic Top Ten List for Study
Abroad Program Directors

KARL M. PETRUSO

UNIVERSITY OF TEXAS AT ARLINGTON

I have had the privilege of looking at study abroad from both sides over the past forty years, as an undergraduate who spent his junior year in Greece in the late 1960s and thereafter as organizer and director of study abroad programs for four American universities in six countries, beginning as a graduate student in the mid-1970s. In designing these programs, my aim has always been to maximize the academic experience for students. My approach has been one of trial and error, retaining the activities that have worked to my satisfaction and discarding the ones that have not. I offer the following suggestions with the hope that some at least might be of value to colleagues new to study abroad. And I trust that readers will indulge my counting them down in David Letterman fashion, ending with the suggestion I consider both most compelling and most gratifying.

It will be obvious that some academic disciplines, courses, and syllabi are more amenable to these suggestions than others (no. 4 might not be completely applicable to intensive language-learning courses, for example). Finally: while most of the programs I have directed over the years have been for honors students, the observations and suggestions that follow are pertinent to non-honors courses and study abroad initiatives as well.

NUMBER 10

Participating in a Study Abroad Program Is a Privilege, Not a Right

Study abroad is not for everyone. Directors should seek to identify students who will benefit the most from the experience *and* will play nicely with others. The study abroad programs I have directed have all been intense as well as intensive. The application process is not a mere formality; I require an essay in which the applicants address their interest in the country or culture as well as the topics of the courses to be taught. All applicants are interviewed, and they must submit a comprehensive physician's certification attesting to their physical and emotional ability to participate in all activities of the program. The group members spend a great deal of time together, much of it in close quarters, and they do a significant amount of hiking, both on city concrete and in difficult, often remote terrain and in unpleasant weather.

NUMBER 9

Students Have Many Reasons for Wanting to Study Abroad, and Some of These Are Unexpected

For every student who espouses an academic interest in the country or region, there is another who could (but rarely is bold enough to) make a very different case. Some motives are charming, even arresting, even if not all are persuasive.

In the process of interviewing a student for a program in Greece, I was pleased to hear him say that he had lived in the country a few years previously and had visited many archaeological sites that were on my syllabus. I asked him which sites impressed him the most, but he could not remember the name of even one or, in fact, anything distinctive about it. As the interview drew to an end, he asked how much time off the students would have per week and followed that with a question about how long it took to travel by public bus to a coastal town north of the program's base, Athens. It eventually emerged that he was hoping to rekindle a romantic relationship with a woman who lived in that town. Needless to say, he was not offered admission.

In reviewing applications for a program in Ireland, my colleague and I read one from a young man whose father was born on that island but had never returned, and the father had recently and suddenly passed away. The student saw this study abroad opportunity partly as a way to both honor his father's memory and connect with his own family roots. My colleague and I decided to offer him a position even though he was not the most academically prepared student in the applicant pool. During the trip, he did good and conscientious work, and he turned out to be one of the most enthusiastic participants and, unexpectedly, emerged as a leader among his classmates. This experience convinced me that balancing academic and other motives for study abroad makes for a diverse and interesting roster of participants. In the end, many kinds of students can benefit—and not only in academic terms—from a study abroad experience.

NUMBER 8

Be Clear about the Nature of the Program

Each year, one of the several orientation sessions sponsored by the director of my university's study abroad office begins with this question: "What do you most want to get out of this experience?" The students are given a few minutes to think and jot down their thoughts, and then they are asked to read the top two or three entries on their lists. Every year, without fail, many (sometimes most) students respond, "to have fun," or "to have a good time."

Ever the wet blanket, I have developed a pointed response: "*I want to have fun, too, and I guarantee you that we will. But this is first and foremost an *academic* program, and I expect you to perform academically to the best of your ability.*" This message is reinforced by having several formal class sessions and discussions on campus before departure, with a good deal of assigned reading (much of it of a basic get-acquainted-with-history/chronology/geography nature). The reading assignments demand that participants invest some time in memorization, an unpopular activity I find increasingly rare among undergraduates today. To reinforce the academic nature of the program, the instructors administer a quiz for each course before departure to ensure that the students arrive at the destination with some minimal level of common knowledge about the country as well as—perhaps equally significantly in the context of this suggestion—a grade on record.

NUMBER 7 (RELATED TO NUMBER 8)

Fold the Overseas Component into Something Larger in Scope and Longer in Duration

The in-country component should be part of a course, taken prior or concurrently, or, at the very least, the course should incorporate on-campus lecture and discussion components as well as an orientation, brownbag lunches, film series, receptions, and other social activities, both before and after the trip. In recent years, at least one student in each of the international programs has established a Facebook group so that all participants can become acquainted with one another before the program begins and share flight information. (The participants never travel to the countries of destination as a group in order to provide the students with an exhilarating, confidence-building experience before the in-country work begins.)

NUMBER 6

Engage Students in the In-Country Component Well before Departure

While the courses offered are typically in traditional lecture format, the instructors have each student prepare an oral presentation 10–15 minutes in duration for each course, for delivery in country, on archaeological sites, historical sites and/or events, or works of art in a museum. They must complete all their research prior to departure and provide their classmates with a handout summarizing their findings and providing a seminal bibliography. Some presentations are role-plays. The students also journal and blog; these activities are highly recommended and occasionally required. Upon returning to campus, the students prepare a formal research paper on each of their presentation topics, taking advantage of what they learned abroad, for submission at a later date.

One component that has successfully gotten students out and about on their own quickly is a scavenger hunt with twenty destinations, all of which are to be located and visited in the first few days after arrival. Students must bring back proof of their treks, for which they can earn a few points of extra credit. Examples: In Athens, they must travel to the central market on Athinas Street and take a digital photo of a foodstuff they have never seen at home; in Dublin, they must visit a pub and interview the bartender about why Guinness is superior to Bud Light; in Paris, they must find the Shakespeare & Co. bookshop and bring back a bookmark; in Edinburgh, they must take a photo of themselves at the top of the Walter Scott monument. Students typically do their scavenging in small groups and approach the task both conscientiously and systematically. In the process they learn about the host city and its public transportation system while building their confidence to navigate unfamiliar terrain. The best thing about the scavenger hunt is that they enjoy it. I have never heard anyone complain about this purposefully arduous assignment, which in itself I regard as noteworthy.

NUMBER 5

Encourage Students to Use Internet Resources Well before Their Departure

At the very least, instructors should give assignments to browse the web versions of English-language newspapers in the country to be visited and to track particular issues of political or cultural interest or of current economic concern. Students enjoy considerable latitude on this assignment, and often they follow a topic related to their academic majors or pastimes.

The venerable hobby of shortwave radio listening—which is how I learned about the world in my adolescent years—has morphed into a much less esoteric phenomenon in recent years. Thousands of foreign radio stations now stream on the Internet and can be tuned in on the students' computers. Participants often find it enjoyable to listen to the traditional music of the country they will soon visit. I always take a small AM/FM/SW radio with me when I travel abroad, and I encourage students to do the same.

NUMBER 4

Avoid Sitting in Classrooms.

I repeat: **Avoid sitting in classrooms.** Do not do in country what can be done in a classroom back on campus. Travel as much as possible and as far as the institution's and the students' budgets permit. A program that calls itself "study abroad in France" should not be confined to Paris with afternoon sojourns to Chartres and Versailles. Paris is not France. On the UT Arlington honors study abroad programs, 100% of the class sessions are held at the places being studied (sites of historical, archaeological, or natural significance), and they are often outdoors. The students are warned before departure that they will do their work in any weather. They are told to bring clipboards or stiff-backed notebooks so that they can write standing up, as well as foul-weather gear and, of course, sensible shoes.

(Did I mention: "Avoid sitting in classrooms"?)

NUMBER 3

Give Students Downtime, but Not Very Much, and Encourage Them to Make Good Use of It

UT Arlington students usually have one day off per week, and instructors suggest strongly that they not stay in their rooms, watch TV, or sleep. They have the rest of their lives to watch TV and sleep, but they have very little time to explore the country they are visiting.

NUMBER 2

Encourage Students to Use Photography to Explore—Specifically, to Create a Narrative of Their Experience Abroad

Hobart and William Smith Colleges and Wofford College have long emphasized the pedagogical power of photography by encouraging their students to create audio slide shows with PhotoStory for Windows or iPhoto for Apple and hardcover photo essays or albums produced by Shutterfly or blurb.com on a theme or story of personal interest in order to memorialize their experience.

Digital cameras are now ubiquitous, but the quality of the far-too-many images that students produce is typically terrible. Before departing for France a few years ago, the program leaders scheduled a mini-seminar by a professor of photography who gave the students a primer on theme, composition, subjects, and point of view to get them to think about learning through photography. I then expressly and sternly prohibited them from taking hackneyed snapshots of their classmates mugging in front of the Eiffel Tower. (The hundreds of thousands of these pictures that have been uploaded to Flickr are only a fraction of the total that have been shot. Don't get me started on this.)

AND MY NUMBER 1 RECOMMENDATION FOR DIRECTORS OF STUDY ABROAD PROGRAMS

Encourage Students to Think about Travel as a Transformational Human Phenomenon Rather Than Merely Focusing on the Way Their Travel Experience Is Affecting Them Personally

Most professors who take students abroad do so because they have had profound international experiences of their own. For many, their lives were changed by their own undergraduate study abroad. *These directors get it.* And for many educators, one of the most satisfying pedagogical experiences they can have is to see their students get it and to hear them say upon their return home that they cannot wait to go abroad again. But these personal experiences are part of a much larger phenomenon, and they are meaningful in a pedagogical sense only if they are situated within a larger context.

At home, I occasionally teach a graduate course on the archaeology of exploration, travel, and trade that ranges chronologically from the Stone Age to late Classical antiquity in the Old World. The class examines the technology of travel, including the invention of wheeled vehicles, boatbuilding, and watercraft propulsion in antiquity; archaeological evidence for early long-distance trade networks; domestication and use of horse, ass, and camel; knowledge and power that derive from travel in early societies; and the early history and impact of tourism, which is currently a hot topic among cultural anthropologists. I have adapted several of these topics to the undergraduate level and consider them in the courses I teach abroad. Indeed, in a recent trip to France, my colleague and I made travel the *theme* of the program—and this is what I want to recommend to colleagues as a fruitful point of departure for considering how students encounter other places and peoples. For the courses I have taught in both Scotland and France (dealing with Stone Age through Roman archaeology in those regions), I assign a book written ca. 300 BCE that survives only in quotations by later authors. The author was Pytheas, an intrepid explorer from the Greek colony of Massalia (modern Marseilles). Pytheas journeyed from his home on the Mediterranean north to the English channel, hopped a boat across to Britain, explored the tin mines in Cornwall, circumnavigated the island, and sailed arguably as far west as Iceland.[1] In a recent program in France, my colleague, Dr. Kimberly van Noort, a professor of French, taught a course on travel literature about France from medieval times to the twentieth century. One of our objectives in that program was to get students to stand in particular places where other foreign visitors have stood throughout history—visitors to France with motives both nice and not so nice (exploration, commerce, pilgrimage, crusade, invasion, military occupation)—and to refract their own observations and experience through those of authors who preceded them. It was particularly moving, for example, to stand on Omaha Beach in Normandy, gazing out on the English Channel on a drizzly and foggy afternoon, our backs to hulking, disintegrating concrete German artillery emplacements, and discuss letters written home to loved ones by American GIs who took part in the D-Day landing in June 1944.

There are many other ways to tease out perceptions of and attitudes toward travel, especially among participants who are out of the U.S. for the first time. I ask students to think about *going* there as opposed to *getting* there and to consider something that people in modern times have sadly come to expect and even take for granted, namely speed and convenience, the demand for which has eclipsed almost every other sensation associated with long-distance travel.

Passengers typically board an eastbound plane at home in late afternoon or early evening, have a drink and a meal, watch a movie that more often than not flopped in the theaters, nap fitfully, wake up groggy and cranky a few hours later for breakfast, and soon thereafter touch down sometime in the morning of the next day in a very different place, quite some distance across the world. They disembark in weather and landscape that are very different from the place they departed. The sights, the smells, the languages, the music, the dress, and the street signs are different. And aside from the minor disorientation that travelers experience, they think hardly anything of it.

What passengers never do, however, is reflect on the wondrous dislocation that the miracle of modern air travel has just visited upon their bodies. And this dislocation takes place in the span of time equal to a single overnight at home. A 2003 television commercial for British Airways was a perfect case in point: a man is shown tucking himself into a bed in Times Square in New York City in the evening.[2] The sun sets. The screen briefly goes black. When dawn comes a few seconds later, he awakes in the same bed, which is now in Piccadilly Circus. He hops out and goes purposefully on his way, utterly oblivious to the enormous change in environment. Both distance and time have been entirely obliterated. The viewers are made to envy this fellow—after all, he flew business class, so he could stretch out and enjoy that rare and elusive thing, a solid night's sleep on a long-distance flight.

People are, in short, jaded about travel. This jadedness has become increasingly interesting to me as an archaeologist whose discipline permits him the luxury of both wondering about and wandering about the distant past. In antiquity—indeed, for the entire history of the human species up until about sixty years ago—all people traveled at a human pace and scale. Getting to one's destination simply took as long as it took. No time zones existed. Jet lag discomforted no one. Distant journeys might take years to complete, and since life expectancy was much shorter than it is today, such trips often consumed a significant portion of a traveler's time on earth. And one can only speculate about how the gradual changes in landscape and cultures through which long-distance travelers moved affected their conceptions of the world.

What people are missing in the modern world is experiencing the process of going there. What air travel has given sojourners with respect to savings in time it has taken away from them in terms of the sensation that they are, in fact, *traveling*. Tremendous efforts are made by air carriers to render trips as antiseptic as possible. The several movies; the window shades, the many music and talk audio channels; the inane video games; the meals and snacks; the alcohol; the data-rich projection of route map, time to destination, airspeed, and outside air temperature on the ubiquitous, inescapable video screens; the gratuitous merchandise in the fat glossy catalog in the seat pocket; and the opportunity to consume duty-free yet still pricey nonessentials: all of these items and activities exist to distract passengers from the reality that they are hurtling through the atmosphere at a speed and an altitude that their ancestors even a century ago simply could not conceive. I have found the topic of dislocation to be an endlessly compelling entrée into steering students to think about other aspects of their lives—life being, after all (as educators never tire of telling our students as well as themselves), a journey. And what more immediate and dramatic opportunity to raise the topic with students than a study abroad program?

A FINAL POINT

One final point, and a related topic for another essay: travel writing is an infinitely rich genre—rarely explored by college students, in my experience—that can leaven any academic course taught abroad, whatever its discipline. Insightful and provocative works from many eras, like the *Gilgamesh Epic*, Homer's *Odyssey*, and Book II of *The Histories* of Herodotus, who recounts his wide-eyed experience of visiting Egypt in the fifth century BCE, offer significant perspectives on every country and people in the world. I will mention only two more recent assigned readings that students have enjoyed discovering: Mark Twain's venerable *The Innocents Abroad* (which is remarkably timely and familiar in our irony-and-snark-soaked culture), and, in a similar vein, the travel essays of Twain's direct literary descendant, P. J. O'Rourke, in works such as *Holidays in Hell*.[3]

I for one have come around to the view that much learning about the meaning and power of place comes through the experiences of others, especially the writings of persons more adventurous, tolerant, perceptive, and articulate than I. The theme of travel as a human phenomenon is one that I will continue to explore in future study abroad programs and is one that I warmly recommend to colleagues.[4] Moreover, I hope that this phenomenon comes foremost to my students' minds in decades to come when they reflect upon their study abroad experiences.

NOTES

[1] A scholarly but very readable reconstruction of Pytheas's voyages and the world he inhabited is that by Barry Cunliffe, *The Extraordinary Voyage of Pytheas the Greek*. New York: Penguin Group USA, 2002.

[2] Video at <http://www.youtube.com/watch?v=U67fM2eJeSM>.

[3] As noted above, the topic of travel and tourism has become a focus of study among cultural anthropologists as well as researchers in many other disciplines, not least as a result of concerns with the ramifications of globalization (witness the large and diverse roster of scholarly conferences on the subject at <http://conferencealerts. com/tour.htm>. A useful anthropological gloss on this subject is Sharon Bohn Gmelch, ed., *Tourists and Tourism: A Reader*. Long Grove, IL: Waveland P, 2004. All directors of study abroad programs will find especially illuminating the participant observation-based contribution by George Gmelch to that volume: "Let's Go Europe: What Student Tourists Really Learn" (Chapter 25, pp. 419–432).

[4] The following works are particularly recommended to faculty who wish to configure a study abroad program around the theme of travel as a human phenomenon: Lionel Casson, *Travel in the Ancient World*. Baltimore: Johns Hopkins UP, 1994; Alain de Botton, *The Art of Travel*. New York: Vintage Books, 2002; Maxine Feifer, *Tourism in History from Imperial Rome to the Present*. New York: Stein and Day, 1985; Eric J. Leed, *The Mind of the Traveler from Gilgamesh to Global Tourism*. New York: Basic Books, 1991; and Susan L. Roberson, ed., *Defining Travel: Diverse Visions*. Jackson: U of Mississippi P, 2001.

CHAPTER 17

A Delicate Balancing Act: Maximizing the Short-Term Study Abroad Experience

KAREN LYONS

UNIVERSITY OF NEBRASKA-LINCOLN

Creating an effective and valuable short-term study abroad program requires energy, patience, research, familiarity with the locations to be explored, and knowledge of available resources. The faculty leader must balance a number of program elements in such a way that the tension among those elements challenges the students and allows for cultural experiences and reflection, combined with solid academic exploration. Doing so is an exciting and rewarding challenge for the faculty member as well as for the students, encouraging lifelong learning for all.

The short-term study abroad experience is both advantageous and limiting. A short-term study abroad program:

- Accommodates many students who are invested in very structured majors and who cannot spend a semester or a year abroad;

- Facilitates an international experience for students who have not traveled much and may be uncomfortable with new circumstances;

- Assuages parental concerns because a faculty sponsor accompanies students;

- Assists students who have limited time or funding; and

- Eases students into an international situation.

Some of the assets of a short-term study abroad program are also liabilities:

- The amount of time and thus the number and variety of cultural and academic experiences are limited.

- The cost of the airfare is quite high relative to the duration of the trip.

- The opportunity to meet new people and to explore communities and the daily life of the foreign site can be difficult in a short period of time.

- The temptation to make the trip a whirlwind tour is strong; doing so may sacrifice quality for quantity of experience.

Despite the limitations of short-term study abroad programs, they can be successful and valuable to students and faculty leaders in many ways. The three key issues in establishing and completing an effective program are academics, preparation, and logistics. All are critical, but in many ways, logistics frame academics and preparation, a situation that is probably the reverse of a semester- or year-long study abroad experience. These three points, if arranged appropriately, will rescue a program from being a tourist venture and enable it to be an exceptional experience for students.

ACADEMICS

By definition, a short-term honors study abroad program must include a solid academic component. Quite simply, the subject matter, regardless of the discipline, is the reason for constructing the program. Additionally, almost of necessity, interdisciplinary facets are involved in the form of cultural experiences. A leader can meet this central need in any number of ways, and the topic of the program will frame the academic approach. For instance, if a three-week program focuses on the architecture of Florence, Venice, and Rome, not only will the students study the appropriate buildings, but they will also experience the food, probably public transportation, and perhaps attitudes toward women. On the other hand, a program lasting three weeks in England and focusing on the King Arthur legend may include not only experiencing Arthurian sites but also observations on the ways in which certain areas have capitalized on the story (a bar in Tintagel, for instance, serves "Excali-burgers"). Regardless of the fringe benefits the cultural experiences afford, the heart of the program will be the academic component: literature, history, architecture, farming methods, community planning, ecology—whatever that may be.

The travel experience may come during or after a course to which it is tied; it can incorporate the academic component completely in the time period during which it occurs, or it can be a mixture of the two. Pre- and, if possible, post-program meetings are valuable to prepare the students for the experience and provide them time and opportunity to process what they have experienced. Meetings prior to departure can include a variety of approaches, but it is desirable that students know each other at least a bit before leaving, so some sort of icebreaker can be effective, particularly with a large group. Not surprisingly, food tied to the location to be explored generally serves this purpose well. Requiring students to make presentations is more effective than frequently used or common icebreakers. Honors students tend to identify people by the content of their presentation, such as a talk on Trinity College; this approach is more likely to keep the focus academic than is hearing people's favorite color, pet's name, or hometown. These presentations on sites, historical figures or events, or cultural expectations also prepare students for the travel experience itself.

Students must obviously be aware of the academic requirements and expectations before departure. Those items can be a bit more difficult to frame and explain than they are in a standard classroom course, but they can also be more rewarding and perhaps more creative. Whatever the format, tying the program to a solid curriculum, with goals and outcomes that meet institutional and honors standards, is critical. One of the most effective requirements is a reflective journal. Students will probably need coaching in what this is; they may well blog or keep diaries, but to ask them to write about their experiences thoughtfully may be a new challenge for them. A journal entry that is an itinerary of a day is not reflective; writing about the ways in which a site visit or lecture ties into the subject matter and what they have learned about that subject matter, however, is valuable. Research requirements are also viable in this context; however, students do need to have a solid focus in this regard before departure. Blogs or discussion groups online are also possible although Internet access can be limited in some areas; thus the faculty member must know that accessibility before including those elements in the program. Those activities also require students to have appropriate equipment with them—smart phones with data plans that can access overseas Internet connections or laptops with appropriate Wi-Fi or hard-wire connections. Students may also find Internet cafés in some areas, but those generally require payment per hour.

Allowing time during the program for students to pursue the most rigorous academic components is also essential. For a short-term program, the temptation to insist that students see everything possible is overwhelming. If students are required, however, to keep reflective journals (not diaries) or to complete research, providing adequate time for those activities is essential. Expecting students to write journals on a bus or train or late at night or to conduct research quickly in a library setting when they are unfamiliar with that library is unrealistic. If journals are required, adequate time for reflection is also necessary. When students are fluctuating between being tired from major time zone changes and being excited by their first experience abroad, thinking and reflecting may not come quickly or easily.

Scheduling group time to discuss the experiences during the program is also helpful; coming together each evening in a hotel or hostel lobby or for a meal together provides an opportunity for raising issues about what students have seen that day and encouraging free discussion that will help students to process what they have learned. Journal prompts may also be helpful although they need to be thought-provoking or they can lead to superficial and banal comments. They can also limit students' ideas; having the freedom to pursue individual interests and thoughts or use creativity within the reflective journal, particularly later in the program, is preferable. If institutional policy allows flexibility, students do not necessarily have to complete work within the timeframe of the travel itself: they may do so later when they have had time to evaluate and synthesize material and reflect on the experience. Obviously, the faculty member must set a reasonable due date in this case, depending on assignments. A research paper, for instance, might have a later due date than a reflective journal because additional research could be necessary upon return.

Allowing some flexibility in what sites students visit and what activities require their participation can also be valuable although doing so can result in students gravitating toward tourist sites rather than toward those that are academically valuable. Providing a list of recommended sites can alleviate this problem. Encouraging students to follow their personal interests when selecting some, but not all, of the possible sites they see can also add diversity to the experience for other students. For instance, if a study abroad program centers in Paris, requiring students to visit the Louvre is probably optimum. But the faculty member might allow students to choose between the D'Orsay and the Marmottan: the former houses a goodly number of Impressionist works; the latter houses works by Monet only. Another choice might be Notre Dame or St. Chappelle; of course, seeing both would be ideal. Certainly group time and experience are important, but allowing individual time and permitting the larger group to ebb and flow into smaller groups of students who have similar interests are often quite valuable. This point ties in with the daily group meeting as well; students will discuss what they have experienced during the day, and other students may decide to see the same sites, or conversely, they may decide some sites are not of as much interest as others.

Allowing or even insisting on flexibility means students become more invested in the program because they must do some research on the opportunities ahead of time. This format pushes them to assume some responsibility in determining what sites they want to see individually and, if the faculty member is comfortable with doing so, as a group. If students make presentations to the group beforehand, as suggested above, as a means of getting acquainted, then students can begin to learn who has similar interests and discuss ahead of time what they might see. By using travel guides and visiting websites, students can access information about the features of various sites, opening and closing times, and costs. Although those media are not always completely accurate (in particular, travel guides often provide outdated entry fees), they will give students general ideas about selecting what they should see. (See Appendix 1 concerning guidebooks.)

At the same time, if some sites are essential to the academic portion of the program, the faculty leader must include them in the itinerary. For instance, in London, I require students to visit the British Library, a site that they would probably not think to include. When they see the Museum's Treasures Room with its original illuminated manuscripts; First Folios of Shakespeare; Magna Carta; DaVinci drawings; Gutenberg Bible; and a most compelling exhibit of Beatles lyrics scribbled on napkins, envelopes, and the back of a child's birthday card, they quickly discover that spending an afternoon there is worthwhile. Additionally, as a cultural experience, I require them to explore Portobello Market, which, while decidedly touristy, exposes the students to a variety of the ethnic groups who populate London. This open-air market is quite different from American farmers' markets, and it provides the opportunity for students to learn that being an American abroad has its embarrassing moments: what they observe is American tourists taking photographs but not participating in the experience of the market itself.

PREPARATION

Preparation for a short-term study abroad program involves numerous components, and primary among them are, of course the academic concerns. The other important factors to consider include cultural, group chemistry, and pragmatic concerns. Preparing students culturally is extremely important, as is priming them on vocabulary, customs, and traveling itself. Part of the educational experience is immersion in the culture, and a short-term study abroad program, particularly to a non-English-speaking country, may unnerve students enough that they cling together rather than engage with local people. Of course, encouraging them to form a strong bond as a group is important because they will be together for the duration of the program. The group chemistry needs to be solid; however, students must step out of the group to meet others in situations that allow them to mingle with people and expand their knowledge. Place as Text experiences planned for certain portions of the program, or even basing the program entirely on that method, will help greatly in moving students into the local culture. (See the NCHC monograph *Place as Text*, edited by Bernice Braid and Ada Long.)

In particular, pragmatic preparation is extremely important. Issues familiar to participants who have traveled internationally are not necessarily on a non-traveler's radar. Such points as clothing needs, institutional policies, general country customs, money and exchange rates, the complexities of airline travel, and safety measures must be addressed. Discussing these issues as a group with all participants, even with those who have traveled extensively, is critical. Seasoned travelers can help those who are not. Providing a handout or establishing a website, rather than relying on students to discover information on their own, is optimal. (See Appendix 2 for some specific suggestions.)

Solid preparation for a short-term study abroad program also involves holding several meetings prior to departure. At least one of these sessions should be almost entirely social to ensure that students know each other's names and are familiar with the people who will travel with them. Once again, food can be effective in these events. High tea, for instance, before leaving for England can put students in a receptive frame of mind. Light-hearted movies about the destination country or informal sessions with students who have previously been to the country are other possibilities. The event(s) should be relaxed, perhaps with coffee table books or photo albums for students to peruse. Particularly for a shy student who has traveled very little, this preparation is important. Students can and do become homesick during short-term programs, and knowing someone with whom they can talk or someone who can cheer them up is helpful and may relieve the leader of that responsibility. Good relationships within the group are essential to a successful program. Certainly the students should form bonds, but the faculty members are an essential part of the group and should insert themselves into the developing group dynamic.

LOGISTICS

A successful short-term study abroad program requires careful planning and thoughtful analysis of the goals so that the travel arrangements interface smoothly with the goals. Balancing such aspects as the cost of transportation for the group with the ease of reaching sites, the cost of entry fees with the importance of the sites, group time with individual time, and scheduled time with free time are all important considerations.

To avoid delays and wasting valuable time on logistical issues upon arrival, everything from entrances to sites to transportation to meetings with faculty or researchers at local institutions must be in place before departure. Having a Plan B for many of the events in the itinerary is also wise because airline or train delays, strikes, demonstrations, or differing cultural perspectives of time can interfere with Plan A.

Because a short-term study abroad program is limited, balancing quality and quantity is a central concern. Deciding which sites to visit and how long to spend at each site is the challenge. The "If-it's-

Tuesday,-it-must-be-Belgium" temptation is strong, and balancing the depth students will gain from spending significant time at one important site with the breadth and diversity of taking in three or four sites, albeit superficially, is an example of this dilemma. While sacrificing one for the other will necessarily occur, quality supersedes quantity. Taking students to a few sites and allowing in-depth exploration will be more effective than quickly visiting too many sites. Deciding which sites to include in the program requires a good deal of thought because the faculty member will undoubtedly have many ideas and be unable to include them all. In some instances, the faculty member may want to involve students in the decision-making process. For example, when the focus of the program is British literature and the base is London, students may be consulted about whether to travel to Winchester and Bath, with their Jane Austen connections, or to Stratford and Shakespeare country. The faculty member must, however, frame the bulk of the program, making decisions about the sites that are most important to include.

If the study abroad program involves visiting several different places in a short period of time, using efficient methods of transportation is essential. The temptation to save money by using public transportation is strong. Sometimes that decision works well, but the faculty leader must be familiar with the way the transportation system works and know the potential problems that may arise. Being certain in advance of the costs of public transportation is critical, and purchasing tickets in advance often reduces costs. Of course, traveling by public transportation usually takes longer than does traveling by private transportation; spending a full day to move from one place to another may consume time that could be used more effectively. If acclimating students to using public transportation is one of the program goals, however, then that time is not wasted.

Balancing cost with effectiveness and efficiency is often a challenge; the disadvantage of private transportation is usually increased cost. Private transportation may mean a mini-bus with driver, who may act as tour guide. This option is usually the most expensive since student fees ultimately support meals and housing for the driver if overnight travel is involved. The itinerary may also be compromised by complications such as limits on the length of time that the driver may be on the road legally or the driver's lack of familiarity with locations. Adding the cost of private transportation, however, may be worthwhile if students are able to visit important sites that add richness to the experience but are not easily accessible otherwise. Alternatively, the faculty member may elect to drive if the group is small enough. If traveling by private transportation involves hiring a van and driving, knowing institutional policies concerning insurance and liability is critical, as is knowing the faculty member's personal automobile insurance provisions. This venture can save money but often puts a good deal of stress on the faculty member, especially if driving involves large or unfamiliar vehicles, touring back roads, driving on the left, backing up a diesel van on a hill to accommodate a tractor, and navigating roundabouts with quirky signage.

One of the most effective ways to limit transportation costs and the aggravation of packing up belongings to change hotel accommodations frequently is identifying a central location where the group can spend several days and venture forth for daytrips to important sites. In that case, public transportation often becomes a valuable asset. Using private transportation sporadically or joining established tours to include less accessible sites may be another way to balance cost and efficiency.

Local tour guides can enhance students' experience immensely, but they can be expensive. Although using a tour guide may increase program costs, given the guide's local expertise, it may, in fact, save money.[1] Finding a good guide involves careful research and planning. The guide should have solid information about the sites of importance to the program, should be able to suggest other points of interest as well as a sensible itinerary that is not too exhausting, and should be familiar with appropriate places for rest stops and food.[2] Finally, the guide should enjoy working with college students and be open to the numerous questions that honors students will pose. Internet research followed by extensive correspondence with several possible guides is wise before selecting one. Even better, if the faculty member can meet and consult with a tour guide about logistics, costs, timing, and other pragmatic and educational issues before planning the program to assess the guide's abilities and attitudes, the tour guide's contribution to the program will be enhanced.[3]

Careful planning and good logistics also help considerably with enculturation as well as balancing quality and costs in lodging. Home stays are a valuable way of exposing students to local life and may be less expensive than other alternatives. They also separate the students from one another and force them to become more self-reliant. Of course, home stays are often time-consuming and difficult to arrange, and if a home stay falls through, serious problems can arise. Using bed and breakfasts or hostels rather than hotels can accomplish almost the same goal. B & B hosts are generally interested in people and eager to meet and visit with the students. Although honors students often charm their hosts, in either the home stay or the B & B, students must understand local customs and be able to discuss important concerns such as food allergies or dietary requirements in the appropriate language. In the case of serious food allergies or dietary requirements or restrictions, the faculty member may want to meet individually with students and assist them in learning vocabulary and emergency procedures.

Hostels, B & Bs, and hotels vary considerably in quality; checking carefully before booking space is important. A hostel can be wonderful, but one that has lukewarm water barely dripping from the faucet and bugs in the shower is not a welcome experience on the first night overseas. A good B & B can be delightful, but one without food nearby for other meals is problematic, particularly if the group does not have a vehicle at its disposal. Hotels can be marvelous, but the quality of facilities can vary widely. Whatever the lodging situation, students should be aware of what to bring or expect to purchase or rent. For instance, hostels often do not provide towels although some may rent them. Because the quality of the lodging contributes heavily to the success of the program, the faculty member should scout these locations in advance if possible.

Balancing the schedule is another critical element of program planning. An effective daily schedule may begin with a good breakfast and conversation about the day's activities, followed by one or two activities, some personal time in the afternoon, dinner, and one evening activity. Alternating a full day with a more relaxed one may prevent mental and physical overload, which occurs quickly for students in unfamiliar places. Doing so will also allow time for journal writing or other academic work, for students to visit with one another and help each other process what they have seen and done, and for some personal choices of experiences to pursue. Keeping a consistent daily schedule is not necessarily desirable; however, having regular meal times and focusing the program on quality rather than quantity will help to maintain good morale and create a successful experience for all involved. (See Appendix 3 for a sample schedule.)

Students, even social students, need time alone, particularly during a program that is intensive and compact. Balancing the need to socialize and to interact with others in the program and with local people with the need for reflection is critical to ensure that everyone in the program, including the faculty member, functions at the highest possible level. Allowing students to plan personal time during the trip for whatever purpose, whether it is a walk in a local park or shopping for souvenirs, will help to alleviate frustration and exhaustion. While a little frustration in the face of challenge is good, scheduling everything very closely; keeping students in vans, buses, or trains several days running; or marching quickly from site to site in a large city and consequently exhausting them will almost certainly lead to illness, personal frustration, and discord within the group.

CONCLUSION

A short-term study abroad program can be a valuable educational experience for students. Program planning must start with academics, but preparing students for the experience—academically, culturally, and pragmatically—is critical to the success of a short-term study abroad adventure. The faculty leader must pay careful attention to program logistics, too; program directors must balance quality and quantity, cost and efficiency, and cost and quality. The ideal program will be neither too concentrated nor a whirlwind; instead, it will provide students with an experience from which they will grow immensely and which they will never forget.

NOTES

[1]To my surprise, while leading one short-term study abroad program, email conversations with the host/tour guide enabled the group to rearrange the itinerary, saved the students nearly $300 apiece, and allowed an extra day in London.

[2]This point seems obvious; however, during one program, I used a tour guide who virtually refused to stop for rest stops, telling women students to duck behind bushes. I had to explain why this approach was unacceptable, an awkward experience for all involved.

[3]I have had varied experience with tour guides. During one program, we were provided a driver who was supposed to be a tour guide but who was completely unfamiliar with the itinerary and the locale. I have also had an extraordinary experience with a wonderful guide; he was also a B & B host whom I found on the Internet and with whom I corresponded in-depth before hiring him. He appreciated honors students' curiosity, got along extremely well with students, possessed a wealth of knowledge about the sites integral to the program, was open to suggestions about the itinerary, and made positive suggestions.

WORK CITED

Braid, Bernice, and Ada Long, eds. *Place as Text: Approaches to Active Learning.* 2nd ed. Lincoln: National Collegiate Honors Council, 2010. NCHC Monograph Series. Print.

APPENDIX 1

Guidebooks

Guidebooks come in a variety of sizes, configurations, foci, and helpfulness. I have no fewer than fourteen guidebooks for London and Great Britain. Some are replete with color photos; some have no photos whatsoever. One is slightly over 100 pages; another is nearly 700 pages. Some have interesting historical and cultural information while others concentrate on tourist sites. Several include information on climate, money, tipping, emergency procedures, using telephones, and purchasing theatre tickets. One focuses on walking tours, one on Arthurian sites. Choosing one guidebook that will cover everything is difficult if not impossible.

During the preparation stage, I prefer thorough, in-depth books that include the most famous sites as well as information on interesting, less famous displays and materials. Information on history, culture, and accessibility are valuable before the program begins. Although these guides are often quite heavy and the airlines have severe weight restrictions, I carefully select the one best-suited to the program to bring along for group reference during the program.

For daily excursions, however, I find a pocket-sized guide more useful. While these guides often concentrate on the "Top 10" visited sites or on tourist attractions such as shopping or children's interests, they usually include the most important sites, often with accompanying maps of local areas, the city, and the subway system. They also generally include the best means of reaching the sites, and they comfortably fit into a pocket or bag.

One disadvantage of printed guides is that they may be wrong about fluid details like entry fees and opening and closing times. Checking the Internet for that information before leaving is wise.

Spending an afternoon in the travel section of a library or bookstore before purchasing one or more travel books is time well used. Some institutions and public libraries have good collections of travel books.

Before leaving, I require each student to purchase and carry a good map, preferably laminated, of any major city the group will explore for an appreciable length of time, and I strongly suggest that each person bring a pocket guide as well. I also advocate that people bring different guides in order to expand the variety of information available to the group.

APPENDIX 2

Preparing Students

Providing the following information before departure will give students the confidence to undertake some exploration and enculturation on their own:

- Food and tipping;
- Drinking policies (yours and the institution's);
- Local customs and behavioral expectations;
- Vocabulary that may cause confusion;
- Vocabulary necessary for health and safety (food allergies, medical conditions);
- Public restrooms (particularly restrooms that require payment);
- Public transportation;
- Money, exchange rates, and the costs of various items at the travel destinations;
- Safety issues (e.g., carrying money and passports wisely, watching for pickpocketing in crowded areas, knowing which locations to avoid);
- Your policies, if any, concerning students' use of a buddy system;
- Emergency policies and procedures.

Many students also need a fair amount of guidance about some or all of the following topics:

- Budgeting for the program (food, entry fees not covered, etc.);
- Exchanging money;
- Using debit/credit cards (currently Discover credit cards are not accepted overseas) and using overseas ATMs safely;

- Making international telephone calls, including the cost impact of Smartphone use;

- Selecting clothing and shoes appropriate for the climate, location, and activities (discourage loud American gear);

- Packing (including the importance of packing light, what to place in carry-on and checked luggage, what to leave at home, TSA requirements);

- Understanding hotel, hostel, and B & B accommodations and amenities;

- Selecting travel guides and maps for destinations.

APPENDIX 3

Sample Schedule

England:
Exploring King Arthur's Genesis

Sunday, May 5
Depart Omaha.

Monday, May 6
Arrive Heathrow @ 6:00–7:00 a.m., pick up by host. Winchester, Arthur's military headquarters, Great Hall, (ersatz) Round Table, Winchester Cathedral, Jane Austen's grave and memorial, Cathedral Library to see medieval manuscripts. Water permitting, the crypts. Time permitting, the Bishop's Palace, and the Westgate Museum if it is open. On the way to Glastonbury, climb South Cadbury Castle, the most likely site of Camelot. Arrival in Glastonbury late afternoon, check into the B & B, dinner in a local restaurant (included in the price of the B & B). The group is together for most of the day—they may separate in Winchester Cathedral.

Tuesday, May 7
(Optional Tor climb at sunrise/sunset on most days.) Tour Wood-henge, Avebury, West Kennett Longbarrow, Silbury Hill. Lunch on the road. Visit Stonehenge at sunset. Dinner in a restaurant or take-away upon return to Glastonbury. The group is together for the entire day.

Wednesday, May 8
Tour Glastonbury Tor, Chalice Well Gardens. Lunch picnic in the garden meadow. Visit Glastonbury Abbey and meet with Arthurian historian Geoffrey Ashe. Dinner take-away, meeting in the B & B. This day involves no travel—we will also have some time to separate and explore Glastonbury individually, write, and relax a bit.

Thursday, May 9
Early breakfast followed by visit to Tintagel, St. Nectan's Glen, Boscastle. Lunch at Tintagel, dinner possibly in Boscastle. Arrive back in Glastonbury late evening. This day is a full day of travel.

Friday, May 10
Travel to London via Cheddar Gorge. Arrive mid-afternoon. Possible theatre performance that evening. Dinner hinges on evening activities. This day is a partial day of travel.

Saturday, May 11
Temple service for those who wish to attend, and/or Portobello Market in the morning, choice of museums in the afternoon. Group meeting before dinner. London walk or theatre in the evening.

Sunday, May 12
Church service for those who wish to attend and/or the British Museum in the morning and the "Most Curious Tour," 2:00–4:00 p.m. Group meeting before dinner. London walk or theatre in the evening.

Monday, May 13
British Library Treasures Room in the morning, free time in afternoon, choice of museums to be determined individually. Group meeting before dinner. Theatre or London walk in the evening.

Tuesday, May 14
Full day in Oxford. Lecture at the Centre for Medieval and Renaissance Studies (CMRS), Bodleian Library tour, lunch at the Eagle and Child. Dinner/group meeting on return to London. Possible London walk or theatre in the evening.

Wednesday, May 15
Free day in London, choice of museums to be determined. Group meeting before dinner. London walk or theatre in the evening.

Thursday, May 16
Depart, mid-morning.

Friday, June 7
Final reflective journal due.

Important Points About This Schedule

- This study abroad program is an extension of a junior-level honors seminar, "Cultural Phenomena and the Arthurian Legend," which is taught in the spring each year. Students who participate have taken the course, or if they have not, they have demonstrated adequate academic background to participate, such as coursework in British literature or history. It is limited to honors students.

- Balance in this itinerary is central: group time vs. individual time, scheduled time vs. free time, required event vs. individual choice, quality time spent at sites rather than seeing a large number of them.

- For the first four nights, the group stays in a B & B, and the host is also the tour guide.

- The first two days are hectic and filled constantly.

- The third day in Glastonbury allows for more flexibility. While everyone visits the sites, students separate at them and have time for reflective writing, which is especially attractive in the Chalice Well Gardens and the Abbey, weather permitting.

- The B & B host is extremely generous in allowing the group to use the dining room for dinners. Students often buy at least one dinner at the Glastonbury co-op, pooling resources and contributions, which helps to reduce costs.

- The "Tor at sunrise/sunset" is optional—the experience is quite interesting and many students opt to climb the Tor (which is a challenge) several times at different times of day. In the morning, the students always hope to see the "mists of Avalon," which do exist and after which Marion Zimmer Bradley named her text, which is assigned reading in the class.

- The fourth day, the day of travel to Tintagel is long, but students have the opportunity to sleep in the van, which helps them to catch up a bit and avoid illness. The activities on that day, however, are strenuous.

334

- Both the B & B and the London hotel furnish full English breakfasts, vegetarian if desired. Students usually bring granola bars, trail mix, and other snacks for an inexpensive lunch.

- The only requirements in London are the British Library and Portobello Market; the latter is open only on Saturday. Students ebb and flow in groups following that, depending on their interests. The students come together each evening and share what they have seen. I do encourage students to see the Tate Britain, which contains a number of famous pictures associated with the legend, and to find the Temple of Mithras, which is associated with one of the versions of the legend they read.

- All students visit Oxford, where UN-L has a direct connection with CMRS, and students explore the city as well as have a lecture on Oxford history or the Arthurian legend.

- Otherwise, students are free to see museums, participate in London Walks, pursue other interests (bookstores tend to be popular), or visit memorials. Afternoon tea usually fits into the schedule.

- Most students opt to see one or two plays at Shakespeare's Globe, where we are "groundlings" for an extremely reasonable price. Tickets are purchased in advance to avoid sell-outs, and the group arrives an hour ahead of the opening time to secure standing room near the stage. This time often provides an opportunity to share ideas and suggestions and/or to meet other people who are also in line.

- This program has been well honed; this itinerary represents the seventh time it has been run. Nevertheless, something changes every time it is offered, usually for the better.

PREPARING TOMORROW'S GLOBAL LEADERS

Honors International Education

PART IV:

MODEL HONORS INTERNATIONAL COURSES

MODEL COURSE 1

Hiroshima Peace Study
(3 credits)

This interdisciplinary course is planned around a 13-day trip to Hiroshima and Nagasaki, Japan, where the U.S. dropped atomic bombs in August 1945. Students read works of fiction and poetry addressing the A-Bombs' aftermath, pursue individual projects that examine or interpret A-Bomb experiences, and carry out fieldwork assignments and volunteer work at the Hiroshima Peace Memorial Museum and Park and Nagasaki Peace Memorial Museum. In both Hiroshima and Nagasaki, the students have opportunities to listen to the A-Bomb survivors' stories and interview them. At Hiroshima National Peace Memorial Hall for the Atomic Bomb Victims, the students use archival materials and a database for their research. Through the presentation at the end of the semester, the students participate in the dissemination of Hiroshima's peace message.

Contact
Kyoko Amano, Associate Professor of English and Associate Director of the Honors College, University of Indianapolis <amano@uindy.edu>.

Disciplines
English, education, and nursing.

When
May.

Faculty
Team-taught by Kyoko Amano, English, and Nanci Vargus, Education, or Cheryl Shore, Nursing.

Enrollment
12, primarily first- and second-year students.

Major Learning Outcomes

The primary goal is to understand universal human concerns through an examination of the peace message of Hiroshima and Nagasaki and to participate in the dissemination of that message.

Required Readings

Ibuse, Masuji. *Black Rain*. Trans. John Baster. Tokyo: Kodansha International, 1994. Print.

Kosakai, Yoshiteru. *Hiroshima Peace Reader*. 6th ed. Trans. Akira and Michiko Tashiro. Hiroshima: Hiroshima Peace Culture Foundation, 1988. Print.

Elective Readings and Viewing Materials Used for Students' Class Reports

"A-Bomb Drawings by Survivors." Hiroshima Peace Memorial Commission. Web. 18 Feb. 2013.

Children of Nagasaki. Dir. Keisuke Kinoshita. Hori Production. 1983. DVD.

Coerr, Eleanor, and Ronald Himler. *Sadako and the Thousand Paper Cranes*. New York: Puffin, 1999. Print.

Hiroshima: A Mother's Prayer. Dir. Motoo Ogasawara. Hiroshima Peace Memorial Museum. 1990. DVD.

Hiroshima Peace Memorial Commission. *The Spirit of Hiroshima*. City of Hiroshima, 1999. Print.

Maruki, Toshi. *Hiroshima no Pika*. Trans. Komine Shoten. New York: Lothrop, Lee & Shepard Books, 1980. Print.

On a Paper Crane: Tomoko's Adventure. Great Plains National Instructional Television Library. 1987. DVD.

Records of the Nagasaki Atomic Bombing. Nagasaki Atomic Bomb Museum. Web. 18 Feb. 2013.

Assignments

- Report to the class (books or films chosen from the list above) and a 4-page written version.

- Journal: a thoughtful reflection of activities, including field (research) work and/or volunteering.

- Field research at the Hiroshima National Peace Memorial Hall for the Atomic Bomb Victims.

- Final paper: (4 to 6 pages) based on field work in Hiroshima, participating in the dissemination of Hiroshima and Nagasaki's peace message and demonstrating understanding of human concerns.

- Presentation to the campus community, approximately 10 minutes long, based on the final paper.

Itinerary and Major Activities

- Hiroshima: Peace Memorial Museum and Park, Hiroshima Castle, Radiation Effect Institute, United Nations Institute for Training and Research, Hiroshima Peace Institute, Hiroshima National Peace Memorial Hall or the Atomic Bomb Victims, Shukkei-en Garden (observe A-Bomb trees, meet with Hiroshima City University students, listen to the A-Bomb survivor's story and interview the survivor).

- Miyajima Island (off the coast of Hiroshima): Itsukushima Shrine, hike Mt. Misen.

- Nagasaki: Nagasaki Peace Memorial Museum; tour Nagasaki, listen to the A-Bomb survivor's story and interview the survivor.

- Kyoto: stay at a monastery (Shunko-in Temple); visit temples, shrines, and castles; Japanese Tea Ceremony by a tea master; lectures on Buddhist funeral readings (as it relates to Ibuse's *Black Rain*); and a meditation by Rev. Taka Kawakami.

Course Strengths

The trip to Hiroshima enhances the content of the books students read and the documentary films they viewed previously in class. The students have opportunities in Hiroshima and Nagasaki to listen to and interpret A-Bomb survivors' stories and interview them. Also, there will be lectures by peace-keeping/conflict-management specialists from the United Nations Institute for Training and Research and the Hiroshima Peace Institute, as well as lectures by scholars from the Radiation Effect Institute. The guided tours of Hiroshima and Nagasaki include A-Bomb sites that are not open to the public.

Community-Based Leadership:
Visions of Hope from South Africa
(3 credit hours)

This course provides a firsthand encounter with the lives of diverse communities and peoples of South Africa. Students are given an active laboratory to put into place the leadership theories and concepts studied in a classroom context, and they have multiple opportunities for interpersonal engagement with peers, professors, community leaders, and college students in South Africa. The course combines research with a service component. Our South African hosts have identified two populations in critical need that we assist: orphaned teen heads of households and elderly women who have primary care responsibility for grandchildren. The commonality for both populations is the loss of parents and children to HIV-AIDS.

Contact

Kevin Dean, Professor of Communication Studies and Director of the Honors College, West Chester University of Pennsylvania <kdean@wcupa.edu>.

Disciplines

Political science, communication, history, and theology.

When

Spring term: weekly two-hour class sessions during the semester and a twelve-day international experience in South Africa. During the first portion, students receive intensive training in methodology, strategies, and related technology in conducting a community-needs assessment. During the second portion, students are immersed in the history, culture, political/social, and theological context of contemporary South Africa.

Faculty
Team-taught by two faculty, Kevin Dean, Professor of Communication Studies, and Dr. Laurie Bernotsky, Professor of Political Communication; supplemented by guest speakers.

Enrollment
18–26 students, freshmen-seniors.

Major Learning Outcomes
- Skills in research methodology.

- Knowledge of leadership theories.

- Capabilities of leadership skills.

- Heightened awareness of students' role in a global society.

- Personal commitment to community service.

Required Readings
Thompson, Leonard. *A History of South Africa*, 3rd ed. New Haven, CT: Yale UP, 2001. Print.

Tutu, Desmond. *No Future Without Forgiveness*. New York: Image, 1979. Print.

Wooten, James. *We Are All the Same*. New York: Penguin, 2004. Print.

Assignments
All students keep a leadership journal (daily entries during the international portion of the class) in which they reflect on a given daily prompt and offer their own insights into each day's experience. They also conduct a community-needs assessment project. Working in pairs on in-depth, 90-minute interviews with individuals identified by our South African hosts, each team conducts a minimum of two interviews with students alternating roles between interviewer and scribe. Each team produces a full transcription of each interview.

Itinerary and Major Activities
A nine-day stay based in Cape Town, an ideal laboratory setting. The city houses institutions of higher education and health research centers and represents a critical agricultural region to support the

country's economic base. It is also cradle to some of the most dramatic moments in the country's struggle with apartheid.

While in the Cape Town area, students are given opportunities to interact with South African students, educators, theologians, politicians, environmentalists, journalists, and artists to develop skills and share a vision to build a better society. Days are split between presentations and small-group discussions with leaders representing particular areas and field trips giving participants firsthand experience with the diversity that pervades South African life, such as Robben Island, Table Mountain, H.E.L.P. Soup Ministries, Guguletu Township, elementary schools, and mission projects. A day is spent in the Sparrow Village AIDS orphanage.

Because of the critical importance of environmental conservation to the African continent, the final phase of the international program involves a two-to-three-day experience at a game park. Here students have the experience of seeing animal and land conservation while exploring nature's majesty.

Course Strengths

The key to success is the interpersonal engagement students receive through multiple opportunities for personal dialog with cultural others and the personal investment through an intellectual service project requested and shaped by our South African hosts.

Experiencing the New Europe
(6 credits)

This four-week international summer program combines class-room study with onsite experiential learning to explore cultural, political, and economic transformation in an urban context. It is composed of two courses:

Explorations of Modernity, which explores the culture and collective experience of people in Central Europe—a territory that includes Ukrainians, Poles, Czechs, Slovaks, Hungarians, Austrians, Slovenes, Croats, Serbs, and, historically, the majority of Europe's Jews and Gypsies; and *Urban Research Seminar*, which introduces students to methods of qualitative research used by ethnographers to study the changes in the Polish city of Wroclaw over time.

Exploring architectural remains and the stories of the city's inhabitants, students spend most of their time outside of the classroom, working in groups under the supervision of instructors who use a variety of research techniques—interviews, participant observation, data recording (notes, film, photography, audio recording), and archival and library research. This course culminates in the creation of research papers and presentations at Wroclaw City Hall.

Through its interactive curriculum, Experiencing the New Europe explores how large processes of geopolitical change—the aftermath of WWII, ethnic and national upheaval, the fall of Communism, democratization, European integration—play out in the local setting of a large European city. Wroclaw, an academic and historical center located in southwestern Poland, offers a unique urban and cultural experience for students who are interested in studying European culture, history, and politics.

Contact
Donna Kowal, Director of College Honors Program, The College at
Brockport, State University of New York <dkowal@brockport.edu>.

Disciplines
History, political science, international studies, and cultural
studies.

When
June/July.

Faculty
Team-taught by three instructors.

Enrollment
15 (targeting juniors).

Major Learning Outcomes
A strong emphasis is placed on collaborative and experiential
learning; students confront the complexity of ethnic tension and
geopolitical conflict in a way that is highly personal—by meeting
and interviewing city leaders and inhabitants rather than simply
reading or conducting library research.

Assignments

"Urban Research Seminar" (3 cr.)

Using the urban space of the city of Wroclaw as a laboratory, students investigate how the past interacts with the present dynamics
of a twenty-first-century Central European city. A reading packet is
provided to seminar participants and includes articles by historians,
anthropologists, sociologists, and political scientists. For the course
project, students work in groups and conduct "action research"—
that is, interviews, site visits, observations, and exchanges with academic experts, city officials, and local citizens—to understand the
cultural and social forces that have influenced the city's transformation over time. Students also visit other cities in the region to gain a
comparative perspective of urban spaces. The course culminates in
a student-led tour through a distinct urban space or site designed
to introduce visitors to Wroclaw and tell a story about how its past

connects with its present. Students prepare the narrative for the tour as well as visual materials. For examples of student work, see <http://wroclawonyourown.pl/the-project>.

"Explorations in Modernity: Lessons from Central Europe" (3 cr.)

 Looking at politics through the lens of arts, literature, and film, this seminar examines the culture and collective experience of the region that lies between Germany and Russia. Participants explore the role of writers, poets, artists, and workers in instigating and nourishing modern political movements. In addition to a packet of journal articles, students read *Performative Democracy* by Elzbieta Matynia (Paradigm Publishers, 2009). The city and site visits included in the program enable students to connect their travel experiences with the readings. In addition to participating in seminar discussions, each student develops a proposal for a research paper. Most students choose a topic that intersects with their academic major in order to earn major elective credit. The paper is completed and submitted after students return to the United States.

Itinerary and Major Activities

Participants visit a variety of sites, including architectural landmarks, museums, memorials, castles, churches, synagogues, Jewish cemeteries, and a former Stasi prison. Special attention is paid to areas and ethnic groups that have been transformed by war and the transition from totalitarianism to democracy.

- Destinations in Poland: Wroclaw, Krakow, and Auschwitz-Birkenau (Oswiecim).

- Destination in Czech Republic: Prague.

- Destination in Germany: Berlin.

- World Heritage Sites included in the program: Centennial Hall (Wroclaw), Auschwitz-Birkenau (Oswiecim), Krakow's Old Town, Wieliczka Salt Mine, and Prague's Old Town.

Course Strengths

The program is unique in bringing American and Polish students together to explore the struggle for democracy and peace in Central and Eastern Europe, using the city of Wroclaw as a laboratory for understanding the transformation of Europe. Students have the opportunity to get to know the city and feel connected to the people, in addition to visiting other urban centers in the region.

Monsters and Modernism
(3 credit hours)

This course focuses on the human fascination with otherness that can be traced back to ancient Greece (the Cyclops in Homer's *The Odyssey* and other mythical half-human monsters) and even earlier to the allegorical tales of ancient Egypt and Mesopotamia. Modern otherness is highlighted in the debates surrounding identity politics—the civil rights, feminist, and, in particular, disability rights movements. The course considers the various theories and methods that social scientists employ to examine identity (including lengthy conversations about postmodernism and alternative epistemologies) in an attempt to understand how normalcy is socially determined. Students will take a close look at popular culture, specifically how disability and other differences among individuals are portrayed in film, television, and print media. Students will read and discuss a wide variety of sources, write several substantive papers responding to major class themes, and engage in Socratic dialog during class meetings and in small groups.

Contact
Jack Trammell, Director of the Honors Program, Randolph-Macon College <jtrammel@rmc>.

Disciplines
Sociology, history, and philosophy.

When
January (ten days on campus followed by nine days in Romania and the Czech Republic).

Faculty
Team-taught by Jack Trammell and Tom Inge, American Studies/ English.

Enrollment
10.

Major Learning Outcomes

- Students will become familiar with the approach of Richard Kearney in his *Strangers, Gods and Monsters: Interpreting Otherness* (Routledge, 2002*)* and the deep problems of human nature associated with otherness.

- Students will consider disability as a historical mismatch with monstrosity.

- Students will develop a language for discussing cultural and identity boundaries.

Required Readings

Kafka, Franz. *Metamorphosis and Other Stories*. Trans. Michael Hofman. New York: Penguin, 2007. Print.

Moore, Alan. *The League of Extraordinary Gentlemen*. Vol. 1. La Jolla, CA: America's Best Comics, 2002. Print.

Stoker, Bram. *Dracula*. Ed. Nina Auerbach and David J. Skal. New York: Norton, 1997. Print.

Wilson, Paul, ed. *Prague: A Traveler's Literary Companion*. San Francisco: Whereabouts P, 1995. Print.

Itinerary and Major Activities

- Romania: sites associated with the historic figure of Prince Vlad Dracule in Wallachia and Transylvania (Bucharest, Sibiu, Sighisoara, Bran, and Brasov).

- Czech Republic: sites associated with Franz Kafka and the Golem in Prague.

Course Strengths

The course exposes students to pertinent topics in both literature and philosophy and, through their travels, to the dividing lines between East and West and between the rational and the irrational (or monstrous sublime in Kantian terms).

Topography and Monuments of Ancient Greece
(3 credits)

This course is an onsite examination of the material evidence relevant to our understanding of Greek antiquity from the Stone Age to the Byzantine period (ca. 20,000 BCE–15th century CE). Students examine both the magnificent (palaces, fortifications, temples, sculpture) and the mundane (pottery, coinage, inscriptions, burials). Archaeological evidence is considered in light of ancient epigraphic and historical sources. All lectures and discussions take place on archaeological sites and in museums.

Contact

Karl M. Petruso, Dean of the Honors College and Professor of Anthropology, University of Texas at Arlington <petruso@uta.edu>.

Disciplines

Archaeology, anthropology, and history.

When

Early summer (three weeks, late May to mid-June).

Faculty

Karl M. Petruso. The course is coordinated with a second 3-credit course, Ancient Greek Mythology and Civilization, taught by Charles Chiasson (Classics Program). All students enroll in both courses.

Enrollment

12–16.

Major Learning Outcomes

- Students will understand the major phases in the development of material culture in Greece from the Paleolithic period to late classical antiquity, with a focus on the Late Bronze Age and Classical period (ca. 1500–400 BCE). They will develop an ability to recognize stylistic evolution in architecture (particularly temples) and art (stone sculpture and pottery painting).

- Students will understand the impact of the physical environment (climate, landscape, and natural resources) on the development of culture throughout antiquity by traveling through the Mediterranean on foot, by coach, and by boat.

- Students will understand the history of technology in this part of the world from the period of hunting and gathering through the invention of agriculture to the rise and evolution of several complex societies.

- Students will, through their visits to many archaeological sites and museums, gain an appreciation of aesthetic, pedagogical, and political decisions that are made in the course of determining how the history and culture of a people are presented to the public.

Required Readings

Readings are assigned from primary sources (including Homer, Herodotus, and Thucydides) and inscriptions as well as from modern archaeological and historical scholarship. Texts in past offerings have included William Biers, *The Archaeology of Greece* (Ithaca: Cornell UP, 1996); James Whitley, *The Archaeology of Ancient Greece* (Cambridge UP, 2001); Robert Morkot, *Penguin Historical Atlas of Ancient Greece* (Penguin, 1997); John Camp and Craig Mauzy, *The Athenian Agora: A Guide to the Excavations and Museum* (Princeton: American School of Classical Studies at Athens, 2010). In addition, a reader with pertinent scholarly articles, site plans, and reconstructions is provided.

Assignments

All students research a chosen topic before departure and present in country an oral report to the class on a site, monument, or archaeological problem; the report is then reconfigured and extended as a research paper to be submitted later in the summer. There is one quiz before arrival in Greece and a final exam written after the students return.

Itinerary and Major Activities

- The program is based in Athens: detailed study of the buildings on the Acropolis in Athens and in the Athenian Agora; visits to Athens museums with important holdings of archaeological materials, including the National, Acropolis, Agora, Kerameikos, and Byzantine Museums.

- Day trips out of Athens by hired coach to the battlefield and tumulus of the Athenians at Marathon, the Sanctuary of Artemis at Brauron, and the Sanctuary of Poseidon at Sounion.

- Overnight voyage by steamship to Crete to visit the Minoan palaces of Knossos, Phaistos, and Mallia as well as the Bronze Age and classical sites of Gournia, Arkhanes, Vathypetro, Tylissos, Aghia Triada, and Gortyn.

- Eight-day trip to the Peloponnesos and Central Greece: the Sanctuary of Demeter at Eleusis, the Mycenaean palaces and citadels of Mycenae and Tiryns, the Sanctuary of Asklepios and theater at Epidauros, the Franchthi Cave, the Early Bronze Age palace at Lerna, the ancient city of Sparta and the Sanctuary of Artemis Orthia, the Byzantine city of Mystra, the Mycenaean palace at Pylos, the Sanctuary of Zeus at Olympia, and the Sanctuaries of Apollo and Athena Pronaia at Delphi.

Course Strengths

This three-week program is travel-intensive. It is modeled on the venerable summer program of the American School of Classical Studies at Athens, which for many decades has introduced graduate students and college and university faculty specializing in classical studies to ancient Greek culture through its surviving architecture, arts, inscriptions, and artifacts of daily life, in historical context. The program demands a good deal of hiking in countryside and city, in any weather, reinforcing the principle that the country itself is the classroom. Special effort is made to encourage students to understand and appreciate the locations of ancient fortifications, palaces, cities, towns, and sanctuaries within the landscape, and to consider the economic, political, environmental, and religious traditions that determined their establishment and evolution.

Scholars' Semester in Oxford
(17 credits)

The Scholars' Semester in Oxford (SSO) is for students who want to study intensively and to a high standard. Students develop their academic writing and research skills while exploring the disciplines and interests of their choice. Students can build a coherent program of study by selecting options within a concentration. SSO serves students primarily in the humanities and some social sciences although students in all majors may apply. Applicants are generally honors and other very high-achieving students. Applicants must have a 3.5 GPA to be considered for the program.

The tutorial is central to the pedagogical approach of SSO and is the heart of undergraduate teaching at Oxford. It is an hour-long conversation between a tutor who is engaged in research and one student who has spent the week reading and writing an essay in response to an assigned, searching question.

SSO students are Registered Visiting Members of the University, which offers substantially enhanced privileges and opportunities over and above being an affiliate of a college, which is the more common approach. They receive a transcript from Wycliffe Hall, University of Oxford.

Contact
Stan Rosenberg, Director, Scholarship & Christianity In Oxford (SCIO), in partnership with Wycliffe Hall, University of Oxford <stan.rosenberg@wycliffe.ox.ac.uk>.

Disciplines
Art history, classics, English language and literature, history, modern languages, musicology, philosophy, psychology, and theology.

When

Michaelmas (Autumn) term: early September to mid-December; Hilary (Spring) term: early January to mid-April.

Faculty

Individual tutorials are taught by Oxford academics. The British Studies core course and faculty-led seminars are team-taught. Approximately 120 faculty deliver tutorials.

Enrollment

55 students per term (semester or year). Juniors, seniors, and graduate students are the target population.

Major Learning Outcomes

SSO students enroll in a primary and secondary tutorial, the British Studies Core (Landscape) course, and an integrative seminar (or thesis in the case of second-term students).

1. Tutorials (9 semester credits: 6 for the primary tutorial and 3 for the secondary tutorial). Students enroll in two: a primary meeting weekly and a secondary meeting fortnightly. Each tutorial has its own particular aims and objectives. In addition, there are aims and objectives that transcend the subject matter. (See below.) Students seek to develop their ability to find their own voice as writers within their discipline, not simply relating the views and findings of others, but using them to develop their own understanding and argument. Students develop their ability to:

   - master a subject in a short period of time, acquiring knowledge of both primary and secondary texts and learning to distinguish clearly the function of each;

   - read on several levels at once: in literary texts reading simultaneously for register, voice, tone, and technical competence in the genre or in historical texts reading simultaneously for findings and method;

   - defend or emend their views in the tutorial in the face of sustained questioning;

- write persuasively and engagingly, following the conventions of their own discipline;

- produce written work of high quality.

2. British Studies core course (4 semester credits). Students develop their ability to:

   - read and understand the British landscape through a sound knowledge of British culture;

   - see the impact of historical and biographical context on literary texts; philosophical and theological ideas; and works of art, architecture, and music;

   - differentiate between history, myth, and heritage preservation and examine critically what they see in historic sites and museums in Britain and elsewhere;

   - pose purposeful questions about the past and answer them imaginatively;

   - see through the eyes of people from other eras and other countries as a means of understanding Britain in past periods and of developing a critical approach to universalist rhetoric;

   - assess often incomplete evidence about the past critically and know what can legitimately be inferred from it.

3. Thesis (4 semester credits). Students should develop their ability to:
   - pose purposeful academic questions and answer them imaginatively and appropriately;

   - assess evidence critically and understand what can legitimately be inferred from it;

   - find their own voice as a writer within their discipline, not simply relating the views and findings of others, but using them to develop their own understanding and argument;

   - design and execute an independent research project.

Itinerary and Major Activities

Study in a system, structure, and pedagogy profoundly different from those of higher education in the U.S. The program is primarily based in Oxford but with field trips to Bath, Coventry, Hampton Court, Portsmouth, Salisbury, St. Albans, and Winchester. Optional field trips to the Cotswolds, Dorchester, the Lake District, London, and Wales. Occasional trips to Europe including Auschwitz, Bologna, Ravenna, Rome, and Venice.

Course Strengths

Learning critical-thinking and writing skills, including how to accept substantial criticism in order to improve and how to develop their own voices as writers. Students write approximately 150 pages in 15 or 16 essays over the course of the term. Textbooks are not used; rather, students work only from research materials, such as monographs, articles, and book reviews. Students learn not to depend on or echo authorities, including their tutors, but to come to their own conclusions, and they learn to defend their positions and amend them as evidence and analysis warrant. For these reasons, the program provides excellent preparation for graduate and professional school.

Youth Culture/Contemporary Youth:
The Making of a New Italy
(15 credits)

This course addresses youth identity and, more broadly, the identity of a country navigating extreme demographic changes. Students engage deeply with the complex interplay of the younger population in Rome and the influence of the nation state and its investment in maintaining the illusion of one cohesive "Italian Identity." Students work together and interact with onsite partners as well as youth groups to learn about youth identity and national identity through a combination of classroom instruction and excursions to schools; community, ethnic, and arts centers; and nonprofit social organizations.

The credits are distributed as follows: background in immigration and education policy in Italy and preparation for service-learning placement (10 credits); language instruction (3 credits); independent research projects related to service learning (2 credits).

Contact
Julie Villegas, Associate Director of the Honors Program, University of Washington <villegas@uw.edu>.

Disciplines
Cultural studies, English, migration studies, and education.

When
Winter term (early January to mid-March).

Faculty
Team-taught by Julie Villegas and Manka Varghese, Education. Partners and guest lecturers include teachers in the Italian public school system, members of political organizations who work directly with Italy's youth, and leaders of nonprofit and educational institutions

who influence decisions about the services and programs provided to Italy's youth.

Enrollment

16–20 honors program and education students.

Major Learning Outcomes

- Identifying key social issues pertaining to youth, education, immigration, and culture.

- Engaging thoughtfully in the service sites.

- Developing project topics related to students' service projects.

- Viewing the city as art (i.e., seeing as a writer and artist would, utilizing metaphors in the creative process).

- Learning a variety of social science and humanities methods.

- Developing team processes.

- Learning about Roman history, art, culture, cultural studies, and politics.

Required Readings

Cahill, Susan, ed. *The Smiles of Rome: Literary Companion for Readers and Travelers.* New York: Ballantine, 2005. Print.

Forgacs, David, ed. *Italian Cultural Studies: An Introduction.* Oxford: Oxford UP, 1996. Print.

Grillo, Ralph, and Jeff Pratt, eds. *The Politics of Recognizing Difference: Multiculturalism Italian Style.* Farnham, UK: Ashgate, 2002. Print.

Hanley, Lisa, Blair Ruble, and Alison Garland, eds. *Immigration and Integration in Urban Communities.* Baltimore: Johns Hopkins UP, 2008. Print.

Jeffrey, Craig, and Jane Dyson, eds. *Telling Young Lives: Portraits in Global Youth.* Philadelphia: Temple UP, 2008. Print.

Lakhous, Amara. *Clash of Civilizations Over an Elevator in Piazza Vittorio.* New York: Europa, 2008. Print.

Orton, Marie, and Graziella Parati. *Multicultural Literature in Contemporary Italy.* Madison, NJ: Fairleigh Dickinson UP, 2007. Print.

Wong, Aliza S. *Race and the Nation in Liberal Italy, 1861–1911: Meridionalism, Empire, and Diaspora.* Basingstoke, UK: Palgrave Macmillan, 2006. Print.

Itinerary and Major Activities

A unique component of this program is participants' involvement in service projects. Students work with schools and community and social welfare organizations as well as nonprofit artists' collectives. The research projects/topics that students choose for their final assignment align with their service projects. Throughout the program, students are asked to reflect on how youths' lives and their intersection with institutions compare with what is happening in the United States, especially in Seattle.

The course also includes excursions to main historical sites of the city with instruction in both ancient and contemporary art in Rome and the surrounding area (the Pantheon, Vatican City, the Colosseum, the Contemporary Art Museum, the Forum Romanum, and Ostia Antica), as well as a weekend trip to Naples.

Course Strengths

- Interdisciplinary curriculum.

- Community partners.

- Service learning and research (individually as well as in small groups).

- Course blog with student blogs attached; video logs; weekly written reflections.

- Final presentations to an audience composed of Roman teachers, community leaders, students, and local friends of the University of Washington Rome Center.

French Communication and Culture
(3 credits)

This two-part sequence focuses on the development of interpersonal, interpretive, and presentational skills through access to authentic materials and participation in collaborative work with native speakers of French. During the year, students work closely with a class in France in a collaborative project. Each student has at least one French partner. The students communicate in real time, exchange emails, and discuss cultural issues. Some of the special features of this course include frequent correspondence with French students via email, Twitter, and Facebook; videoconferencing with webcams and microphones; and live chat sessions. American students travel to Marne la Vallée (this component is optional) to visit their French correspondents during spring break.

Contact
Lara Lomicka Anderson, Associate Professor of French and Applied Linguistics, University of South Carolina <lomicka@sc.edu>.

Discipline
French.

When
Fall and spring semesters.

Faculty
Team-taught by Lara Lomicka Anderson and Stacey Benoit of École Nationale des Ponts et Chaussées (ENPC).

Enrollment
10–12.

Major Learning Outcomes

- Building and honing interpersonal, presentational, and interpretive communication skills; increasing vocabulary and fluency in French.

- Discovering and learning about French culture through native speaker partners, classes at school, and educational visits.

- Developing better understanding of oneself and the other, building critical-thinking skills; furthering intercultural experience.

Assignments

Students prepare a final portfolio (an organized collection of evidence used by teachers and students to document the growth of a student's learning and efforts towards the accomplishment of specific learning goals). The portfolio contains quizzes, email exchanges, examples of Twitter posts and Facebook discussions, homework, and complete transcripts of out-of-class chats completed by the student in the fall, along with his or her own analysis of the extent to which that work reflects progress made and goals achieved during the semester. The portfolio is an exercise of reflection; students are urged to be honest, critical, and reflective in their responses.

Itinerary and Major Activities

Students travel to France for 10 days during spring break. The major destinations and activities are the following:

- Highlights in Paris and Vincennes: École Nationale des Ponts et Chaussées, Louvre, Orsay Museum, Hotel de Ville (town hall), Eiffel Tower, Fragonard Perfume Museum, Chateau de Vincennes, Carnavalet Museum, Victor Hugo Home, guided tour of Revolutionary Paris, and Pompidou Modern Art Museum;

- Interactions with classes: ENPC English classes, Romainville elementary school, sports classes;

- Cultural visits: organ concert at Notre Dame Cathedral, cheese tasting, raclette dinner, chocolate and tea tasting, French film evening, and open-air market.

Course Strengths

- Offers a non-traditional way to learn languages, beyond the textbook, as students learn French with and from peers who are native speakers.

- Incorporates efficient use of technology (Skype, email, Twitter, Facebook, and iPod Touch) to facilitate communication and language learning outside class and to build community.

- Fosters personal connections with native-speaker partners who make learning French real, authentic, and meaningful.

- Fosters intercultural communication.

- Allows students to travel to meet partners and experience the other country after five months of virtual collaboration.

Cultures in Contact
(3 credits)

This course is designed to introduce students to a specific world culture (in this case the people of Belize) through a variety of methods. The readings include sociological, economic, historical, and fictional accounts of the country. The objective is to learn about Belize while also learning how to approach, study, and engage with a culture other than one's own. Students learn to be acutely aware of their ethnocentrism and the cultural lenses through which they examine difference. In so doing, they become familiar with current events and issues (both historical and contemporary) facing the people of the country. Understanding the complexity of issues surrounding cross-cultural contact is a major goal of the course.

Contact
Jesse Peters, Professor of English and Theatre, University of North Carolina, Pembroke <peters@uncp.edu>.

Disciplines
English, sociology, economics, and history.

When
Spring semester.

Faculty
Jesse Peters.

Enrollment
6.

Major Learning Outcomes
In many ways, this course is an exercise in what Mary Louise Pratt refers to as the "contact zone." She writes:

> I use [this term] to refer to the space of colonial encounters, the space in which peoples geographically and historically

separated come into contact with each other and establish ongoing relations, usually involving conditions of coercion, radical inequality, and intractable conflict. . . . By using the term 'contact,' I aim to foreground the interactive, improvisational dimensions of colonial encounters so easily ignored or suppressed by diffusionist accounts of conquest and domination. A 'contact' perspective emphasizes how subjects are constituted in and by their relations to each other. It treats the relations among colonizers and colonized, or travelers and 'travelees,' not in terms of separateness or apartheid, but in terms of co-presence, interaction, interlocking understandings and practices. (6–7)

Ultimately, students enrolled in this course gain new perspectives and strategies for approaching all types of cultural contact. They become comfortable negotiating differences and adapting to change, whether geographic or philosophical.

Required Readings

Bolland, O. Nigel. *Colonialism and Resistance in Belize: Essays in Historical Sociology.* Benque, BZ: Cubola, 2004. Print.

Geertz, Clifford. *The Interpretation of Cultures.* New York: Basic Books, 1997. Print.

Pratt, Mary Louise. *Imperial Eyes.* London: Routledge, 1992. Print.

Sutherland, Anne. *The Making of Belize: Globalization in the Margins.* New York: Bergin and Garvey, 1998. Print.

Thompson, Peter. *Belize: A Concise History.* Oxford, UK: MacMillan, 2004. Print.

Assignments

- Blackboard discussion journal.

- Individual essay.

- Panel presentation.

- Contact essay.

- Midterm and final exams.

Itinerary and Major Activities

The course includes a one-week trip to Belize either over spring break or immediately following spring commencement. The destinations include Jaguar Preserve (Mayan Village Center), Lamanai (Mayan Ruins), Hopkins (Garifuna), Crooked Tree (Creole), and Caye Caulker (Rasta/Island Life).

Course Strengths

This course stems from a philosophy of reflective engagement with other cultures. It encourages international travel but also pushes students to move beyond the position of "tourist." It draws on the ideas of Mary Louise Pratt and is infused with the strategies of the City as Text™ methodology. This framework can be layered over any travel/cultural class in honors education.

Intercultural Leadership
(3 credits)

This seminar-style, community-based learning course introduces students to an array of leadership paradigms arising from non-Western societies such as those found in Australia, Native America, and Mexico. The course includes two components: a distance-learning module and an eleven-day community-based learning module on Mexico's Yucatan peninsula. Through readings, discussions, assignments, and a service project in the Mayan village of Yuncu, students explore, analyze, observe, interact with, and reflect upon non-Western leadership models in the literature and in practice.

Contact
Loree Crow, Associate Director for Honors, University of Northern Colorado <loree.crow@unco.edu>.

Disciplines
Anthropology and leadership.

When
Early June to late July (6 weeks online followed by 11 days in the Yucatan).

Faculty
Team-taught by two anthropology and leadership instructors.

Enrollment
7–12 upperclassmen. The course is open not only to honors students but also to Leadership Program students and those from other disciplines on campus at the instructors' discretion.

Major Learning Outcomes
Students develop abilities to
- describe examples of non-Western leadership;
- observe and identify elements of non-Western leadership models;

- compare and contrast Western and non-Western leadership paradigms;

- evaluate the efficacy of particular elements of non-Western leadership models for their own leadership contexts (workplace, school, community).

This course is highly individualized and relies heavily on student reflection. Students are expected to initiate regular (i.e., weekly) communication with the director. Activities include video lectures, reading assignments, student research, and multimedia assignments.

Students in the Intercultural Leadership course join others in a Peace College Mexican Civilization course to run a summer day camp for residents in Yuncu. The camp's activities include games, English language lessons, singing, and playing soccer for the younger children; activities for older individuals include English lessons, computer training, and a collaborative photovoice-style project. Participants in this project take our students on tours of their village, photograph aspects that are "close to their hearts," and create PowerPoint presentations with photos and narrative.

Required Readings

Allston, Lee J., Shannan Mattiace, and Tomas Nonnenmache. "Coercion, Culture, and Contracts: Labor and Debt on Henequen Haciendas in Yucatan, Mexico, 1870–1915." *Journal of Economic History* 69 (2009): 104–37. Print.

Bevington, Gary. *Maya for Travelers and Students*. Austin: U of Texas P, 1995. Print.

Bordas, Juana. *Salsa, Soul, and Spirit: Leadership for a Multicultural Age*. San Francisco: Berrett-Koehler, 2007. Print.

Carr, Joe P., and Witynski, Karen. *The New Hacienda*. Layton, UT: Gibbs Smith, 2003. Print.

Cramer, Mark. *Culture Shock! Mexico: A Guide to Customs and Etiquette*. Portland, OR: Graphic Arts Center, 2002. Print.

Huck, George Ann, and Jann E. Freed. *Women of the Yucatan: Thirty Who Dare to Change Their World.* Jefferson, NC: McFarland, 2010. Print.

Julien, Mark, Barry Wright, and Deborah Zinni. "Stories from the Circle: Leadership Lessons Learned from Aboriginal Leaders." *Leadership Quarterly* 21 (2010): 114–26. Print.

Northouse, Peter G. *Leadership: Theory and Practice.* 5th ed. Los Angeles: Sage, 2010. Print.

Assignments

- Online response questions.

- Leadership interview.

- Dimensions of culture questionnaire and analysis.

- Narrative and leadership.

- Photojournal project.

- End-of-semester critical reflection.

- "Embracing Community Symposium" slide submission.

Itinerary and Major Activities

Most days are spent at the Service-Learning Kids' Camp with picnic lunches and dinners cooked by the participants with occasional cooking lessons from Maya women. The students also have the opportunity to visit Loltun cave, an archaeological site, and the Maya ruins at Uxmal. The final day includes snorkeling followed by dinner on the beach at Puerto Morelos.

Course Strengths

This course combines intercultural leadership theory with an experiential-learning and service-learning project in a Mayan village. The students have six weeks of study online before journeying to the Yucatan. The team-taught aspect of combining the expertise of Anthropology faculty with Leadership faculty also makes this program a stimulating academic experience for students from all disciplines.

Special Topics in Marine Biology and Animal Behavior

(3 credits)

This course introduces students to marine biology in the Caribbean. The first week is spent at St. Francis College, where students discuss assigned readings on the ecology of coral reefs, large marine mammal behavior, and the Virgin Islands. They also participate in field trips to the New York Aquarium and the American Museum of Natural History. During the second week of the course, students and faculty travel to the Virgin Islands Environmental Resource Station (VIERS) on St. John, the Virgin Islands. The students explore the natural environment through hiking and snorkeling and learn about practices designed to sustain the natural environment.

Contact
Kathleen Nolan, Chair, Biology and Health Promotion Department, St. Francis College <knolan@sfc.edu>.

Disciplines
Biology and psychology.

When
Two weeks in January or May.

Faculty
Team-taught by Kathleen Nolan and Kristy Biolsi.

Enrollment
Twelve students, primarily honors biology and psychology majors.

Major Learning Outcomes
• Observe and analyze the biology and ecology of coral reefs, including changes in coral reefs.

• Analyze large marine mammal behavior.

- Compare and contrast tropical, temperate, and arctic marine ecosystems.

- Assess strategies for sustaining marine ecosystems.

- Analyze the connections between Caribbean culture and history and marine biology and animal behavior.

Required Readings

Davidson, Osha Gray. *Fire in the Turtle House: The Green Sea Turtle and the Fate of the Ocean*. New York: Public Affairs, 2003. Print.

Mowat, Farley. *A Whale for the Killing*. Mechanicsburg, PA: Stackpole Books, 2005. Print.

Assignments

- Book reports.

- Journals.

- PowerPoint research presentations.

Itinerary and Major Activities

The destinations include the New York Aquarium and the American Museum of Natural History in New York City, and the Virgin Islands Environmental Resource Station (VIERS) in St. John, the Virgin Islands. Major activities include guided hikes and snorkeling in coral reefs and mangroves in St. John.

Course Strengths

The course is experiential and hands-on. The students travel to the places that they read about, and they see a wide variety of plants and animals, including several varieties of mangroves, cacti, palms, and other tropical plants as well as fish, corals, sponges, sea stars, squid, turtles, and sharks. They learn about strategies for living sustainably within their environment.

ABOUT THE AUTHORS

ELIZABETH BAIGENT is Reader in the History of Geography at the University of Oxford. She is responsible for course design and academic standards for the Scholars Semester in Oxford, a program of SCIO: Scholarship and Christianity in Oxford. She has numerous peer-reviewed publications in history and geography.

BERNICE BRAID is Director Emeritus of the University Honors Program, Long Island University Brooklyn. A past president of NCHC, she has worked with the Honors Semesters Committee since its inception and invented City as Text™ to serve as the integrative seminar in interdisciplinary, site-specific programs. She has facilitated sixteen Faculty Institutes in the U.S., Spain, Germany, Mexico, Puerto Rico, Italy, and Greece, and she has worked as consultant on faculty development initiatives in the U.S., Puerto Rico, and Czechoslovakia. Currently, she is Director of Core Seminar at LIU.

ELLEN B. BUCKNER is Professor in the College of Nursing, University of South Alabama (USA). She was the founding coordinator of the Honors in Nursing Program at the University of Alabama-Birmingham and has been instrumental in developing a nursing honors program at USA. She has facilitated undergraduate research, service-learning, and study abroad opportunities for honors students. She is a Councilor for the Council on Undergraduate Research and Regional Coordinator for the Honor Society of Nursing, Sigma Theta Tau International. She is a past member of the NCHC Board of Directors.

KAYLA BURTON graduated from Morehead State University and will continue her education at North Carolina State University to earn her MA in British and American Literature. Burton has completed research projects concerning obstacles to studying abroad, as well as pieces concerning Alice Walker's *The Color Purple*, Ovid's

Metamorphoses, and Samuel Taylor Coleridge. She has presented her research at the Kentucky Honors Roundtable, the Kentucky Philological Association, and the Celebration of Student Scholarship at Morehead State University.

PHAME CAMARENA is Director of the University Honors Office and Professor of Human Development and Families Studies at Central Michigan University. He was the CMU faculty representative to the American Council of Education meetings on Internationalizing the Curriculum, and he also serves as the faculty advisor for the CMU Student Fulbright Program. He led the initial development of the Los Niños de Oaxaca Project in Mexico.

HELEN COLLINS is a graduate of Central Michigan University Honors Program with a Bachelor of Arts degree, Political Science: International Relations major. She was a first-year student participant in the Los Niños de Oaxaca Program and has completed an internship in Bolivia, working with an NGO whose mission is eliminating poverty and promoting sustainability.

KEVIN W. DEAN is Director of the Honors College and Professor of Communication Studies at West Chester University of Pennsylvania. He is the chair of the Pennsylvania State System of Higher Education Honors Directors. A former National Kellogg Fellow, Dean has lectured on leadership development in Scotland, China, Russia, and South Africa. He earned his PhD in Public Communication from the University of Maryland.

MISCHA DEKKER earned his graduate degree in the Research Master Philosophy at Utrecht University and Research Master Social Sciences at the University of Amsterdam. He completed his undergraduate degree in Human Geography and was a student in the Utrecht University Honors Program.

CHRISTOPHER J. FROST is Dean of the School of Arts and Sciences at St. Joseph's College in Patchogue, New York, and Professor Emeritus, San Diego State University. He previously served as

Associate Dean of Undergraduate Studies at San Diego State University and Associate Director of the University Honors Program at Texas State University. A Fulbright Scholar in Romania and a Fulbright International Lecturer in Morocco, he has written several books and numerous articles that cross both disciplinary and cultural boundaries. He has led over a dozen study abroad programs on three continents. Frost completed his doctorate in Psychology and Interdisciplinary Studies at Boston University.

CHRISTINE HAIT is a professor of English at Columbia College in South Carolina, where she regularly teaches honors courses. She has published articles on American writers Kay Boyle and Katherine Anne Porter, and her scholarly interests include film and popular culture. She enjoys the opportunity teaching in honors gives her to create courses that reflect her interests in both film and literature.

LYGIA HOLCOMB is Assistant Dean for Graduate Clinical Programs and Associate Professor at the University of Alabama at Birmingham. She also has a faculty practice in the School of Nursing Nurse-Managed Center as a Family Nurse Practitioner. She organizes and participates in missions, college courses, and collaborative research in Honduras. Holcomb is active in many professional organizations and is a past-president of Nu Chapter of the Honor Society of Nursing, Sigma Theta Tau International. In 2008 she received a Special Recognition Award from the Municipality of Puerto Cortes following her many mission trips there. In 2009 she was appointed a PAHO/WHO Collaborating Center Scholar.

CECILE HOURY is Assistant Dean for Continuing Education at the Robert Stempel College of Public Health & Social Work at Florida International University. Houry also teaches an upper-division, community service-research seminar for FIU Honors College. Houry is a member of the NCHC International Education Committee and has presented papers at several NCHC conferences. Born and raised in France, Houry earned her doctorate in History from the University of Miami.

TIMOTHY L. HULSEY is Associate Provost of the Chancellor's Honors and Haslam Scholars programs at the University of Tennessee-Knoxville. He previously served as Dean of the Honors College at Virginia Commonwealth University. He has led study abroad programs in Canterbury and Oxford. Hulsey holds a PhD in Clinical Psychology from the University of Tennessee and completed pre- and post-doctoral fellowships at Dartmouth Medical School. He is the co-author, with Christopher J. Frost, of *Moral Cruelty: A meaning and the Justification of Harm*.

MICHAEL B. JENDZURSKI earned a BA in Kinesiology from West Chester University of Pennsylvania (WCU), and he is currently a graduate student in Communication Studies at WCU. Michael is president of Omicron Delta Kappa and past president of the WCU Honors Student Association. He participated in four WCU Honors College service-learning programs in South Africa.

KIM KLEIN is Director of the University Honors Program and Professor of History at Shippensburg University in Pennsylvania. A past member of the NCHC Board of Directors, she also serves on the NCHC International Education and Honors Semesters committees. She has led honors study abroad and service-learning programs in Belgium, France, and the Dominican Republic. She earned her PhD in History from the Johns Hopkins University.

PHILIP KRUMMRICH is Director of the Academic Honors Program and study abroad programs at Morehead State University. He has participated in international programs in Spain, Austria, Costa Rica, and Mexico. He earned his PhD in Comparative Literature from the University of Illinois, and he has taught college classes in languages, literature, and honors for more than thirty years.

CHANTEL R. LUCAS graduated from Columbia College in 2012. She is studying for her master's degree in Media Practice for Development and Social Change at the University of Sussex as a Rotary Ambassadorial Scholar. With a concentration in documentary film, her interests include investigating media technologies in an increasingly globalized landscape. Chantel was a student in Columbia College's honors seminar, "Paris, Film, and Literature," and she participated in the subsequent study abroad program in Paris.

KAREN LYONS is Associate Director of the University Honors Program and a member of the faculty of the English and Women's and Gender Studies departments at the University of Nebraska-Lincoln. She serves on the NCHC Publications Board and Portz Committee. She has led several short-term study abroad programs in England and one in Ireland (where she learned almost all of the pitfalls cited in her chapter). She earned her PhD in English from the University of Nebraska-Lincoln.

CORINNE D. MANN is Coordinator of the French Program and Co-Director of the Gender and Women's Studies program at Columbia College, where she has served on the Honors Program Advisory Committee.

LISA MARKUS is pursuing a master's degree in Nursing at the University of Pennsylvania. She served as the Honors Program Coordinator at Butler University's Center for High Achievement and Scholarly Engagement where she advised students on ways to integrate their international studies with their honors program requirements, including their thesis requirement.

JILL MCKINNEY is Associate Director of the Center for Global Education at Butler University, responsible for sending domestic students abroad, helping faculty coordinate overseas programs, and assisting international students from partner universities abroad. She earned an MA in Cultural Anthropology from Ball State University and an MS in Effective Teaching and Leadership from Butler University.

MARY KAY MULVANEY is Director of the Honors Program at Elmhurst College in Elmhurst, Illinois. She is an English professor with a specialization in rhetorical theory and composition pedagogy. She designs, organizes, and teaches short-term international courses in a variety of locations including England, France, Germany, Poland, and the Czech Republic. Many of her courses employ City as Text™ methodology. She currently serves on the NCHC Board of Directors, and she is a past chair of the NCHC International Education Committee.

A. MINH NGUYEN is Professor of Philosophy, Associate Director of the Honors Program, and Coordinator of the Chautauqua Lecture Series at Eastern Kentucky University. A Vietnamese-born philosopher specializing in the philosophy of mind, he has also published in the areas of Chinese thought and Japanese aesthetics. He currently serves on the NCHC International Education Committee and Diversity Issues Committee.

KARL M. PETRUSO is Dean of the Honors College and Professor of Anthropology at the University of Texas at Arlington. He is an archaeologist specializing in the prehistory of the eastern Mediterranean. He has organized, directed, and taught in study abroad programs and archaeological field schools in Greece, Egypt, Portugal, Scotland, France, and Ireland. He is a member of the NCHC International Education Committee.

KAREY SABOL directs international initiatives for the Division of Undergraduate Studies at San Diego State University, where she also coordinates the honor society, Scholars Without Borders. Sabol has been on the forefront of promoting campus-wide study abroad outcomes assessment at SDSU, presenting on student learning abroad to faculty and administrators and leading study abroad assessment efforts for Undergraduate Studies. She served as a Peace Corps volunteer in Jordan from 1998–2000.

MARY ANN STUDER is Dean of the McMaster School for Advancing Humanity and Director of the Carolyn M. Small Honors Program at Defiance College. She designs and conducts faculty and student training for all international initiatives supported by the college. Studer has traveled with nearly one hundred fifty students to over twenty countries in the last ten years. She has been named a

McMaster Fellow to Belize each year since 2005 and has supported over seventy-five community-based research initiatives there.

JUSTIN T. VAN DIJK earned his graduate degree in International Research Master Human Geography and Planning at Utrecht University in the Netherlands. As an undergraduate, he participated in the Honors College at the Faculty of Geosciences at the same university, where he majored in Human Geography and Planning and minored in Philosophy. He is a junior lecturer in Human Geography and Planning at Utrecht University.

ANNE M. WILSON is a professor in the Chemistry Department at Butler University, specializing in organic chemistry. She recently completed a six-year stint as the director of Butler University's Honors Program. In her fifteen years at Butler, Wilson has mentored thirteen undergraduate theses and over forty undergraduate research projects.

MARCA WOLFENSBERGER is Professor of Excellence in Higher Education and Society at Hanze University of Applied Science Groningen in the Netherlands. She is also the honors director of the Geography and Planning Department at Utrecht University. She is an NCHC-Recommended Site Visitor. She has published several research articles on honors education in academic journals. In her latest book, *Teaching for Excellence—Honors Pedagogies Revealed* (Waxmann 2012), she compares honors teaching strategies in the United States and the Netherlands.

JOHN ZUBIZARRETA, the 2010 Carnegie Foundation/CASE U.S. Professor of the Year for Baccalaureate Colleges, is Director of Honors and Faculty Development at Columbia College, South Carolina. He is a past president of NCHC and SRHC, and his books include first and second editions of *The Learning Portfolio: Reflective Practice for Improving Student Learning* (Anker, 2004; Jossey-Bass, 2009) and *Inspiring Exemplary Teaching and Learning: Perspectives on Teaching Academically Talented College Students* (NCHC, 2008), co-edited with Larry Clark.

NCHC Monographs & Journals

Assessing and Evaluating Honors Programs and Honors Colleges: A Practical Handbook by Rosalie Otero and Robert Spurrier (2005, 98pp). This monograph includes an overview of assessment and evaluation practices and strategies. It explores the process for conducting self-studies and discusses the differences between using consultants and external reviewers. It provides a guide to conducting external reviews along with information about how to become an NCHC-Recommended Site Visitor. A dozen appendices provide examples of "best practices."

Beginning in Honors: A Handbook by Samuel Schuman (Fourth Edition, 2006, 80pp). Advice on starting a new honors program. Covers budgets, recruiting students and faculty, physical plant, administrative concerns, curriculum design, and descriptions of some model programs.

Fundrai$ing for Honor$: A Handbook by Larry R. Andrews (2009, 160pp). Offers information and advice on raising money for honors, beginning with easy first steps and progressing to more sophisticated and ambitious fundraising activities.

A Handbook for Honors Administrators by Ada Long (1995, 117pp). Everything an honors administrator needs to know, including a description of some models of honors administration.

A Handbook for Honors Programs at Two-Year Colleges by Theresa James (2006, 136pp). A useful handbook for two-year schools contemplating beginning or redesigning their honors program and for four-year schools doing likewise or wanting to increase awareness about two-year programs and articulation agreements. Contains extensive appendices about honors contracts and a comprehensive bibliography on honors education.

The Honors College Phenomenon edited by Peter C. Sederberg (2008, 172pp). This monograph examines the growth of honors colleges since 1990: historical and descriptive characterizations of the trend, alternative models that include determining whether becoming a college is appropriate, and stories of creation and recreation. Leaders whose institutions are contemplating or taking this step as well as those directing established colleges should find these essays valuable.

Honors Composition: Historical Perspectives and Contemporary Practices by Annmarie Guzy (2003, 182pp). Parallel historical developments in honors and composition studies; contemporary honors writing projects ranging from admission essays to theses as reported by over 300 NCHC members.

Honors Programs at Smaller Colleges by Samuel Schuman (Third Edition, 2011, 80pp). Practical and comprehensive advice on creating and managing honors programs with particular emphasis on colleges with fewer than 4,000 students.

If Honors Students Were People: Holistic Honors Higher Education by Samuel Schuman (2013, 256pp). What if Honors students were people? What if they were not disembodied intellects but whole persons with physical bodies and questing spirits. Of course...they are. This monograph examines the spiritual yearnings of college students and the relationship between exercise and learning.

Inspiring Exemplary Teaching and Learning: Perspectives on Teaching Academically Talented College Students edited by Larry Clark and John Zubizarreta (2008, 216pp). This rich collection of essays offers valuable insights into innovative teaching and significant learning in the context of academically challenging classrooms and programs. The volume provides theoretical, descriptive, and practical resources, including models of effective instructional practices, examples of successful courses designed for enhanced learning, and a list of online links to teaching and learning centers and educational databases worldwide.

NCHC Monographs & Journals

The Other Culture: Science and Mathematics Education in Honors edited by Ellen B. Buckner and Keith Garbutt (2012, 296pp). A collection of essays about teaching science and math in an honors context: topics include science in society, strategies for science and non-science majors, the threat of pseudoscience, chemistry, interdisciplinary science, scientific literacy, philosophy of science, thesis development, calculus, and statistics.

Partners in the Parks: Field Guide to an Experiential Program in the National Parks by Joan Digby with reflective essays on theory and practice by student and faculty participants and National Park Service personnel (2010, 272pp). This monograph explores an experiential-learning program that fosters immersion in and stewardship of the national parks. The topics include program designs, group dynamics, philosophical and political issues, photography, wilderness exploration, and assessment.

Place as Text: Approaches to Active Learning edited by Bernice Braid and Ada Long (Second Edition, 2010, 128pp). Updated theory, information, and advice on experiential pedagogies developed within NCHC during the past 35 years, including Honors Semesters and City as Text™, along with suggested adaptations to multiple educational contexts.

Preparing Tomorrow's Global Leaders: Honors International Education edited by Mary Kay Mulvaney and Kim Klein (2013, 400pp). A valuable resource for initiating or expanding honors study abroad programs, these essays examine theoretical issues, curricular and faculty development, assessment, funding, and security. The monograph also provides models of successful programs that incorporate high-impact educational practices, including City as Text™ pedagogy, service learning, and undergraduate research.

Setting the Table for Diversity edited by Lisa L. Coleman and Jonathan D. Kotinek (2010, 288pp). This collection of essays provides definitions of diversity in honors, explores the challenges and opportunities diversity brings to honors education, and depicts the transformative nature of diversity when coupled with equity and inclusion. These essays discuss African American, Latina/o, international, and first-generation students as well as students with disabilities. Other issues include experiential and service learning, the politics of diversity, and the psychological resistance to it. Appendices relating to NCHC member institutions contain diversity statements and a structural diversity survey.

Shatter the Glassy Stare: Implementing Experiential Learning in Higher Education edited by Peter A. Machonis (2008, 160pp). A companion piece to *Place as Text*, focusing on recent, innovative applications of City as Text™ teaching strategies. Chapters on campus as text, local neighborhoods, study abroad, science courses, writing exercises, and philosophical considerations, with practical materials for instituting this pedagogy.

Teaching and Learning in Honors edited by Cheryl L. Fuiks and Larry Clark (2000, 128pp). Presents a variety of perspectives on teaching and learning useful to anyone developing new or renovating established honors curricula.

Journal of the National Collegiate Honors Council (JNCHC) is a semi-annual periodical featuring scholarly articles on honors education. Articles may include analyses of trends in teaching methodology, articles on interdisciplinary efforts, discussions of problems common to honors programs, items on the national higher education agenda, and presentations of emergent issues relevant to honors education.

Honors in Practice (HIP) is an annual journal that accommodates the need and desire for articles about nuts-and-bolts practices by featuring practical and descriptive essays on topics such as successful honors courses, suggestions for out-of-class experiences, administrative issues, and other topics of interest to honors administrators, faculty, and students.

NCHC Publication Order Form

Purchases may be made by calling (402) 472-9150, emailing nchc@unl.edu, visiting our website <http://www.nchchonors.org>, or mailing a check or money order payable to: NCHC • University of Nebraska–Lincoln • 1100 Neihardt Residence Center • 540 N. 16th Street • Lincoln, NE 68588-0627.   FEIN 52–1188042

	Member	Non-Member	No. of Copies	Amount This Item
Monographs:				
Assessing and Evaluating Honors Programs and Honors Colleges: A Practical Handbook*	$25.00	$45.00		
Beginning in Honors: A Handbook (4th Ed.)	$25.00	$45.00		
Fundrai$ing for Honor$: A Handbook*	$25.00	$45.00		
A Handbook for Honors Administrators	$25.00	$45.00		
A Handbook for Honors Programs at Two-Year Colleges*	$25.00	$45.00		
The Honors College Phenomenon	$25.00	$45.00		
Honors Composition: Historical Perspectives and Contemporary Practices	$25.00	$45.00		
Honors Programs at Smaller Colleges (3rd Ed.)*	$25.00	$45.00		
If Honors Students Were People: Holistic Honors Higher Education	$25.00	$45.00		
Inspiring Exemplary Teaching and Learning: Perspectives on Teaching Academically Talented College Students*	$25.00	$45.00		
The Other Culture: Science and Mathematics Education in Honors	$25.00	$45.00		
Partners in the Parks: Field Guide to an Experiential Program in the National Parks	$25.00	$45.00		
Place as Text: Approaches to Active Learning (2nd Ed.)	$25.00	$45.00		
Preparing Tomorrow's Global Leaders: Honors International Education	$25.00	$45.00		
Setting the Table for Diversity	$25.00	$45.00		
Shatter the Glassy Stare: Implementing Experiential Learning in Higher Education	$25.00	$45.00		
Teaching and Learning in Honors*	$25.00	$45.00		
Journals:				
Journal of the National Collegiate Honors Council (JNCHC) Specify Vol/Issue ___/___	$25.00	$45.00		
Honors in Practice (HIP) Specify Vol ___	$25.00	$45.00		
Total Copies Ordered and Total Amount Paid:				$

Name_____ Institution _____

Address _____

City, State, Zip _____

Phone _____ Fax_____ Email _____

*Print-on-Demand publications—will be delivered in 4-6 weeks.

Shipping costs will be calculated on the number of items purchased.

Apply a 20% discount if 10+ copies are purchased.